D0871730

# Suicide: Inside and Out

# David K. Reynolds and Norman L. Farberow

**University of California Press**

Berkeley · Los Angeles · London

1976

University of California Press
Berkeley and Los Angeles, California

University of California Press, Ltd.
London, England

# CONTENTS

v

# FOREWORD

Over a quarter of a century ago, when I served as director of the Yale Psychiatric Institute and Hospital, we admitted as a patient the social anthropologist, William Caudill. Dr. Caudill, however, was only simulating patienthood and his cover was protected from discovery by patients and staff by a secret administrative collusion. The results of that investigative endeavor to understand the inside of the hospital was published under the title, *The Psychiatric Hospital as a Small Society.*

The present work goes considerably beyond that first attempt to convey the subjective sense of being in the small world of an asylum. In the first place, it is a specific study and not a general one. It is focused on the suicidal person and on the situational structure and processes of the suicidal watch. It is preceded by an objective assessment of looking at the situation and its behavioral interaction from the position of the uninvolved "outside" observer. Like the early study, it is characterized by the use of the expert self to experience the subjective impact of the social and cultural environment, but it also is enhanced by a debriefing feedback from personnel after the patient role experience was ended and had been disclosed.

The present investigators call their method "experimental research," necessitating the adoption of a situationally determined identity and living within a setting in association with other role-identified persons, including in this instance patients, staff, and different kinds of visitors.

One of the most impactful findings of this work is the reinforcement given to the importance of the social and cultural setting in the subjective construction of one's identity. So predominant does this "situational identity" or "situated self" become that the investigator himself came perilously close to acting out a situationally determined suicidal ideation.

This book puts together what contemporary behavioral scientists seem determined to keep asunder. The students of subjectivity will be reminded that the subjective sense of self is constructed largely out of the information wittingly and unwittingly provided by the immediate sociocultural and interpersonal setting. The behaviorists will understand that the other side of environmental control is the subjective environmental appraisal and analysis resulting in either subjectively perceived self-enhancement or subjectively interpreted self-defeat. This study of the microculture of a hospital, a small society, could be a paradigm for the study of the whole society.

Edward Stainbrook, M.D., Chairman
Department of Human Behavior
School of Medicine
University of Southern California

# PREFACE

This book is based on a study of suicidal patients and of suicide observation status in two Veterans Administration (VA) neuropsychiatric (NP) hospitals. It is unique in that we used not only the traditional means of analysis of records, observation, and interviewing of both patients and staff to gather our data but, in addition, the anthropologist on our team (DKR), assuming the identity of a depressed, suicidal patient, entered a VA hospital. Thus we have not only the formal and informal perspectives from staff members and patients but the very personal account of a researcher-patient. The degree to which these perspectives and experiences reflect those found generally among staff and patients in psychiatric hospitals must be individually evaluated by each reader. On the basis of the response of others to our preliminary reports, we feel that many of our findings can be generalized for neuropsychiatric hospitals within and outside the VA system.

Our theoretical focus has been on the ways in which the role groups in psychiatric wards perceive and organize their experiences. The psychiatric hospital is a "small society," as Caudill (1958) put it, and within it the world view of his role group is both the product and the creator of "reality" for the suicidal patient.

Of course, the way one views one's self, that is, one's self-image, is a nexus for perspectives on one's world. Research has indicated increasing awareness of problems of identity and the "presentation of self" among those labeled mentally ill (Goffman [1959]; Braginsky et al. [1969]; Rosenhan [1973]; Laing [1961]). The problem is characteristically acute for the suicidal patient; for him it has grown to such proportions that the wisdom of the very continuation of the "self" is in question. As a result, the way in which a suicidal person views himself and his world becomes crucial in his decision. Our experiences may help to shed some light on the suicidal patient's world view and what might be called his view of self, or his personal identity.

The book is divided into four parts. The first part reviews the literature and provides background information on previous studies of suicide in NP hospitals.

The second part describes the preparation and organization phase of the study. Data were gathered from several wards of one VA hospital over a period of three months. During this period the researcher presented himself to staff and patients as a "research anthropologist" (a rather ambiguous identity since most of them seemed to equate anthropology with archaeology, if they were familiar with anthropology at all). It was clear, however, that within the dichotomy between staff member and patient, the anthropologist (with his formal title, his freedom of movement, his own keys and hours, and authority to elicit cooperation from the staff) "belonged with" the staff and not the patients. The second part, therefore, emphasizes staff perspectives on suicidal patients and suicidal status. Other researchers (Caudill, 1958; Sudnow, 1967; Salisbury, 1962) have noted that one not only gathers more material from but also tends to see the materials in the same way as those subjects with whom he is identified.

The third part, dealing with the anthropologist's experience qua patient, gives a complementary patient perspective, albeit in a different VA hospital. A second hospital was necessary because the anthropologist's identity as researcher was less likely to be recognized there. In this third part the personal account of suicide status is preceded by a description of the data-gathering strategy called "experiential research" and a survey of other investigations of mental patienthood which utilized this strategy. The researcher's journal account is supplemented by hospital records (nursing notes, psychological test results, etc.) and records of posttreatment meetings with hospital staff members who had had contact with the researcher-patient.

In the final part the information from our outside-insider approaches is pulled together. We offer a broad framework for understanding suicides during and shortly after psychiatric hospitalization and present some suggestions for meaningful prevention.

The staff and the patients at the Veterans Administration Hospital, Brentwood, were all remarkably kind and helpful. We are especially indebted to Dr. Joseph Crockett for making the study feasible and for contributing enlightened observations and comments throughout its course.

We are also grateful to psychiatrists Dr. A. Brunse and Dr. J. Tokar, to nurses Mrs. Grady, Mrs. Soroko, and Mrs. LaCroix, and to the staff members (particularly the nurses' aides) and patients at the Veterans Administration Hospital, Sepulveda, Ward X, who made themselves available for questioning and observation. The necessary organizing of information in preparation for the research could not have been done without their help.

Thanks are owing to Dr. Robert Litman and the Suicide Prevention Center staff who participated in both the preparation and debriefing phases of the study, and to Mary Jorgensen of the Central Research Unit staff for her competent research assistance, especially in preparation of the literature review materials. Grace H. Stimson of the University of California Press did her customary creative and thorough editing of the manuscript. We appreciate the typing of Ms. N. Yamamoto and Ms. E. Kwong. Finally, we could not have carried out this study without the assistance of a grant from the National Institute of Mental Health (no. 22800).

To all those named above, and to the many others who played a role in the study, we owe a debt that can be repaid, in part, only by our best efforts to make this book useful to others like them.

# SUICIDE AND PATIENTHOOD IN PSYCHIATRIC WARDS

Interest in the field of suicide and suicide prevention has shown a tremendous upsurge in the past decade. Not only has the number of suicide prevention centers grown and suicide research expanded in new directions, but also the number of published articles has increased dramatically. For the years 1958 through 1967, the number of published items averaged 130 a year; for 1968 and 1969, the yearly average was approximately 300; and for 1970, it was close to 500 (Farberow, 1972). Yet in spite of this growing interest in suicide one area remains almost devoid of information — the study of completed suicide by hospitalized psychiatric patients.

In 1954 Banen noted that there were almost no studies of committed suicide among psychiatric hospital patients. In 1965 Chapman reported that he had found only five studies (in the English language) on the subject in the preceding ten years (Banen, 1954; Beisser and Blanchette, 1961; Farberow et al., 1966; Levy and Southcombe, 1953; Pokorny, 1960). The situation has improved only slightly in the years since Chapman's study. Farberow et al. (1971) reported an eight-year survey of hospital suicides. As late as 1972 Sletten et al. commented on the unusual paucity of published material on the subject of committed suicides in mental hospitals.

Banen (1954) offers two possible reasons for a seeming reluctance to study suicide in mental hospitals: (1) a possible unwillingness to discuss what could be interpreted as a blemish on hospital records; (2) the scarcity of material available to one investigator. Nevertheless, there are advantages in the study of these suicides, such as the availability of complete patient records and the observations

1

of a staff attuned to psychiatric problems (Beisser and Blanchette, 1961). And, more important, there is a need to understand why patients commit suicide in a psychiatric hospital, for the institutional suicide rate still far exceeds that of the general population.

Mental hospitals have reported various suicide rates over they years. Levy and Southcombe (1953) found that 58 suicides occurred at Eastern State Hospital between the years 1891 and 1949, thus making the suicide rate 380 per 100,000 admissions. At that time the incidence of suicide in the general population was 11.2 per 100,000. Other studies have reported rates ranging from 19 to 2,250 patients per 100,000 (Beisser and Blanchette, 1961). A more recent study (Sletten et al., 1972) found the rate at the five Missouri state hospitals equivalent to 90 per 100,000 cases and further noted that suicide is at least five times more common in the mental hospital population than in the general population. Using "patients treated" as the basis, Farberow et al. (1971) reported a rate of 72. If the average daily patient census is used as a basis, however, the rate increases to about 250.

Beisser and Blanchette (1961) advise caution when comparing these widely varying suicide rates. They state (p. 366) that "fluctuations in rate by years in our own study did not necessarily coincide with fluctuations in other studies. It is evident that such rates by themselves have little meaning for comparison. Suicide rates are meaningful only when considered within the total framework of the individual institution. The myriad of factors which make the institution unique evidently play a role in the suicide rate." It is also apparent that the requirements of each investigator must be examined carefully in order to note the base used to compute the rate of suicide. These bases vary, including patients treated, average daily patient census, number of admissions, number of discharges, and others.

It is not necessary to make comparisons of different suicide rates, however, for one paradoxical question to arise. Why does suicide occur at all in a mental hospital, a place that offers treatment and protection? In an effort to answer this question, several studies have sought to define the characteristics of the suicidal patient. Farberow et al. (1966) found that the suicidal patient in a neuropsychiatric hospital tended to have a more serious form of psychiatric illness; that is, the illness showed more acute phases and the patient exhibited more extremes in behavior, fluctuating from restlessness, hyperactivity, and agitation on the one hand to severe depression, muteness, and withdrawal on the other. Suicide occurred among patients with the more serious psychiatric diagnoses, such as schizophrenia and manic-depressive psychosis, whereas the controls tended to receive more diagnoses of organicity and neurotic disorders. In studies of schizophrenic (Farberow et al., 1961) and anxiety and depressive patients (Farberow and McEvoy, 1966), dependency frustrations were found to be most characteristic of suicides.

Levy and Southcombe (1953) classified 50 percent of the patients who committed suicide as schizophrenic and diagnosed 10 percent as manic-depressives. In 45 percent of the patients there was no evidence of depressive features, either during psychotic episodes or in the premorbid personality makeup. In these cases, suicide probably occurred as a result of auditory hallucinations or delusions. As a possible theoretical explanation for their findings, the authors (p. 510) quote Zilboorg's statement that "the suicidal drive is not dependent on or derived from any traditional clinical entity found in present-day psychiatric nosology, but should be viewed rather as a reaction of a developmental nature which is universal and common to the mentally sick of all types and possibly also to the many so-called normal persons."

According to their 1971 report, Farberow et al. found that the psychotic category embracing 68.6 percent of the population of mental hospitals contributed 85.7 percent of the suicides. The largest subgroup among psychotics includes schizophrenic patients, who were overrepresented in the suicide population by 13.3 percent. The depressed psychotic group is overrepresented by 4.6 percent. Organic diagnoses — acute and chronic brain syndromes — were underrepresented in the suicides. Although such patients make up 21.1 percent of the hospital population, they contribute only 5 percent of the suicides, an underrepresentation of 16.1 percent.

Of the eighteen patients who committed suicide studied by Chapman (1965), sixteen were given final diagnoses of the "most severe degree of disorganization." Fourteen of the sixteen were diagnosed as having schizophrenic reactions, one had a psychotic depressive reaction, and one a chronic brain syndrome. According to Chapman, these findings are in accord with Karl Menninger's formulation of suicide as a fifth order of dyscontrol, representing mental disintegration at its most extreme.

In comparing their suicide patients with a control group, Beisser and Blanchette (1961) found a high frequency of depression combined with a diagnosis of schizophrenia. They also noted a lack of improvement in response to hospital treatment among patients who later committed suicide. In about half of the suicide group (54 percent), Beisser and Blanchette observed that the psychiatric status was progressively deteriorating, whereas the status was improving for only 17 percent. The reverse was true of the control group.

As to whether suicide constitutes a psychotic act, Banen (1954) believes the two opposing schools of thought surrounding this issue can be correlated by accepting the Freudian concept of the death instinct which exists in all humans. That more people do not commit suicide in view of the universality of the death instinct is because of the concomitant counteracting life instinct. Each person develops his own way of handling these two forces, but a logical conclusion is that no one is entirely free of self-destructive tendencies. Thus Banen does not see suicide as a psychotic act, but he explains (p. 355) why more psychotics commit suicide than nonpsychotics:

> Just as the law of gravity applies equally well to the psychotic and the nonpsychotic alike, so do the laws of human behavior. What differs in the two categories is not the basic drives but rather what happens to these basic drives as a consequence of each individual's life experience. There are no large suicide statistics to substantiate this but all the indications are that the rate of suicide is materially higher among psychotics as compared to nonpsychotics. Apparently the world of unreality to which they have retreated is, at least to some, even less acceptable than the world of reality which they have forsaken. Then too, we know that psychotics are governed more by primitive and infantile drives without the benefit of a strong controlling ego capable of judging and weighing contemplated acts and are, therefore, more likely to carry out a suicidal act impulsively.

In attempting to determine why people commit suicide in a mental hospital, the focus thus far has been on the mental status of the patients who kill themselves and the possible theoretical bases for their suicidal acts. The conclusion, regardless of whether suicide is regarded as an inherent drive, an instinct, or a wish to die, would seem to be that those patients who commit suicide in a mental institution are the more seriously disturbed. It would be interesting to know how many of the severely psychiatrically ill patients had been given a final diagnosis before they committed suicide, or to what degree the diagnosis was influenced by their prior suicidal behavior. Beisser and Blanchette (1961) found that more members of their suicide group than of their control group had made previous threats and attempts to take their own lives. Does the knowledge that a patient is suicidal bias the clinician's diagnostic evaluation? At best suicide is a mystifying and disturbing occurrence which may seem plausible only when seen as the act of an irrational mind.

Although the studies mentioned above have focused primarily on the patient's mental status as predisposing him to suicide, the role of the environment has not been ignored. Rotov (1970) integrates the mental and environmental aspects by dividing the factors affecting a patient's suicide potential into two groups. The first group comprises "necessary causes," or causes that make the suicide possible. They include psychosis, depression, social mores in certain cultures, prolonged stressful life situations, brain disorders, and the like. The second group is "sufficient causes," or causes that make the suicide probable. This group includes such additional factors as lack of environmental support, unavailability or inadequacy of therapy, constitutional or temporary ego weakness, various intercurrent stresses, and so on. According to Rotov's model, therefore, outside or environmental influences could increase or decrease the possibility of a patient's killing himself.

The effect the environment can have on a patient's prognosis has been described by Karl Menninger (1963, p. 291): "An individual's adjustment always means his reaction to a reaction to a reaction to a reaction, etc. And when an individual has fallen or wavered, his struggle back to the line of march is often handicapped by the attitudes which have been created in the environment by the development of his illness." When a person enters a mental hospital, his environment becomes that of the hospital. Often this new environment represents restriction and change of activities and a general loss of autonomy. Patients who have expressed suicidal ideation or who have made prior threats or attempts are subject to the additional hospital environmental measures of seclusion, removal of potentially self-destructive articles, shock treatment, and so on. Banen (1954) goes even further, urging that certain physical precautions, such as removal of self-destructive implements from the environment, be taken with all hospitalized active psychotics. All these measures are part of a total treatment program undertaken by staff members to help the patient by preventing him from implementing self-destructive tendencies.

Many precautions, however, may simply represent the hospital staff's fear of failure and fear of responsibility (Rotov, 1970), so that any positive effect preventive techniques may have on the behavior of patients is open to question. Beisser and Blanchette (1961) report that seclusion is used reluctantly and only when necessary in most mental hospitals because of insufficient personnel. Fifty-two percent of patients in their suicide group were in seclusion at the time they committed suicide. The authors conclude that enforced physical isolation can be a frightening experience for many patients. When patients are cut off from human relationships, their only available objects are internalized ones. This fact is especially important for assaultive patients, who may turn their aggression against themselves and commit suicide.

Removal of self-destructive materials may also be of questionable benefit. The patient's need to kill himself is more important than the symbolism of the method chosen (Beisser and Blanchette, 1961). Of concern are the effects of depriving the patient of these means. When sharp instruments and other patentially destructive means are removed from his environment, a patient may still use his shirt to choke himself or stuff toilet paper down his throat. It is possible that the articles removed from the patient's possession are significant symbols of his contact with others, and their removal may be perceived as similar to being placed in isolation, a validation of the patient's loss of human relationships and ability to control his own actions.

Shock treatment is also a doubtful method. Lipshutz (1942) espouses electroconvulsive therapy (ECT) as one means of treating depressed patients, believing that the resultant improvement may be caused by ECT's meeting the patient's need for punishment. There is no evidence, however, that shock treatment has reduced the suicide rate. Levy and Southcombe (1953, p. 505) conclude that, "Although it is generally assumed by psychiatrists and other workers in this field that the introduction of the newer therapies, especially shock treatments, have drastically reduced the actual number of suicides, no definite statistics can be found in this respect in the literature."

Beisser and Blanchette (1961) found that the use of tranquilizing drugs had a decided effect on the number of suicides committed. In 1954, the year these drugs were introduced at Metropolitan State Hospital, Norwalk, California, the suicide rate more than doubled. Aside from pharmacological effects of the drugs, Beisser and Blanchette feel an answer may lie in the attitude of the hospital personnel. Staff members may have felt they could relax their vigilance because the hospital was employing a new, effective treatment agent.

In some cases, hospital treatment at even the simplest level has had negative results. For patients in whom an object loss has resulted in a depressive reaction, hospital treatment may foster dependency upon the institution as a replacement for the lost object (Chapman, 1965). When object relations have been seriously disrupted, dependency needs may not be met or may increase during hospitalization. The combination of overprotection in the hospital and a sense of losing one's identity among the mentally disturbed may further undermine the patient's already low self-esteem.

As shown in the studies discussed above, the attitudes in the environment of a mental hospital patient are reflected clearly in hospital treatment procedures and staff behavior. These attitudes may, of course, be interpreted differently by different patients. Banen (1954) emphasized how important it is for the staff to remain alert and sensitive to the mood, expressed thought content, and behavior of each individual patient. Stanton and Schwartz (1954), in studying the sociopsychological environment of the mental hospital, cautioned that the hospital milieu must be understood in terms of its significance to each patient individually. What one patient feels to be support and a high level of care may be seen as rejection and inefficient procedure by another.

A dramatic example of the effects of hospital attitudes on suicidal behavior is given by Kobler and Stotland (1964). They describe their approach to suicide and emotional disturbances as "field-theoretical" and "psychosocial." For them, suicide incorporates both environmental and intrapsychic factors. Suicidal behavior is viewed as an effort to solve the problems of living. Whether or not an individual actually commits suicide depends largely on the nature of the response by other people to his problems.

The authors theorize that in order for a suicide to occur certain conditions must prevail. A person comes to feel that his future is devoid of hope. He, or someone else, brings the alternative of suicide into his field. He then attempts to communicate his feelings of hopelessness to others in an effort to be reassured that some hope still does exist. The kind of response these others give the individual at this point is critical in determining whether or not suicide will occur. For an actual suicide to take place, a necessary (albeit not sufficient) aspect of the field is a message that the situation really is hopeless and that the individual really is helpless.

For the hospitalized patient, the responses of the personnel to his direct or indirect communications of hopelessness are the crucial part of his field. Unfortunately, such responses often convey an implicit or explicit expectation that the disturbed patient will kill himself. It seems likely that the prevalence of this negative expectation stems from an illness approach that divides people into the prone and the nonprone: "The prone are the sick ones, the weaklings, helpless and worthy of concern rather than respect. . . . And respect has implicit positive expectations; it says: you can cope, you can choose" (Kobler and Stotland, 1964, p. 264).

To illustrate their theory, Kobler and Stotland describe a hospital that, in the first years after its opening, provided a model environment for its patients. The emphasis was on milieu treatment, a concern for the potentially therapeutic value of all twenty-four hours of the patients' day in the hospital. The particular form of milieu therapy stressed was attitude therapy; the ward staff had to behave in certain ways toward each patient as prescribed by the physician. There was constant and free communication between ward personnel and doctors. The overall atmosphere in the hospital was one of confidence in the ability to control the danger of suicide.

After almost nine years, during which time only one suicide had occurred, one suicide attempt and four completed suicides came within a period of six months. The difference in suicide rates in the two time periods was attributed to a difference in the atmosphere in the hospital, not to a difference in patients. The hospital structure had been changing and the attitude of the hospital staff was deteriorating. Staff members felt a lowering of confidence, increased feelings of hopelessness and helplessness, and an acute anxiety about patients who could be viewed as suicidal. They were thus incapable of providing new goals, new social roles, and new identities for the patients: "In their hopeless and helpless state, and finding no meaning in life, the patients struggled still more desperately for purposes. . . . What was offered in the environment of the hospital . . . was the expectation, the fear of suicide. The patients grasped at it as an identity" (Kobler and Stotland, 1964, p. 16). This example shows clearly that staff attitudes do affect patients' recovery and gives specific meaning to Menninger's comment that recovery is handicapped by the attitudes which have been created in the environment." Throughout this book runs the theme that others have a strong impact on our identity, our definition of self. It is only natural that each of us should become the person who fits the web of expectations in his immediate social world.

 # AN OUTSIDER'S
# PERSPECTIVE

The preliminary stage in our research was devoted to gathering and organizing the data necessary to prepare for DKR's sojourn in the hospital. The plan was to acquire as much information as possible about suicidal patients from staff members. We wished to learn their ideas and conceptualizations about suicidal behavior, to see how they interacted with patients, and to observe, insofar as possible, the impact of their concepts and feelings upon those most concerned, the suicidal patients themselves. Our perspective at this stage of the research could be broadly termed "interactionist" in the tradition of Simmel, Cooley, Goffman, and others. We approached our research questions (and other issues that arose in the course of our study) with the tactic of exploring the interactions appropriate to socially defined settings and roles. What were the implicit and explicit social meanings of the actors' interactions? What were the consequences of the socially situated definitions and behaviors in these settings?

We felt is was necessary to compare the description of what actually occurred in the hospital (from an outside observer's perspective) with the interpretations of hospital reality as provided by members of role groups within the hospital setting. Through these comparisons we proposed to grasp the social construction of reality, in this instance the social construction of suicide and suicide observation status in each hospital ward.

## SUICIDE OBSERVATION STATUS

Suicide observation status ("S.O.S.," "special status," "S-status," or simply "status") is a special category applied administratively for the protection of potentially self-injurious patients in many mental hospitals. Usually, formalized rules regarding observation and responsibility for the patient, restrictions on his activity, and even special dress are associated with this status.

Psychiatric opinion varies widely as to the usefulness and legal wisdom of placing patients on S-status. Some psychiatrists routinely place new admissions with suicidal complaints on S-status for two weeks. Others do not use the category at all or use it only rarely, while still others use it as necessary, arguing that placing a patient on S-status in some cases may not only be antitherapeutic, but may also embroil the hospital in additional legal difficulties should the patient kill himself while on status.

## RESEARCH PROBLEMS

Several problems intrigued us as we began to investigate S-status in VA neuropsychiatric hospitals.

1. The problem of privacy and personal space. What are the effects on the suicidal patient of being physically restricted in terms of mobility and of being under constant observation? How does he handle his need for privacy and independence, particularly in the American culture, which supposedly places high value on these aspects of life? Does he retreat inwardly, attempt to escape, project a smoke-screen identity behind which he hides? Does he push for freedom or accept the limits imposed on him?

2. What are the effects of S-status on a patient's self-concept? A suicidal person already has some difficulty with his self-image since he seriously considers destroying himself. When this initial problem is compounded by the social stigma attached to mental hospital patients generally and by the possibility of jealousy and devaluation of S-status patients among their attention-starved patient peers and the already overworked staff members, the result is not likely to be a self-image of great positive valence.

3. How do staff members determine suicidal intent? This question is important, because from the staff's estimation of intent come decisions regarding assignment to and removal from S-status. Having worked in suicide research for a number of years, we were quite sensitive to the difficulties involved in assessing the suicidal tendency. Yet the assessment must be made. From a

purely administrative perspective no public hospital has the facilities to keep large numbers of patients on S-status for long periods of the time because of the heightened demands on staff time and energy.

## THE SETTING

The data for the first phase of our research were collected over a three-month period. Approximately forty hours of observation and interviewing were spent in the VA neuropsychiatric wards under study. Twice that amount of time was invested in discussion and analysis outside the wards. Two progress reports and a summary report were submitted to the building supervisors and the hospital's psychology research director and copies were circulated among ward nursing personnel. Then followed two meetings with the staff during which our tentative findings were presented, implications for communication among role groups in the ward were drawn, and feedback and questions were aired. The result was a mutually satisfying exchange of information between researchers and ward personnel with practical, concrete suggestions for the handling of suicidal patients. The analysis presented below profited from these meetings and, retrospectively, from the suicide "live-in" described in the following section.

At the time, the ward where we made most of our observations stressed attitude therapy in addition to the usual psychopharmacological agents employed in VA neuropsychiatric hospitals. Since it was the only locked ward in the building, patients from the building's remaining three wards were normally transferred to it when they were placed on S-status. Approximately twenty patients, male and female, were housed in the ward. They tended to be young or middle-aged at the time of our study, and they were racially mixed.

As seems to be common in public psychiatric institutions, the ward personnel included predominantly foreign-born white male psychiatrists, native-born white female nurses, and Negro male psychological technicians (hereafter called NA's, meaning "nursing assistants" or "nurses' aides"). The problems of interaction presented by the diversity of backgrounds and communication styles among these role groups were largely offset by ward routine and informal social relationships. But, as we shall see, each role group had its own characteristic way of perceiving suicidality based on the information available to it and its view of the psychological nature of man.

## ROLE GROUPS

### The Psychiatrist

The psychiatrist represented ultimate authority in the hospital to the S-status patient. It was he who put the patient on status and it was he who took him off status. It was the psychiatrist who assigned the patient to the open or the closed ward and who decided whether or not to allow privileged status, that is, whether the patient would be allowed to leave the building, go home on weekends, and so forth. The psychiatrist regulated medication, determined the therapy regimen, and made other decisions on the handling of patients. In performing these functions he usually received advice from and consulted with nurses, aids, and other personnel, but he was also personally and directly accessible to patients. He had information and a perspective not shared by other staff members, and so he sometimes made decisions that countered intermediate levels of counsel.

The ward doctor accepted his responsibility for the care and treatment of suicidal patients soberly and conservatively. As society's ultimate authority in determining a suicidal identity, he was the expert on the danger of suicide. There was, in effect, almost total power vested in the doctor. When he was out of town the immediate responsibilities for S-status patients were delegated to other staff members (e.g., the decision whether or not to allow a patient to attend a hockey game was referred to the social worker handling his case). But everyone, including the patients, knew that movement off S-status and out of the locked ward would be delayed until the doctor returned.

### The Nurse

We know least about the nurse's relationship with the suicidal patient. The nurse was busy in a sense that neither physicians nor aides were busy. She had numerous time-consuming administrative tasks as well as medical responsibilities. She was seen by some patients as the gatekeeper, or as the channel of communication with the doctor. She was a professional intermediary.

Like the physician, the nurse saw herself as having prime responsibility for S-status patients. She had to translate general orders into specific routine practice. It was her responsibility to assign an S-status patient an appropriate bed (near and visible to the nursing station) and to provide adequate experienced aide supervision (using a detail slip) when an S-status patient left the ward. She gathered information about the patient's condition to pass along to the ward doctor.

Of all staff members in the suicide ward the nurse seemed most likely to be the target of the patients' hostility. She was often distant and professional. She had enough authority to be worth hating (the aides just did what she told them to do) yet not enough to make it impossible to appeal to higher authority. She was a sitting duck for hostility, particularly if her firm attitude (as prescribed by the doctor) set limits that were unacceptable to the patient.

## The Aide

While, strictly speaking, the aide might not be of the patient's world he was in it more than any other staff member. He had more opportunity to establish ties with the S-status patient than anyone else except another patient. His formal staff status was on a level that allowed patients to identify with him and open up to him on a friendly basis. Of course, personality factors and the patient's disturbance affected his relationships with the aide.

The informal ties that developed between aides and patients on S-status had potential for both positive and negative effects on the patient's safety. A patient might confide in the aide, alerting him to suicidal ideas or potentially harmful objects. On the other hand, we learned of an aide who failed to check a returning patient's pockets because they were "old buddies." The patient shot himself with a concealed pistol shortly after readmission.

The aide, too, felt he had primary responsibility for protecting S-status patients. After all, it was he who was entrusted with their hour-by-hour observation in and outside the ward.

## The Patient

Relations among patients were extremely variable. A patient who was in good contact with reality was likely to know who was on

S-status and who was not. In fact, a list of the names of patients on S-status was posted at the nursing station in some wards.

One interesting observation (corroborated by our later experiential research) was that two patients seemed to be drawn together by their both being on S-status. These patients had little in common — their disorders were different, their personalities were different, their personal histories were different — yet they were thrown together with only each other for company when they were prevented from attending certain activities (such as occupational therapy) which were open to everybody else. They took an interest in each other's problems, sat together in group meetings, and in general provided each other with sympathetic support. In the process, they exaggerated the similarities of their cases and minimized the differences (without ignoring the differences altogether, however). Their common features — their suicidality and their handling of the problems facing them and the restrictions imposed upon them because of their suicide potential — were uniting factors.

"Getting on," "being on," and "getting off" S-status are the three main chronological stages in the career of the suicidal patient. Each stage presents characteristic problems of decision for staff members and parallel opportunities for the patient to influence those decisions.

*Getting on suicide status.* — Determining whether a patient is potentially self-destructive is a serious undertaking. One cannot rely on physiological signs, though such indications as tears and psychomotor retardation may provide indirect evidence. But even this evidence is equivocal, for psychomotor retardation may invite the evaluation that a patient is too depressed to harm himself. One cannot depend upon cues that may elsewhere be useful in determining the nature of mental disorder, cues such as odd behavior, hallucinations, loose associations, and so forth. In fact, the only two kinds of data which are at all useful in determining whether a person is suicidal or not are what he says about harming himself and what he does about it. Of course, if he is fully bent on killing himself, and if he is in contact with the world in which he is operating, he will do his best to keep such cues hidden so that no one will prevent him from accomplishing his suicide.

In determining whether or not a patient intends to kill himself, the psychiatric staff faces a dilemma which is quite difficult to resolve. Staff members cannot allow the patient to harm himself in order to discover his intent. They must instead rely on easily misinterpreted indirect cues and, most important, on the patient's own statements about his suicidality. If they accept his statements and err, certain pitfalls open up before them; and if they mistakenly reject his statements, other pitfalls await them. The stakes — not only the quality but the very continuation of the patient's life — are always high.

The question must be asked: "Do you feel like killing yourself?" It may be softened and intellectualized into "Have you had suicidal thoughts?" or "Have you been wondering what's the use of living?" but the essence of the query remains. It is asked routinely on admission of a patient and as necessary thereafter. It has been argued that by asking such a question the possibility of suicide may be suggested to the patient and an idea may be planted, but there is no other way of obtaining this crucial datum.

Then the patient's response, whatever it may be, must be evaluated. Evaluation is made within the context of who the patient is and the setting in which he speaks. One can discover some of the criteria for evaluating the truth of a patient's statements about suicidality by simply asking staff members to verbalize them. Some criteria, however, are difficult to verbalize (e.g., "I just feel that he's not telling the truth"), others completely escape the awareness of some staff members (e.g., the criterion of familiarity; see below), and still others are not elicited because they are not socially acceptable responses to the question (e.g., the criterion of potential manipulation; see below).

Before pursuing a formal analysis of criteria used by staff members to evaluate a patient's response to a query about his suicidality let us look briefly at the options of response open to the patient. Essentially he has three possible options: he can say that he intends to kill himself, that he does not intend to kill himself, or that he is uncertain.

The consensus view of the ward staff seemed to be that the patient who said he was suicidal and was telling the truth was a genuine risk and should be watched carefully. The patient who said he was suicidal but was not telling the truth was a "manipulator" and a potential risk if ignored or challenged to harm himself. The patient who said he was not suicidal and was telling the truth was no immediate risk. The patient who said he was not suicidal but was not telling the truth posed the highest risk and might be labeled "crafty" in his attempts to diminish staff members' watchfulness. Finally, the

## TABLE 1

| | I am suicidal | | I don't know | I'm not suicidal | |
|---|---|---|---|---|---|
| | Truthful | Lying | | Truthful | Lying |
| Label | Suicidal | Manipulator | Suicidal | Nonsuicidal | Suicidal, crafty |
| Degree of risk | High | Moderate | High | Low | High |

patient who was in doubt as to his suicidality and was telling the truth was a genuine risk and required careful watching. Apparently, there is no corresponding conceptual category of the doubtful patient who is lying. These categories are summarized in table 1.

There is a tendency for the staff to underrate the suicidal potential of the manipulator and to overrate that of the doubtful patient. The reason for the former is that the manipulator's trustworthiness as informant is in question and so the staff overreacts to his version of the statement "I am suicidal." The doubtful patient again confronts the staff with a situation in which the key input needed for assignment of suicidal risk is clouded. Usually the reaction is conservative and the patient's statement is accepted at face value. In both situations the staff faces the necessity of making an important decision when the crucial (sometimes the only) data input is in a distorted form. One might consider this a problem of data quality control.

Two variables that affect staff members' evaluation of suicidality in a patient are (1) familiarity and (2) the fear of manipulation.

*Familiarity.* — The degree to which a suicidal patient is known to staff members has a great deal to do with their evaluation of suicidal risk. For example, only one of two patients admitted with approximately the same suicidal history was placed on S-status. An aide explained about the patient who was not put on S-status: "Oh, Mr. W. was in before. We know him as well as we know each other." When responsibility for an S-status case was transferred to a nurse or a nursing aide who did not know the patient, the aide exercised far more caution, and adhered more closely to formal S-status rules, than he would have had he been familiar with his new charge. Differences in care were especially marked for patients not considered high suicide risks by aides who knew them personally.

*Manipulation.* — There is a great deal of variation in the personal reaction of staff members to the threat of manipulation. Of course, no one likes to be "conned," but the amount of damage done to a staff member's ego and to his social presentation of a competent self to others seemed to vary from person to person and from ward to ward.

In making evaluations of suicidal behavior as manipulation, staff members took into consideration the timing of suicidal attempts and verbalizations. When a patient was first admitted (and wanted in badly), or was just about to be discharged (and did not want to leave), or if his VA pension benefits were about to be discontinued, or if an evaluation of his condition for purposes of determining his pension level was soon to be undertaken, there was a tendency to view any suicidal behavior as a gesture, minimizing its psychiatric import and maximizing its manipulation potential.

To take a specific example from a locked ward, Mr. W. was taken off S-status and given a laundry detail assignment. This particular assignment was selected because it allowed him to be escorted to and from the work site and it provided supervision while he was on the job. On the first day of work Mr. W. had somatic complaints. On the second day his hallucinatory voices returned telling him to commit suicide. That same day he found, hid, and then turned in to a staff member a piece of broken glass. He was promptly returned to S-status. Three staff members independently professed skepticism of the genuineness of Mr. W.'s suicidal impulses; they said he simply did not want to work. They knew he had planned to visit his sister during the summer, and they suspected that he merely wanted to take it easy until then, all the while accumulating money from his VA disability benefits.

It is possible, of course, to view the patient's need to manipulate as part of his symptom complex. In practice, however, such an evaluation is difficult for psychiatric personnel, in part because going along with the manipulation implies the possiblity that one has been fooled and thus undermines one's own presentation of competence and psychiatric omniscience. One ward psychiatrist saw staff willingness to sidestep the threat of manipulation as an unconscious evasion of treatment responsiblity. But, in practice, he found it rather difficult to reeducate the staff along these lines. Snavely (1968) found that VA hospital personnel who made conservative evaluations of suicide potential and who favored restrictive treatment had had more extensive clinical experience. He suggests that further studies of psychiatric settings as interactive social systems would elucidate the decision-making bias involved in placing patients on suicide status and keeping them under restrictive conditions.

The manipulative motivation inferred by the staff, incidentally, provides a good illustration of the ways patients are unintentionally taught "vocabularies of motive" (Mills, 1940). To give two examples, after Mr. W. had turned in the piece of broken glass, an aide asked him if he was just "conniving" to get off the laundry detail. Conniving was an understandable motive for behaving as Mr. W. had behaved. In another case, Mr. S. after a suicide attempt, was asked if he was "seeking attention." Upon being interviewed later, Mr. S. spontaneously remarked that he had not attempted suicide to gain attention, though he knew some patients did it for that reason. He had also learned that attention seeking is an understandable motivation, from the professional point of view, for suicide attempts.

Patients who are considered manipulators quickly become aware of their being so classified. They face some of the same difficulties encountered by patients categorized as uncooperative. Staff members anticipate angles in the simplest requests and may delay the granting of favors to help bring manipulative patients into line. Mr. C, for example, was noisy, attention-seeking, and manipulative. Everyone on the ward staff knew of his proclivities, as did Mr. C. himself. There was consensus that he might accidentally kill himself in a gesture (a number of staff members and even Mr. C. independently reported this possibility). The manipulative aspect had progressed to a new level — the staff must be watchful, even for gestures, and Mr. C. knew it.

*The variable of setting: unfamiliarity and manipulation in an admissions ward.* — An extreme example of unfamiliarity with patients and the resultant manipulation anxiety was found in the hospital's admissions ward, which by its very nature has problems in dealing with any patient, but especially with suicidal patients. This type of ward has a unique sorting function. Newly admitted patients are temporarily housed there until they have been evaluated and passed along either to (1) wards whose treatment approaches might be beneficial for the patient or to (2) ward psychiatrists whose training gives them a particular interest in a certain category of patient. Evaluation of suicidal potential is one aspect of the sorting function of this ward.

The element of transience profoundly affects social relationships in the admissions ward. Except for those who are repeatedly readmitted, the staff has little opportunity to develop relationships with patients. Staff members also have limited opportunities to participate in the curing and helping process, since patients are transferred from the admissions ward to other wards once the crisis and evaluation periods are over. Similarly, patients in the admissions ward seem to be more isolated from one another than in other wards. Their aloofness is reflected in their lack of interaction, their selection of spaced seating in the dayroom, and their unfamiliarity with other patients when questioned about them.

Since the admissions ward staff remains relatively constant, it is not surprising to find strong in-group solidarity among its members. They seem to become strongly dependent on one another as they seek consistency and stability in the ever-changing flow of patients. It is against this background that the following remarks should be interpreted. DKR's visits to the admissions ward were few and relatively short.

Because unfamiliarity is maximized in the admissions ward one would expect, if anything, overcautiousness in dealing with suicidal patients. Yet worries about being manipulated, combined with familiarity, dominated the admissions staff and colored responses to patients. Amid smiles and laughter, one staff member confessed to telling a newly admitted patient (who had attempted suicide by hanging himself in his garage) that he "didn't try hard enough." Another member retorted that this statement had made the patient feel bad because "the other doctor told him the best he was doing was trying." A third member responded that she had told the same patient he should have cut his throat instead! She softened the statement, however, by adding that she was not in uniform at the time. The whole interaction revealed a strong in-group solidarity and a shared conviction that the patient was not genuinely suicidal. It also suggested a lack of involvement with the patient as a human being worthy of concerned understanding. His case was "easily" handled by "therapeutic doses of antidepressants" and transfer to another ward, where "I hope they keep him long enough this time."

*Summary.* — In general, the most important bit of information available to staff members for determining suicidality seems to be the patient's honest estimate of his own tendency. Again and again, one hears statements such as "Watch Mr. S. closely; he's unpredictable.

He doesn't know if he'll try to kill himself." The following exchange between an aide and a patient is pertinent:

"Why did you cut your wrists?"

"I was feeling low. But I didn't really want to kill myself."

"Now you're bored. You want to go to the library. What if you feel low in the library? Will you tell someone or attempt suicide?"

"I don't know."

Because the patient himself was unsure, the aide saw him as a suicidal risk and kept him in the ward.

*Being on suicide status.* — The formal definition of S-status in this hospital is found in a professional information bulletin issued by the hospital's chief of staff (for the complete bulletin see Appendix A):

Precautions for Assaultive and Suicidal Patients

    (1) *Responsibility for Designation of Patients as Assaultive or Suicidal.* When the admitting physician determines that a newly admitted patient is suicidal or assaultive, he will record this information in his admission note and on doctor's orders. During hospitalization, this determination will be made by a staff physician who will also be responsible for removing the patient from assaultive or suicidal status. The removal order should be countersigned by the unit chief or Chief of the Service.

    (2) *Special Precautions.* Suicidal and homicidal patients will be assigned to a "locked" or "closed" ward. They will be provided with constant supervision by nursing personnel. A list of such patients will be maintained in the ward nurse's office, and all ward personnel will refer to this list at the beginning of their tour of duty.

Instead of following the uniform procedure outlined on paper, however, S-status is, within broad limits, a diverse range of privileges, restrictions, and experiences. The decision to place a patient on S-status, and the limits placed on his behavior while on S-status, are determined by interpersonal negotiations. That is, the flexibility within the system of formal rules governing S-status permits a great deal of social maneuvering by patient and staff. For example, a patient who had to be escorted to and from appointments was nevertheless allowed, in one office setting, to wander out into the hall, into a kitchenette, and into the bathroom unobserved. This degree of privacy granted the patient was based on staff estimates of his suicidality. The ward physician, nurses, aides, and the social worker all agreed that the patient was not actively suicidal. He was expected to come off status the next day.

For other patients, too, the term "constant supervision" is interpreted in various ways by those with immediate responsibility for the patients' safety. One reason for such flexibility is eminently practical. Owing to the limited number of nursing assistants on any shift it is impossible to assign a single staff member to a particular patient during the entire shift. The aides have other responsibilities besides keeping their eyes on suicidal patients. Second, aides find it oppressive from a human standpoint to shadow a patient wherever he goes. They want to avoid pressuring him with constant supervision. The granting of some privacy has practical aspects, too. In order to get their ward work done with minimal disruption aides find it necessary to maintain positive relationships with as many patients as possible. Anyone alienated by continuous observation is a potential source of trouble, and trouble requires the staff's attention in order to restore the status quo and prevents staff members from continuing with the necessary routine work. Obviously it pays off to allow a degree of freedom to patients considered by aides to be good risks.

Furthermore, a number of aides believe that constant watch over a patient is a reminder of suicide (i.e., a symbolic expression that the patient is expected to harm himself). "Don't press 'em," was the rule as verbalized by one NA, "as long as you know where they are."

Third, the hospital nursing education program and the ward philosophy emphasize tactics other than continuous observation for protection of suicidal patients. The tactics include removal of objects that would bring death quickly (such as razor blades, glass, and sharp-pointed objects), positioning aides so that broad areas of the ward can be observed by each of them, and checking on patients who have been out of sight for too long (in bed, in the bathroom, etc.). During training sessions the aides are given practical exercises in making the environment safe so that constant observation of an S-status patient will be unnecessary.

Finally, the aides are sensitive to daily fluctuations in a patient's mood and behavior. They feel that variations and cycles strongly determine the suicidal potential of a given patient at a given time. Thus they have some leeway in easing off in their strict vigil during good periods and can be more alert during dangerous times.

This conception of suicidality as rapidly fluctuating in response to mood and situational pressures seems broadly characteristic of the NA role group. We turn now to a more detailed description of the models of the nature of man, particularly suicidal man, which seem to underlie two role groups' attitudes toward suicide observation status and to underlie, as well, their interactions with suicidal patients.

## TWO MODELS OF SUICIDAL MAN

### Psychiatrists' Model

In suicide wards psychiatrists make their evaluations of suicide potential within a psychodynamic framework. They rely heavily on their interpretations of in-depth interviews and personal history data. The family relationships behind personality patterns of behavior and emotion are the key variables in their understanding of the patient's reaction to stress. Psychiatrists base their evaluations on a model of man which involves relatively enduring, deep-seated personality characteristics that extend essentially unchanged through time. Historical and interpretive depth are emphasized in the kind of evaluation found in the extensive literature on the psychodynamics of suicide. Suicide researchers, too, have typically accepted such a model of man. Later in this section we examine some of the reasons that psychiatrists and suicidologists seem to hold different perceptions of the suicidal man from those of nursing assistants. In our experiential analysis we outline some of the implications for the patient who is confronted with these different understandings.

### Nursing Assistants' Model

In contrast with the psychiatrists' model, the aides' model of man views the patient as more rational, flexible, and situationally responsive. Aides are likely to rely heavily on a patient's daily activity (including speech) and his recent behavior history in the hospital for their evaluations of his suicidality. A few illustrations point up this perspective.

In a group meeting of patients and nursing staff, Mr. C. presented his petition to get off of S-status. He gave his own psychodynamic interpretation of suicide in support of his request claiming that no one (particularly he himself) kills himself impulsively when angry. When the emotional upheaval has passed, after a month or so, an icy calm fills the mind. That is the time for careful planning and a serious attempt at self-destruction. The immediate response of one aide was that Mr. C., though he had certainly raised hell the past week with impulsive angry outbursts, had recently shown restraint. The implication was that if Mr. C. continued to be cooperative he would be removed from S-status. The shift was clearly from an in-depth interpretation to a description of immediate situational behavior.

In another case, the aides more than other staff members seemed to feel that the S-status patient, Mr. W., had manifested a great deal of control over his suicidal "voices." Aides recognized the existence of the voices but "they [the voices] don't bother him so much." The aides noted that when Mr. W. was feeling low it required distracting talk to bring him out of his depression.

The situational aspect of suicidal potential, according to the aides' perspective, is most revealing. They are united in holding that it is the patient's day-by-day adjustment that is important in suicidality. They believe it is possible to get a feel for how the day will go by talking with a patient in the morning or when they first come on duty and gauging their watchfulness accordingly. But since the day's events may change a patient's mood, the aides also consider it important to keep in touch with him. For example, an aide reported that Mr. S. occasionally went around giving away cigarettes from a carton he had bought, apparently in an effort to attract friends and to make peace with the world. The aide predicted, however, that someday Mr. S. would get slapped by someone to whom he had given a gift and that he could, as a result, become depressed and potentially suicidal. Again, from another aide, "We've got to watch him. He's stabilized at a low level but if there's some stress, he might [attempt suicide]." The technical word "stress" may be borrowed but the idea that reacting to events may make a person suicidal is a natural one to the aides.

The aides have reservations about the usefulness of hospital records. A man's behavior is quite changeable and flexible, but the records distort and freeze the behavior so that it conforms more closely to the long-term model employed by psychiatrists. Distortion has various sources. Nursing notes may report behavior out of context; they may report one unusual event in an otherwise quite normal day; they may reflect the nurses' fear of a big and/or hostile patient; or they may be slanted to facilitate staff members' arguments for changed medication or special status. On the other hand, a patient may go to the staff, be very frightened, and intentionally or unintentionally distort his answers, thus appearing sicker than he really is. As the aides point out, everybody feels low at times. A patient may feel good all week, but when the doctor asks him he can honestly reply that he feels bad at that moment (having become depressed only a short time before); the statement to the doctor is the one that goes into the record. Because records are snapshots, not movies, they cannot adequately depict changes that do occur in emotion, attitude, and behavior.

There undoubtedly is a sense in which hospital records, and psychiatric labeling in general, provide support for a more inflexible image of man. And, of course, records can be very misleading. One aide had this opinion about them: "I don't believe in reading too much history — especially records of six or seven years ago. People change a lot." He recalled two patients who seemed to be Frankensteins from their records, but "I never met two nicer guys." Thus records can give a novice a set for responding to a patient which is inconsistent with the flexibility necessary for dealing with him on a day-to-day basis. Aides therefore have a tendency to belittle the value of records.

Aides, like psychiatrists, learn to listen carefully to what a suicidal patient is saying. They take pride in their belief that patients talk less guardedly to them than to other staff members. They feel that because they see a patient every day and can talk to him on his own level, the patient feels freer to open up to them about what is really troubling him. "Some say you've got to be 'professional' to help a patient. Bullshit!" one aide remarked.

Refusal to talk is one of the main criteria by which aides judge the level of suicidality. "He didn't discuss his problems until today" is, for them, a communication indicating improvement in a suicidal patient. Similarly, patients who talk about past suicidal impulses are usually seen as less suicidal than those who do not. The aides interpreted Mr. W.'s revealing the razor blade he found as part of a promotional gimmick in the *Los Angeles Times* and his turning in the piece of glass he found in the laundry as positive signs leading away from suicidal danger. They contrasted Mr. W. with Mr. S., who did not talk about his feelings but in silence attempted suicide.

The sense that experienced aides may have with regard to suicide is unlikely to be described in professional journals. Compilation and formalization of their distilled experience should prove useful, at least as a basis for testing hypotheses and models.

## The Two Models Compared

The roots of the differences in perception of man seem to lie in the educational backgrounds of the two role groups and in their accessibility to limited sets of data. It is clear that both doctors and aides are using the data that are most accessible to them. The doctor has no time to live with the patients (and nursing notes are of necessity poor substitutes for daily experience), and the aide has neither the formal training for in-depth interpretation nor the authority to require the patient to produce the kind of data on which such analysis can be made. Most researchers, like psychiatrists, have not taken the time to live alongside mental patients; the few who have (see below) were uniformly impressed by the situational effects on behavior and mood in psychiatric settings and the flexibility in patients' response's to situational pressures over time.

It is no wonder that the two role groups develop divergent evaluations of the same patient's suicidal potential. It is not unusual for an NA to say, "Mr. X. could have come off S-status two weeks ago," given the differences in perspective. Thus far, in our experience, the psychiatrist's judgment has consistently been the more conservative (see Snavely, 1968). This conclusion is not surprising in view of the doctor's formal responsibility and his implicit assumptions about enduring psychodynamic personality patterns.

We must emphasize, however, that the data-gathering procedures of the two role groups share one feature in common: listening to the patient. The process of listening implies paying full attention to what the patient is saying so as to pick up nuances and subtle meanings. Interpretations of the verbalizations may diverge, but the importance of listening is evident in the social operations of both groups.

Brief contact with ward social workers suggests that they interpret suicidality in a more psychodynamic framework than do the aides, but they also rely heavily on what might be called "extra-hospital situational stress" in determining suicidality. Since information about financial problems, pending divorce, family pressures, and so forth is particularly accessible to the social worker, it is not surprising that such data are considered important.

It is necessary that the data available to each role group be passed on to the others, and to some degree they are. Each group is generally aware of the others' evaluations (at least doctor-aide and doctor – social worker exchanges of information are noticeable). Nevertheless, if one's evaluative procedures minimize the usefulness of others' data and give preference to one's own data, the exchange of data is little more than the superficial communication of accessory information.

## S-STATUS PATIENTS

### Perspectives of Two Patients

1. Mr. S. described this VA hospital as a "good place" compared with other hospitals. The term "good" was not assigned on the basis of the hospital's therapeutic opportunities but on the basis of (1) the number and kinds of recreational opportunities provided and (2) the food. Mr. S saw the disadvantage of being on S-status in much the same light: there were no extra privileges. Here, as when talking with other patients, the particular disadvantages of being on S-status were hard to separate from those associated with being in a locked ward and having no privilege card, restrictions that accompanied S-status but accompanied other statuses as well (e.g.,assaultive patients).

Concerning other patients, Mr. S. remarked that most of them were "pretty far gone" or they were just waiting to get out. The result was that patients left one another pretty much alone. The other patients knew that Mr. S. was on S-status, but he felt that their knowledge neither helped nor hindered his making friends among them.

In passing, it is interesting to note that Mr. S. used "craziness" as a rationale for his suicide attempt. He said he didn't want to die in his last attempt, he didn't want to hurt himself, he didn't want attention; he just went out of his mind, "flipped out," and did it. This explanation seemed to be all that he needed at the moment; that is, he was satisfied with it.

2. Mr. B. was a Negro patient on S-status. He felt caged by the restrictions of status. He threatened to blow up if he was not placed in an open ward soon. He didn't like "to have to ask for a match." He didn't want people to cater to his "every little need." He wanted "medical" treatment. Mr. B. was quite knowledgeable about the conditions of S-status. He knew that he needed two signatures to get off the status. He knew that people on S-status were assigned beds by the door so that they could be watched. And he knew that at night "they come in and check every fifteen minutes. I just watch 'em. Then I get up and go in the dayroom so they can really keep an eye on me in the light." He knew "they are looking over my shoulder" but he pretended not to notice. Sometimes it bothered him, but at such times he got up and walked around. "I don't let on. I just smile."

There was good rapport between this patient and the Negro aides. There was no favoritism or preferential treatment. Rather, the patient and the aides seemed to share an experience base for understanding each other.

Mr. B. shared a freedom fantasy with many other patients on S-status. The fantasy was the belief that the patient has numerous ways to kill himself while on S-status if he really wants to. When pinned down and willing to talk about these generalized ways to kill oneself, one S-status patient actually specified a way. He could, he said, rig wire leads to a light socket and electrocute himself. One aide considered it possible to get a jolt from such a setup but felt that the shock would not be enough to kill a person unless he had a weak heart. At any rate, we first considered the "hundreds of ways" (the large majority of them vague and/or unspecified) to be a device to create the illusion of freedom in an area where, in fact, the S-status patient had little freedom. Later we reversed our position on this matter as a result of our experiential research findings. As a patient, DKR discovered ample time, opportunity, and means to kill himself while on S-status (see pp. 182-183).

## Four Suicidal Patients from Staff Perspectives

1. Miss M. was very quiet. She spent a lot of time lying down. She wished she were dead and was extremely depressed. For the moment she lacked energy to kill herself, but she would become a danger to herself when she became more active. There was wide agreement among staff role groups on this type of S-status patient.

2. Mr. C. was noisy, attention-seeking, and manipulative. Everyone, including Mr. C., was aware of these characteristics. There was also consensus that he might accidentally kill himself in a gesture. (All staff members — and Mr. C. himself — independently informed us of this possibility.) If pushed by the staff, if not taken seriously in his threats, he might also commit suicide to "show us." There was a discrepancy, however, between physician and aides in evaluating the suicide potential of this patient. The aides emphasized the immediate manipulative advantages of Mr. C.'s social posture and so minimized his suicidality except under the circumstances described above.

3. Mr. W. was quiet and coherent. He heard voices and, when asked, was willing to talk about the voices. With emotional flatness he stated that the voices told him to kill himself. Staff and patients agreed tht Mr. W., if given the opportunity, would kill himself while under the influence of the voices. Mr. W. was not a behavior problem in the ward. Nevertheless, he was a most upsetting patient because the staff had no effective control over the voices he claimed to hear.

4. Mr. K., too, was aware that he was on S-status. Some patients respond to their new status by playing games with the aides, hiding and generally creating a disturbance. Mr. K., however, seemed rather to settle down under the protective watchfulness, even to the point of informing staff members of his whereabouts and his destination. Mr. K. told the aide who escorted him to the psychologist's office that he came every month for a lithium study evaluation, sidestepping the acute interpersonal upset that had brought about his admission to the hospital. But the aide knew Mr. K.'s history of a recent suicide attempt and he knew that Mr. K. was on S-status, and Mr. K. knew that the aide was aware of these conditions. Similarly, Mr. K. introduced himself to us as a driver education teacher and physical education teacher at a local college. In fact, he had been a custodian at the college for fifteen years. We learned that Mr. K. also showed the scars from his suicide to other patients in an effort, apparently, to gain prestige. The need for self-image support from his environment led Mr. K. to present himself as normal and distinguished to one audience, the aides and the researcher, and to present himself as dangerous and distinguished to another audience, the patients.

## Getting Off Suicide Status

" 'Never tell a doctor that you're well,' said one patient. 'He won't believe you. That's called a 'flight into health.' Tell him you're still sick, but you're feeling a lot better. That's called insight.' 'You've got to be sick and acknowledge that you're sick,' says Rosenhan, 'to be considered well enough to be discharged'" (*Newsweek*, January 29, 1973, p. 47).

In our experiential research we look at some of the ways by which a patient can present an image that will permit his removal from S-status. Such behaviors and attitudes as maintaining a neat and clean appearance, socializing, insightful and hopeful talk about problems, cooperativeness in ward routine, future planning, active work, and avoidance of behavioral cues to suicide will ultimately result in removal from S-status.

Negotiation between doctor and patient sometimes takes place before the doctor will consider allowing a patient to go off status. One example of this procedure produced a kind of contract between therapist and patient. The goals of the two parties were simply that the patient wanted to get off S-status and the doctor needed assurance that (1) suicidal desires were gone and (2) when and if they returned, the patient would notify him. Both doctor and patient seemed to be aware of the underlying assumption of honesty and trust on both sides. Note the following interactions:

"So you want to go out on a weekend pass?"

"Yes."

"Have you given up your suicidal ideas?"

"No."

"Then I can't let you go out on pass, can I?"

"What do you want me to do, lie to you?"

Mr. C. drove a hard bargain during negotiations for his removal from S-status. The doctor tried to elicit the usual promise that the patient would inform him if suicidal thoughts returned:

"Did I tell you before?"

"No."

"Then I can't promise I will next time — but I'll *try*."

Mr. W. promised to tell the doctor if the voices he was hearing began to tell him to kill himself. But in Mr. W.'s case, as noted before, the staff was uneasy about the unpredictability of the voices. Furthermore, a new stress (breakup with his fiancée) was looming on the horizon. Therefore, since the element of trust could not be relied upon, Mr. W. remained on S-status.

Mr. C. remarked spontaneously that he "figured the doctor trusts me." The doctor had taken him off S-status, put him in an open ward, and allowed him to visist his home in the afternoons with self-medication. Mr. C. was particularly proud of the confidence shown by permitting him to administer his own medication. The doctors trust was promoting self-confidence and self-trust in this patient and was putting him on a path toward development of a self worth keeping alive. As pointed out earlier, the psychiatrist remains one of society's authorized experts in these matters.

The element of trust is displayed and socially reinforced in a ward public ritual called special staffing. At a special staff meeting which decided to grant a patient's request to be removed from S-status the following affirmations were elicited from the patient:

"Suppose the idea to kill yourself comes back, what would you do?"

"I'd talk to you."

"Later in the same meeting the patient was asked about a confrontation with his girl friend.

"If it does make you feel bad, you'll tell me about it?"

"Yes."

"This question-and-answer routine is typical of the public commitment required before a patient is removed from S-status. Violating the trust cannot be justified later by claiming that no such agreement was contracted, since witnesses are present at the public ritual.

Traditional anthropological techniques of participant observation, interviewing, and examination of written records allow some insight into the social meaning of suicide observation status in this VA neuropsychiatric hospital ward. Our perspective as outsiders permitted us to map out the boundaries of reality in this setting and to note some of the taken-for-granted aspects of the structured system. In considering what S-status involved, we did not merely take as given the formal security measures for suicidal patients; rather, we looked at the ways patients were observed and protected while on status. And as we looked, we asked questions, often naive ones, sometimes thought-provoking ones for the staff. When our short research period was over, we presented interim reports to the ward staff. Discussion of our tentative findings prompted staff members to explore with one another their differing perspectives of man, suicide, and suicide observation status.

But we had glimpsed only part of the picture. In the process of conducting our research we had framed still other questions that seemed unanswerable by means of the tactics employed before. We needed an inside perspective on S-status. We needed to be privy to the experience of being suicidal and being watched, being powerless yet being the center of someone's attention. There was only one way for us to obtain the quality of data we believed necessary. That way was to become "suicidal," to be admitted to a psychiatric hospital, and to be placed on suicide observation status.

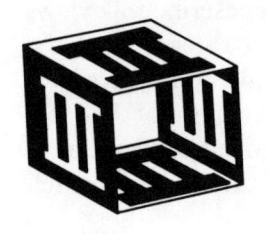

# THE TACTIC OF EXPERIENTIAL RESEARCH — AN INSIDER'S PERSPECTIVE

Suicide is both a personal and a social act. In understanding a suicidal event we cannot afford to ignore either the personal perspective or the social context in which the event takes place. While few would argue with the above statement, suicidologists' tactics for studying these influences have been primarily reconstructive. By "reconstructive" we mean that researchers have had to try to piece together after the fact the psychological and social elements that had precipitated a suicidal act. Through interviews, suicide notes, and other documents they have sought to reconstruct the antecedents of suicide for individuals or for statistical groups. Few clinicians have been able to investigate the social world in which their suicidal patients operate, except through the filter of the patients' recollections. In other words, suicide research (not unlike archaeology) has traditionally operated under the handicap of temporal and spatial distance from the set of phenomena under study.

Experiential research, on the other hand, allows direct and immediate observation of the interacting social and personal worlds of the suicidal person. The researcher is assured of being present and of being prepared to observe critical data. He is privy to the thoughts and associations of his subject. His subject is trained to observe and report on inner and outer events. Preparations can be made beforehand for obtaining from others their perspectives on the subject's suicidality. In only one way can these ideal research conditions be assured: the researcher and the subject must be the same person. Experiential research in suicide requires the investigator to adopt a suicidal identity and to immerse himself in a social milieu in which he is perceived to be suicidal.

33

There has been a tradition in anthropology to describe folk views of life as well as to order data by the analytical categories of the researcher. Within the past decade more formal analytic tactics have been developed for such subdisciplines as ethnosemantics, ethnocognitive analysis, and ethnomethodology. These refined tactics aim at the formal description of the linguistic-cognitive categories in which one's informants organize their world.

A few researchers have used themselves as informants; for example, the method has proven useful in analyzing the domain of American-English kinship terms. An introspective starting point seems justifiable in this instance because one's own categories can presumably be validated, to some extent, by investigation of the categories of other native American-English speakers. The advantages of being one's own informant are obvious. Practical considerations include convenience, cost, motivation, and so forth. Theoretically, although self-deception remains a hazard (a problem encountered in all research, of course), the possibilities of mistakes in communication and of deception between the researcher and a separate informant are eliminated. Not all research problems, however, have scientifically trained participants who can and will call on their own experience to become expert informants. The usual remedy is to find informants/interviewees who can and will offer information to the researcher.

Often the suicidal patient who is experiencing social pressures of one kind or another is not trained to analyze the interpersonal origins of the pressures he is experiencing and to report systematically their effects on his psychological state. The traditional participant-observer anthropologist, who may be aware of what appear to be impingements of the social milieu on the psychological functioning of a suicidal patient, finds it awkward to interrupt an interaction to inquire of a patient how it is affecting him. The point is simply that one who wishes to study the interaction of society, culture, and the individual need not stand at a distance to do so. He can do the studying from the inside in a process called experiential research. The process includes adopting the identities of various persons, living in the settings associated with these persons' roles, and reporting his observations of what occurs within him and outside him. In a sense, such a researcher makes himself into his own expert informant.

The idea is hardly a new one. The impulse behind the legendary king who periodically donned peasant dress and mingled with his subjects to keep abreast of popular opinion is closely related to our own tactical interests. In the social sciences a number of researchers have put on patient uniforms and lived in psychiatric wards (Caudill, 1958; Goldman et al., 1970; Deane, 1961). We have focused a bit more carefully, perhaps, on the methodology of experiential research, and we have added refinements by checking on the reliability and validity of our findings. But our aim remains the same as that of other researchers: to gain insight into a social world by experiencing it. A trained observer's ability to look at both his environment and his own reactions to that environment is a potentially useful tool in social science research. The interface between his social milieu and his psychological functioning is explored directly by the very psychosocial being in which these vectors merge.

Ours is not the only study in which experiential research techniques have been employed. Caudill (1958), Deane (1961), Reynolds (1969), and Rockwell (1971) have demonstrated the usefulness of such techniques in providing insights and training experiences. The roots of experiential research lie in phenomenology, psychodrama, and role playing, and in the symbolic interactionism of sociology. Its aim is to describe social and individual realities and the ways in which these realities interrelate. The major test of this technique has been in mental hospitals, possibly because in that setting the social realities of staff role groups and the individual realities of mental patients come into sharp perspective.

The method repeatedly asks two equally weighted questions: "What seems to be going on within me?" and "What seems to be going on within the individuals and collections of individuals around me?" The researcher oscillates from introspection to observation to participation. Experiential research differs significantly from the participation-observation technique of traditional anthropological work. Anthropologists usually focus on the persons under study. Personal insights may be offered incidentally (e.g., Bowen, 1954; Chagnon, 1968), and attention may be paid to the role of the anthropologist in affecting the data he gathers and to the effects of fieldwork on him. Nevertheless, despite Margaret Mead's claims that the anthropologist is his own most sensitive instrument, few anthropological attempts have been made to legitimate the study of the convergence of anthropologist and cultural system. Anthropologists seem to be either other-conscious or self-conscious, but rarely both, and even then they fail to use the two "facings" simultaneously to gain insight into individual-in-culture problems.

Moreover, rather than occupying or creating a role of outsider-observer, the experiential researcher exists within the system in a role that is already an accepted feature of that system. In this instance he is seen as a patient, not as a nonmember of the system who has entered it for the purpose of investigating some issue or problem. His presence therefore causes less disruption to the social system than does the intrusion of a foreigner.

## Advantages of Experiential Research

The writings based on experiential research have proven to be rich in detail, providing data that make a personal impact on the reader. The reader finds himself invited to test the researcher's observations against his own experience. To some extent we pursue this course with all research writings and with literary productions as well, yet the reality-grounded nature of experiential research yields a markedly readable output.

As a hypothesis-generating device this method is among the best (Caudill et al., 1952), partly because the investigator is positioned in an unfamiliar role that forces him to ask questions and study interrelationships among variables in order to survive and function in that role. Because the hypotheses are firmly grounded in experiential reality, they cannot be formulated on the remote abstract level where untestability, dilution, or distortion prevails.

A further advantage of experiential research is the almost immediate applicability of results. In much social science research a major translation must take place to make the findings pragmatically useful. Experiential research operates so close to the level of the participants that many of the insights find immediate acceptance and adoption.

Philosophically, there is clarity in experiential research. It is overtly perception-oriented research; that is, it admits openly that findings have been filtered through the experience-distorted perceptions of the researcher. Although all research faces the same predicament, self-awareness in experiential research focuses attention on the researcher's biases and requires methodological efforts to account for their effects on the research. The same is not always true of other forms of research, despite the lip service given to the underlying possibilities of experimenter distortion.

Finally, the era we live in is becoming more sympathetic to the need to recognize experiential knowledge and integrate it into our armamentarium for understanding man. With countless arguments from LSD users, black Americans, Vietnam veterans, and others that "You can't really know what it's like if you haven't experienced it," there is a clear need to begin to assimilate this sort of knowledge into a useful framework.

### Problems of Experiential Research

The major theoretical problems of experiential research lie in the areas of replicability and generalizability. These problems, however, are not insurmountable, as we shall see. But the reports coming from experiential researchers are fundamentally personal accounts of experiences in particular settings. It is impossible to replicate these experiences even in the limited sense that any research finding can be replicated. The instrument (i.e., the investigator) changes and cannot be duplicated, and the unique social setting evolves. Supplemental information of another type is necessary to evaluate validity, reliability, and generalizability of findings.

Another problem is that of time and effort commitment. Experiential research requires living in over a considerable period of time. To find investigators who are willing to devote a large block of time to this kind of research may pose a problem. The difficulty is exaggerated by the potential danger to one's physical person and psyche. In our study, for example, "David Kent" faced the dangers of playing a role of depression, of the potential effects of medication, and of the possibility of communication difficulties should he wish to terminate the study abruptly. Assuming a stigmatized role such as that of a mental patient may be enlightening in many ways, but it is not pleasant. One is likely to be comfortable in the familiar and respected role of teacher, researcher, therapist, or administrator, or in a combination of these roles. It is difficult to find people with both adequate training and sufficient motivation to engage in research of the type we are describing.

In order to overcome some of the difficulties inherent in so subjective a method of research, we have gathered supplemental information and have utilized additional data-perspective sources in our subsequent research. Two obvious plans suggested themselves: (1) simultaneously placing more than one experiential researcher in a single social setting, occupying the same role class, and (2) placing the same researcher in several roles in several settings. Both possibilities gave us a reference point for "calibrating" the research instrument: (*a*) by comparing its "readings" with those of another instrument and (*b*) by examining its readings in several situations for systematic commonalities and gaps. (These refinements in method will be reported in a forthcoming publication on suicidal behavior in aftercare facilities.)

Another way to detect bias is to make a systematic effort to list conscious expectations of the researcher prior to entering the setting. If he finds no more than he expected to find, one may entertain reasonable doubts as to the generalizability of his results (not necessarily their validity), given his set and its associated behavior. But when unexpected and contraexpected results appear as well, one can feel somewhat more comfortable with the outcome of the research.

In our study, naively taken and blindly scored psychological tests, psychophysiological changes, introspective accounts (including unexpected material judged by experts as possessing validity), and recorded observations by hospital personnel were convincing testimonies to the genuineness and typicality of the depression David Kent was feeling. Also, in our study, we conducted subsequent interviews and discussion meetings with various ward groups in order to assess their views of Kent. We uncovered interesting information on the ways he was like or unlike other depressed, suicidal patients. Such postmortem analysis, however, embodied the danger of selective memory because by that time staff members were aware of David Kent's other identity. Fortunately, the official hospital records of Kent's hospitalization provided an unchanging standard for evaluating the staff members' postexperience analyses.

In the long run one can never assess the reality of this type of personal experience. Some aspects of experience are so seriously distorted when translated into language forms that perhaps a better strategy is to communicate the means by which the experience was achieved and allow the reader to experience those events (or similar events) himself, a kind of "experiential operationalism." Yet, given the researcher's social science background for perceiving and conceptually locating his experiences, we feel that much can be translated into usable social science data.

*Ethics of Experiential Research*

The problem of ethics enters into experiential research. In at least two studies (Barry, 1971; Caudill, 1958) the research identity of the investigator was not known to staff members until after the patient had been discharged. Deception is not always necessary, but if an investigator is likely to be treated differently should his alternate identity be known, concealing that identity is preferable to revealing it. There are several ways of handling the ethical problem. In our study, staff members were told that a researcher-patient would pass through their ward sometime within the next twelve months. They did not know which patient it would be or exactly when he would make his appearance. After the project had ended every staff member was contacted individually or in a group. Aid and support for this particular experiment were enlisted from everybody (after initial defensiveness or anger on the part of some personnel) through (1) explanation of the project's goals; (2) utilization of staff members' perspectives to help interpret Kent's recordings of events (thus shifting their role from "subjects of investigation" to "investigators"); (3) offering findings that could be used to make the ward a more livable place for all concerned; and (4) getting to know (or to reknow in a new context) staff members on an informal basis, meanwhile communicating a nondistant, noncritical, nonthreatening personal posture.

Individuals and social settings vary. We were fortunate in having the staff members accept the project beforehand on the basis of the assurances of their respected unit chief. In other situations it may be necessary to give more details before personnel will accept the study. Researchers may be rejected because of rigidity, hostility of the staff, or the inability of the investigators to win trust and confidence from others. As in all research, means and ends must be examined carefully so that the research goals are not achieved at the expense of undermining the freedom and trust of the other participating persons. It is taken for granted that the researcher himself will adopt his new identity without coercion and in full awareness of the risks involved. In our study, for example, the anthropologist-investigator had to sign a release absolving the Veterans Administration of responsibility should he suffer any negative or harmful effects.

The identity of the particular ward is not revealed here even though the hospital has undergone considerable change since our research was conducted and the ward no longer exists as a single administrative unit. The area the ward formerly occupied has been subdivided into specialty units, and staff and patients have been assigned to other wards.

## Why Experiential Research for This Particular Problem?

There are a number of alternate research approaches reported in the literature which attempt to deal with some of the issues of our study. In one approach, reported by Levinson and Gallagher (1964), a period of observation and interviewing led to the construction of a questionnaire which was administered to a sample of 100 patients. By this means the authors aimed at eliciting the patients' own conceptions of their patienthood. Such an approach, however, must be evaluated in the light of the findings of Braginsky et al. (1969), who demonstrated that patients may respond to questionnaires in terms of the impression they wish to convey to authority figures in order to achieve certain perfectly rational goals.

In another approach (Hyde, 1955), several group discussions about the life of patients were recorded. The groups were composed primarily of hospital attendants and the patients' experiences are described as seen through the eyes of psychiatric aides. This approach has obvious advantages and shortcomings.

In yet another research approach found in the literature patients or ex-patients describe life as it is lived in an NP hospital. In fictionalized or autobiographical form (Kesey, 1962; Kaplan, 1964; Boisen, 1960; and Peters, 1949), these sources provide perhaps the finest, richest description of the patient's world. The writers of such accounts, however, are a very select subsample of the patient population. Furthermore, none of the books cited was written about the experience of admission to suicide status at a VA neuropsychiatric hospital — the specific research problem at hand.

Finally, various combinations of participant observation have characterized most of the sociological and anthropological work on hospital wards. Salisbury (1962) sought to establish a "new type of role not formally recognized on the ward" (p. 4). This role was intended to minimize identification with any other existing role group. In exchange for acceptance and information, the observer acted as an alternative communication channel, a source of information, a runner of errands, and generally as a helpful service person.

He discovered that, over time, he was perceived as a member of one or another of the role groups commonly found in the wards; in particular, he found himself treated as a patient, although differences seemed to be noted (e.g., he had ward keys) and behaviors adjusted accordingly. Salisbury noted his own bias toward perceiving ward events as a patient, especially when he compared his interpretations of ward procedures with those of a sociologist who had worked more with attendants at the same hospital. Goffman (1961a) passed himself off as a recreation assistant, living with patients during the daytime, "avoiding sociable contact with the staff and the carrying of a key" (p. 9). He sought to describe the patient's perspective on his institutional situation.

Sudnow (1967), in a study of the social interactions and shared meanings surrounding death and dying in two hospitals, used formal and informal interviewing and observation to gather his data. He was asked to wear a resident's lab coat at one hospital, an attire that proved to have both advantages and disadvantages for his research. Being taken as a resident saved him from being questioned about his presence and his purposes, but with the assumed authority came inferred responsibility and requests from patients and their families. One suspects also that the authority associated with the resident's role created a social distance between Sudnow and the patients which limited the flow of information crucial to this kind of study. Sudnow unobtrusively took notes and made recordings which he later wrote up. He found concealed wireless and tape recordings to be almost useless because of the high background noise within the hospital.

Caudill and Stainbrook (1954) used interviews, observation, and verbatim recordings without participation in the patient role. As he later reported, however, Caudill (1958) found that his formal role as an anthropologist helping in the activities program soon came to be perceived differently by different role groups in the wards. Evidently, it is not a simple matter to establish the precise role identity desired.

The research approach most like our own is discussed by Fritz Redlich in the foreword to Caudill's book (1958) and is treated in detail in Caudill et al. (1952). Since it bears directly on what we call experiential research, its relative merits and disadvantages must be examined. Caudill spent two months as a patient in a small psychiatric ward. Redlich (in Caudill, 1958, pp. 8-9) describes the disadvantages he perceived in the method: the observer identifies with patients and ceases to observe them objectively; ethical problems face the researchers; the research is psychologically difficult for the observer and, subsequently, for the staff.

Caudill (1958, pp. 14-15) presents a somewhat more balanced perspective, noting the discomfort associated with the deception, the strain of maintaining his alternate identity, and the one-sidedness of his perceptions. On the other hand, he comments here and elsewhere (Caudill et al., 1952) on the richness of the data, the discovery of new problems and issues to be researched by other methods, his heightened sensitivity to patients' experiencing of time and boredom, their reactions to staff authority, and so forth.

The issues raised by Caudill and Redlich were faced squarely in our research. The possibility of arousing negative responses among staff and patients was anticipated and balanced against the insights such a study would give into a VA hospital ward's handling of suicidal patients. The psychological consequences for the observer were weighed against his desire to undertake the study, his estimate of the potential benefit it might have for patients, and his prior training and experience. These issues were far from simple, but in our estimation the balance tipped heavily toward the usefulness of the undertaking.

In summary, the literature contains an array of research tactics employed in the study of psychiatric wards. There seems to be general consensus that assuming the role of patient results in identification with the role and adoption of the patient world view (see also Riley, 1963, p. 72). This is precisely the area in which study is essential because there is little systematic information about and much practical import in the impact of suicide observation status on the patient.

It is not surprising that the experiential researcher strongly identifies with the role group of which he becomes a member. His bias is obvious: How well does the system meet his needs and those of his fellows? But as he oscillates back and forth between identities and as he receives input from management and staff members during post-hospital debriefing sessions, the viewpoints from which he observes and makes sense of the social system (and his functioning within it) increase in number and variety.

Each alternative means of investigation has its own limitations and biases. Researchers are particularly sensitive to the systematic

and purposive distorting of information fed to the outside participant-observer (e.g., Salisbury, 1962); to the lack of checks on the
biases of patients who give accounts of their hospital experiences
(e.g., Kaplan, 1964; Peters, 1949); to distortions caused by the
artificiality of settings in which data are obtained by interviewing
individuals or recording focused group discussions (e.g., Hyde, 1955);
and to literary simplification and overstatement in novels based on
personal experience (e.g., Kesey, 1962; Green, 1964). Whenever a
research problem demands the dual bias of a social scientist seeing a
particular aspect of the world through the eyes of a member of a
particular role group, then experiential research may well be the
most suitable method. Through such research one more multifaceted
interface between society and the individual can be charted.

## Experiential Research of Others

Experiential research has been used sparingly in psychological and
psychiatric research. Although it is hard to find reports specifically
concerned with suicide, we did find accounts of experiences of
patienthood in neuropsychiatric hospitals. The personalized aspect of
experiential research receives appropriate emphasis, but admittedly it
is difficult to generalize.

Generalization may be possible after a sufficient number of
experiential studies have been conducted and reported. Within the
past twenty years a number of reports have emerged dealing with the
experiences of investigators living in as patients in psychiatric hospitals. They reveal an impressive degree of consistency despite differences in academic background, varying kinds of hospitals and wards,
and the range of openness of the researchers in reporting their
alternate identity to others in the setting. Some researchers took
medication; others did not. Some were known to patients on the
ward before the live-in period; others were not. Some were mistakenly taken to be patients; others were not. The ward stay was as
short as a day (Mueller and Sherman, 1969) and as long as two
months (Rosenhan, 1973). The background and purposes of the
studies varied. Yet, despite differences in procedure and purpose, the
researchers' observations and experiences were remarkably similar.

What the consistency of results seems to mean is that situationally imposed pressures in many psychiatric institutions are sufficiently strong to provide highly similar experiences despite all sorts

of divergencies in background variables. The psychiatric hospital is clearly an extreme example of strong influence within the milieu, but it lends support to a perspective of human functioning which emphasizes man's situational flexibility, that is, his tendency to act and respond in situationally determined similar ways regardless of personality structure, personal-historical events, and formal educational background.

Nine accounts of attempts to learn the perspectives of mental hospital patients by temporary immersion in psychiatric patient life are reviewed in detail. These studies were carried out by nurses (Mueller and Sherman, 1969), halfway house volunteers (Wellmet Project Proposal, 1969), a sociologist (Deane, 1961), a psychiatrist (Rockwell, 1971), several psychologists (Goldman et al., 1970; Weitz, 1972; and Rosenhan, 1973), an anthropologist (Caudill, 1958; Caudill et al., 1952), and a journalist (Barry, 1971). Since we came across these references (i.e., all but Caudill's study) only after our own live-in research was completed, the similarities between our conclusions and those of others do not mean that we were influenced by the experiences of others.

1. *Nurses* (Mueller and Sherman, 1969). – Newly appointed nurses at the VA Hospital in Downey, Illinois, were invited to spend a day in the patient role as part of their orientation. Mueller and Sherman collected summaries of impressions from thirty nurses who had elected to spend eight hours in the closed ward for women.

The nurses, dressed in street clothes with valuables removed, were admitted to wards in units other than their own. They were identified to the patients as nurses visiting the ward. Many nurses were anxious about the proposed role shift and all felt some discomfort while living as patients.

The nurse-observers found that the psychiatric patient is exposed to demeaning cues from others, particularly staff members. These cues undermine the sense of self-worth in patients, who become withdrawn, form coalitions for identity protection, are uncooperative with ward personnel, and exhibit suicidal behavior. Examples of improper staff conduct are reported by Mueller and Sherman: "Some nurses sense and write of the lack of respect some staff members unconsciously convey to patients. When one nurse attended a patients' singing group, the therapist requested a solo from someone in the group. Another patient suggested that the newcomer sing. The therapist was condescending while asking the nurse about her previous experience in singing before groups, but he insisted that she sing now. Later that day, after discovering he had not been talking to a patient, he apologized and said, 'I didn't realize you were a nurse!' " "The doctor's rounds seemed very impersonal and impressed me as an 'I don't really care' attitude." "I notice personnel speak to patients in a rather brisk, curt manner at times." "As a patient I just felt degraded somehow." This demeaning aspect of hospital life is exaggerated by the frequency with which events over which the patient has no control happen to him: "All [the nurses] commented on the admission shower, saying they were taken to shower rooms and their clothes removed and they didn't know what was happening. I think this situation impressed upon me the fact of having activities in which patients can have some voice instead of already being planned for them." '

The regimentation of institutional life attacks one's self-concept: "I felt inferior to the people with keys and a little degraded at the thought of being herded in a group wherever we went." "Another ward routine that to me would become annoying is the lining up of patients to go on their details and excursions. I can't put it into words or express it clearly as I can't quite understand my feeling about it, but somehow this too is undignified." "I had the feeling of being a prisoner as we walked through the tramway in single file." "Also I felt a lack of responsibility for my behavior for we were told what to do and led from one activity to another." "My second reaction was that all decisions would be made by someone else. Not the small ones, but the larger ones that we are used to making, and somehow this makes a person lose some of their confidence in themselves."

Being locked in and being dependent on others for even minor satisfactions can undermine one's self-confidence: "What's it like to be on the other side of a locked door, to be deprived of your keys, to depend on someone else for everything you want or need?" "Having to ask for a light for each cigarette probably curtailed the number of cigarettes I smoked during the day." The nurse who made this last statement traded self-deprivation for self-esteem.

The most common dissatisfactions expressed by the nurses were connected with the facilities the patients had to use; the lack of privacy in the toilets was particularly humiliating. "One of the most uncomfortable experiences I had during the day was when I used the patients' lavatory. There were no screens in use and every time someone opened the door, you were exposed to a good share of the dayroom." "I did not go to the bathroom all day long as I do not need an audience. I don't see how the patients do it." The toilets were not the only disturbing aspect of the physical environment. "One patient commented that hospital clothes are very demoralizing and that the bars on the windows frightened them the first few days." "Another thing that bothered me was the smoke-filled day-room." ". . . the gym suit wasn't bad but the shoes or slippers I wore seemed rather dirty and repulsive but this must be how many patients feel so I went ahead."

Possessions that were functional as well as meaningful in symbol-izing one's identity are taken from the patient. Several nurses men-tioned the frustration of being deprived of their keys. Another wrote: "The thing that bothered me most during the day was that I did not have my watch. This small personal item I missed more than anything." The effects of patienthood on a person's sense of time are discussed in more detail later, but in having her watch taken away, the nurse lost more than a timepiece; she lost a "personal item." "Already I was beginning to feel with longing the loss of my 'worldly possessions' as keys, uniform, and cap."

When institutional routines are paramount the individual needs of patients must be deferred. Several nurses had the disquieting experience of having to wait for a needed object. "Several times I had to ask the aide for the cards. I probably would have given up after the third time except that I was desperate for something to keep me occupied." "I asked a nursing assistant to ask the nurse if I could have an APC, but the nurse had gone to a meeting — I had to wait. . . . Now I'll be able to understand demands of a patient who is constantly asking for just a plain APC for headaches."

What were the feelings of some of the nurses as they encountered "crazy people," strangers who were sometimes loud, sometimes violent, sometimes grossly irrational? "There were several hyper-active patients and though this did not bother me, I felt that it would have affected me if I had to listen to it day after day." "There were several patients who were quite talkative, using loud, unacceptable language. This made me quite uncomfortable and from my observa-tions also disturbed some of the less aggressive patients." "There were several times that I was frightened by the actions of the other patients, even with some knowledge of psychiatric conditions. How do the others feel with no inner knowledge?" "It is very depressing and revolting to continually watch some of the actions of the very sick patients. I can see how a person could become worse just by being in the same room with some of the other ones."

Despite the upsetting mannerisms of some patients, the newly admitted patient-nurse felt a strong need to be recognized, to be accepted, by her fellow patients. But in this strange place, in the newcomer's role, many found themselves ignored, isolated, and lonely. "The patients for the most part ignored me, much as they might a new patient." "No one had spoken to me since I had entered the dayroom. I was beginning to feel like a stick of furniture, or maybe I should say, I felt transparent since no one seemed to see me or know that I was there. Someone had started a jigsaw puzzle and left it unfinished. I began to work on it. After ten minutes or so a patient came and asked if I was a new patient. I felt like yelling with joy. At last someone had spoken to me. After she came up others began drifting over. One sat down to help me with the puzzle. I then began to feel like I was a real visible human. . . . I will long remember the boredom and the loneliness I experienced during my day as a patient." "While sitting there I kept wondering or rather hoping someone would come up and say something." "Somehow, I felt very lonely most of that time because I was ignored by all of the patients except 'Wilma.' . . . The nursing assistants and the student nurses, I am sure, were aware of who I was but none of them introduced themselves." "People who were not working on this ward just look through the patients like they didn't even see them!"

The nurses experienced perceptual and value changes even in the relatively short time of their hospital stay. The most common change was in the sense of time passing, a perceptual change closely related to the lack of activity and to the feeling of boredom associated with patient life. "One thing that impressed me was the boredom of just staying on a locked ward." "At long intervals there weren't many activities . . . and just sitting in the dayroom made me a bit tense and nervous and a little uncomfortable." "I felt and think the patients also feel, that the time really drags with only T.V., magazines, etc. to occupy their mornings. . . . All seemed to enjoy this activity period which passed very quickly and expressed regret at returning to the ward with its relative inactivity." "The thing that impressed me most about the whole day was the lack of something to do." "I decided, I can't take this, I am going to ask to leave. I looked at the clock and much to my amazement I had been there exactly fifteen minutes."

"I felt uncomfortable at having no purpose except to sit and exist." "I kept watch on the clock and it seemed to stand still." "I kept checking my watch. . . . First I checked my watch, then the clock, then read a little. Time just stood still."

Unusual feelings and disorientation bothered some of the nurses. "When I entered the dayroom, a feeling of confusion and strangeness crept over me." "I was unprepared for the feelings of complete apathy that I felt, simply by becoming a part of the ward situation. Here I was, supposedly of sound and alert mind and body and I felt totally immune to anything life had to offer me here."

In so short a period identities began to shift, values began to change. What was unimportant and taken for granted before came to be seen in a new light. "I have always thought myself a lazy person, but today I realized that no matter how much I dislike work, I could never dream of being so lazy as to take idleness as compared to doing any work no matter how hard!" "These activities (such as going for a walk) which we as nurses think are useless are very important to the patient." Several remarked on the increased importance of smoking and the need for a coffee break under conditions of enforced idleness. For example, "I never before realized how anyone could smoke one cigarette after another, but after sitting idly for a while, I decided it was better than nothing at all to do."

The strange feelings aroused by the nurses' initial contact with ward life were accompanied by the growing recognition of how little they knew about how to "get along" in the ward. "I think, though, acting as a patient really made me realize how important it is to orient patients to the ward, to let them know what the setup is, and spend a lot of time with them during the first week or two after admission." "This experience proves to me that the new patient must get individualized attention to help her to adjust to the hospital atmosphere." "I would have liked the nursing assistants to introduce me to a few of the patients so that I wouldn't have had to introduce myself." "I wasn't introduced to any other patients. Even though I wasn't a real patient I wasn't shown the bathroom, or the water fountains, the dining room or the dayroom."

There is a solution for the loneliness and ignorance of the new patient. It is what we have come to call "the patient coalition," an informal self-protective cooperative association of patients devoted to making hospital life endurable. Early in the stay of many nurses, fellow patients made brief contacts to size up the newcomer. Patients noticed a new face in the ward. "A nursing assistant commented, 'Several of the girls asked me who you were.' . . . .She stated one patient remarked that I was 'sitting too still to be a patient'; . . . they had been observing my behavior." Almost immediately patients sought information (not necessarily from the newcomer himself) about her identity, and, in exchange, they offered information about ward conditions. Sometimes the initial contact was almost immediate, but for at least six of the nurses it was preceded by a long period of being ignored. In those instances the contact was made only after the nurse began to read, page through a magazine, work a puzzle, write a letter, or knit. It was as if the ability to become involved in some activity was the signal that the nurse was approachable, that is, capable of sane social intercourse.

Sometimes newcomers were informally "adopted" by experienced patients. An old-timer would take a newly admitted, inexperienced patient under her wing in exchange for company, esteem, and whatever future benefits such an association might offer. "Then, when dinner was called, she 'buddied' me into the dining room, preceded me in line, showed me the ropes and saw to it that I got what I was entitled to." "I again sat with Mrs. V. On the way back to the dayroom, Mrs. V. turned to me and said, 'Guess you're my pet now.' . . . I was somewhat amazed to find that being locked in did not bother me and I felt fairly at home as these two patients took me 'under their wings.' " "First thing that was noted of surprise to me was the way the more alert patients helped and encouraged the more withdrawn with getting fixed up for the day — hair combed, makeup, proper clothing, etc. — but as the day wore on it became apparent that these same people could be quite aggressive in ordering the others around the ward throughout the day."

What does a patient have to offer in a social exchange? Sympathy, encouragement, information — but very little else. Particularly in terms of material goods, patients have little to give except for cigarettes. "One patient immediately inquired, 'Are you new in this building?' Truthfully, I answered, 'Yes, this is my first day.' Whereupon she began to tell me about watching out for my purse (I had none); also 'Susie is not to be trusted, she reports you.' . . . While writing a personal letter several patients whispered to me to be careful of what I wrote as it would be censored. . . . I had extra attention from several of the patients (during a game session) so that I sat at the 'right table to get a present,' which I received." Of course, with some basic information at hand the patient can begin to make personal adjustments to the inconveniences of the ward. Two nurse-patients found bathrooms with more privacy outside the ward. Several initiated activities to alleviate their boredom.

Thus far we have emphasized the negative, identity-disrupting aspects of patienthood and the adjustments necessary to protect oneself from their effect. The nurse-patients also found positive, self-enhancing activities in the wards. What stood out as high points in their experience? "When students did manicures and shampoos and sets, the whole mood changed." "The beauty shop is an excellent idea for this ward. Some patients were more expressive here than any other place known to me. Was it because it simulated an actual beauty shop and [provided] a touch with reality?" "One nice thing about the beauty shop, I thought, was that they offered coffee to the patients while their hair was being done. The patients seemed to appreciate this immensely." "This time . . . [the ward nurse] sat down in front of a group of five or six patients and carried on a conversation with them. She seemed friendly and helpful with patients and was a bit of sparkle in the long day." "I rang the bell since I had no key and felt somewhat relieved when the nurse smiled at me. It was at this moment when I realized how important a smile can be to a new patient." "The doctor made rounds and spoke to me. I was still cherishing every bit of attention I could get." These activities had one thing in common. They all expressed recognition of the patient occupying socially acceptable roles, such as beauty shop customer, friend, shopper, and even patient (in the sense that one's doctor demonstrates concern about one's health).

As in most institutions mealtime became a positive experience out of all proportion to its importance in ordinary life. Only one nurse made a negative comment about the meals. Several remarked that the ward atmosphere seemed more relaxed, more positive in feeling tone, after meals.

Yet in spite of their partial success in seeing the ward as a patient might, the nurses were frequently reminded of their nonpatient identity. The artificiality of their position made the experience unreal and, for some, less valuable than it might otherwise have been. The contrast between their temporary adoption of patienthood and the patients' lives struck several nurses. " Dr. B. stopped at my chair, while on her morning rounds. The personnel member accompanying her quickly told her I was a nurse. I don't know if I could have taken the 'questioning' of an intake staff." "Probably the reason it did not bother me was the fact that if it became unbearable, all I had to do was holler 'help' and I would be let out."

The restricted time element substantially limited the nurses' feel for ward life. "One woman stated that she thought we should spend two weeks in order to get a true picture." "I, however, had the assurance that I could go home in a 'short' time. That is the only reason that I finished out the day. I thought, 'If these people can stay here day after day with no end in sight, I can at least attempt to conclude this one day."

Most nurses felt that, in order for them to have a more realistic experience, their nursing identities should have been concealed from the patients and the ward staff. "This experience would probably effect more true enlightenment on what a patient's day really is like if the staff on the ward — and especially that part of it that is constantly with the patients — were not informed that this was not just another patient; because by their knowing, there is a sentiment of unspoken kinship or mutual understanding that 'you know and I know' that is just a temporary thing, which greatly eases for the staff-member-turned-patient-for-a-day the probable feelings of anxiety, stress and strain that a real patient would suffer. But, of course, done without general staff knowledge, it would greatly increase the threatening and/or traumatic aspects of it for the person being 'patient' and probably much more so than most of us would care to experience." Although Mueller and Sherman believe that "fooling the staff and patients serves no useful purpose" and might later cause difficulties for confused patients when they encounter the nurses occupying their proper nursing status, we suspect that there would be few volunteers and fewer who would complete a day's experience as a patient if the protection of being known as nurse by both staff and patients were removed.

With their experience time-limited and their nursing identities revealed to patients, some nurses felt it difficult to adopt the patients' world view. "I couldn't shake the feeling that I was a nurse, and feel wholly like a patient. I kept wanting to be supportive and initiate conversations." Apparently, this desire is associated with the nursing role and not with the patient role. "The most vivid thoughts I had at that time were probably guilt feelings. Here I was sitting around reading in a room full of regressed patients. I wanted to go over and talk to them but felt that I should keep the passive role."

Again, we learn something about this nurse's perception of the roles of patient and nurse and about the difficulty of behaving appropriately as a patient.

2. *Clinical psychologist* (Weitz, 1972). — William Weitz, a clinical psychologist, spent a twenty-four-hour period as a patient in Walter Reed General Hospital as part of his internship. His identity was made known to anyone who asked him directly, but he was dressed in the blue pajamas of the patient.

Perhaps Weitz's two most revealing findings have to do with the powerlessness of patients, its effects on their adaptation to the ward, and the identity change that he sensed going on within himself. He described the dependent, impotent position into which the patient is maneuvered. "I found the loss of control over my own life to be the greatest threat; . . . traditional ward situations do not permit patients to have much control over their eventual fate. Rather, major decisions about the patients' lives are largely determined by the ward doctor and other ward personnel" (p. 153). "Suddenly tremendous feelings of anger overwhelmed me as I sensed a loss of personal control over my life. . . . I was jealous of those staff people who could come and go on the ward, those individuals with a sense of their own freedom" (p. 152). Along with anger and resentment came efforts to reassert some independence. "I found myself utilizing various means to attempt to regain some sense of freedom and personal control. I now believe that the habitual questioning of ward administrators by hospitalized psychiatric patients is not simply a sign of manipulation and excessive dependence, but rather it may be an attempt by these individuals to achieve some sense of personal involvement in their life decisions, even in the most limited ways" (p. 153).

The researcher, on the basis of his own experience, questions the pathological labels attached to normal responses within a peculiar environment. The sense of being different and the knowledge that he was soon to leave the hospital provided Weitz with some boundaries for his feelings of powerlessness. "Although interacting with the other ward patients, I felt somewhat alone. It was in this pensive mood that I started to question if my experiences were common to the other ward patients. My thoughts drifted to the next morning when I would be free to leave the ward. Feelings of comfort accompanied my thoughts of regaining a sense of independence and the ability to make my own life decisions. I found it important to maintain these thoughts, as they gave me something to grasp on to during my feelings of loss" (p. 152).

Weitz, like other researchers, found a paradoxical recognition of personal change and identification with fellow patients despite knowledge of his unique status as a researcher. "Instead, I spent my day in activities consistent with the status of a ward patient, only I was not 'playing a patient' but was actually beginning to feel like one. In fact, people who were not aware of my reason for being on the ward were unable to differentiate me from other ward patients. As significantly noted, I was not pretending to play the role of a patient, but found myself caught up in actually experiencing myself as one. My reactions on the ward were very much different from what I had anticipated, for I found it difficult to escape from the constraints which I felt as a patient" (p. 152). As we discovered in other accounts as well, the identity change was accompanied by sleep disturbance. "When the lights were finally turned out, sleep was difficult. The day had seemed so long; yet I was unable to escape into sleep" (p. 152). Inability to sleep may be related to the fear that giving up control of one's consciousness to sleep will result in loss of identity and one will wake up a different person, perhaps even an insane person.

3. *Sociologist* (Deane, 1961). — William Deane, a sociologist, became a patient in a psychiatric ward for schizophrenic patients for a one-week period. He was well known as sociologist and group therapist to some of the patients and to all the staff. But his discharge date was unknown to him and he was taking medication in small amounts. His reactions to patienthood are congruent with those already reported.

He describes the pervasive boredom of patienthood. "First of all, a ubiquitous routine and sameness characterize most days. . . . In spite of the brisk and inclusive regulation of patient life, leisure time constitutes a fairly large proportion of the waking day" (p. 62). "On the second day, I became aware of a sense of huge boredom. The day dragged endlessly. . . . My spirits sagged during the hour and a half of waiting to go. . . . I had the same feeling of endless time" (p. 64).

The waiting is a consequence of the fact that the patient's life is dominated by routine. ". . . the job to which each patient goes generally requires the same sort of routinized, scheduled activity that other major areas of his life require; . . . the routine life is enforced by supervision. This is not heavy-handed or unfriendly and does not operate too obviously. Yet it is perfectly clear that 'paid help' are always present to insure an orderly existence" (p. 62).

The routine forces dependency and a sense of personal impotence and frustration. "I told Miss L. that I . . . wanted to smoke first. She told me that I would have to wait until 10 A.M. to do this. This irritated and frustrated me. . . . The difference [between regulated, routine life inside the hospital and outside it] is in the greater inclusiveness of routine and regulation in the hospital, and in the further fact that the patients themselves have very little part in determining their own routine supervisory needs, or regulatory conditions. These are imposed at the convenience of the staff in the interest of efficient, economical management with minimal risk and must be observed by the patient whether he sees any sense to them or not" (p. 64). The pattern is obvious. Events happen to the patient; others make decisions, set up or cancel scheduled events, and so forth.

There are few opportunities to make meaningful decisions in one's life in the ward. When they do occur, they stand out as worthy of description. "The ward attendant wanted to know which service I wished to attend. I said that I didn't care, but that if I had to make a choice, I would go to the Catholic service" (p. 67). Other reactions include attempts to manipulate the system as a gesture of retaliation and defiance. "What scheming to beat the system I attempted was designed to reduce sensory deprivation — to eat fast and get more food, to drink my coffee quickly and get another cup, to go to group therapy and get some extra cigarettes" (p. 68). Such meager efforts can have important symbolic value in preserving a vestige of self-esteem. Other attempts to cope with powerlessness lead to withdrawal or hostility. "For example, there was some withdrawal from active participation, as shown by my early retiring, frequent drowsiness, and indulgences in fantasy. There was considerable projective hostility directed toward the staff and my wife. I was hostile, also, about rules and regulations, particularly those pertaining to smoking, and I resented certain activities in which I was asked to participate" (p. 68). Resentment and paranoia accompany the impotent dependency of patienthood.

Values change as one adopts the patient role. Apparently insignificant symbolic gestures have an important bearing on a patient's day; little nuisances become disproportionately large in consequence. "However, since the film was showing on one camera only, there were frequent interruptions of reel changes. This annoyed me far out of proportion to the short interval of time involved" (p. 66). Cigarettes and food, commodities taken for granted in the everyday world, began to have a special impact on Deane's hospital life. "In the group therapy meeting, I felt very depressed. It appeared that Dr. G. had not brought any hospital cigarettes, and one of the things I had been looking forward to was the opportunity to smoke two or three extra cigarettes. . . . One of my major reasons for not wanting to go [to the movie] was the fact that I wouldn't be able to smoke during the movie. I was not then aware that one could smoke after returning from the movie, so it seemed to me that there would be an unbearable period of time between about 6:45 P.M., the time of the movie, and the next morning, during which I couldn't smoke" (pp. 65-66). "Two or three times patients either asked me for cigarettes or I offered them. This reduced my previous supply and was a source of anxiety" (p. 66). Cigarettes play an important role in social interaction in psychiatric wards. As noted earlier, they are one of the few commodities patients can offer in social exchanges.

Deane recounts his relationships with other patients. He was, of course, aware of the psychological and social limitations of his fellow patients. "Should . . . [the patient] be interested in reading or playing cards, for example, his interest might soon be threatened by the lack of variety of the literature or the limited capabilities of the other patients for playing cards. . . . I discovered that I had some actual fear of living with 'crazy people,' that beneath the facade of my consciously enlightened attitude toward mental illness there existed an emotional acceptance of popular folklore about the 'madman' " (p. 63). "Sitting at my left during the movie was a large rawboned patient who constantly repeated several complicated movements. . . . This had no effect upon me, however, I was not annoyed by it but only interested in slyly observing the stereotyped motions" (p. 66).

Despite differences, the need for social contact draws the researcher into the patient subculture. "Raymond [a fellow patient] bustled around and introduced me to everyone. I began to feel benevolent and gay. I talked with all the men, who were extremely friendly and complimentary toward my stay. . . . I felt elated but restless. . . . I had found . . . [a particular manic patient] wearying but now I talked with him eagerly and felt a great fellow feeling with him. His incredible ramblings seemed to make more sense than before." As Deane was about to leave the ward, "I recalled that I owed a cigarette to Wood and one to Russell, so I paid them back. I had three cigarettes left, and I gave these to Sherring, who was pacing the hall. I shook hands with all the men and had difficulty holding back tears" (p. 67). The patient coalition, as we have called it, provided him with essential support during his hospital stay, and it was with genuine sorrow that he severed his equalitarian ties with the real patients at the end of the week.

In Deane's case, again, despite experiences that set the researcher apart from other patients, we find basic personality and identity changes accompanying patienthood. These changes occurred even though there were differentiating cues for the researcher's social role. They began with an explanation to the patients of just what Dr. Deane was doing. "These conditions surrounding my stay made it clear to the patients on 1 South that I was not 'sick.' They were told that I wished to come into the hospital and live as a patient in order to better understand the patient" (p. 61). The news was "warmly received" by the patients. "I was somewhat self-conscious, feeling distinct and different from the patients. The patients, as a whole, however, seemed to be well aware of my coming, and all who expressed themselves to me felt that it was a good idea" (pp. 63-64). Reminders came that Deane was not a genuine patient. "On Monday night, I asked Mr. Byrd for a light at 8:15 P.M. For a moment he looked a little embarrassed, and then said, 'If you want me to really treat you like a patient, I can't let you smoke after 8 P.M.' Interestingly enough, I felt no resentment toward him at all" (p. 66). Deane felt no resentment at the restriction, we feel, because he had ultimate control over its imposition. That is, the phrase "If you want me to . . ." placed responsibility for the decision on Deane's own shoulders. Such signals of inferred competence are rarely offered the ordinary psychiatric patient. Elsewhere Deane describes his inner debate on whether or not to ask the ward attendants to reimburse him for the cigarettes he had given other patients. He decided not to, but the point, as before, is that it was his option to ask or not, an option not afforded the regular patient.

Psychological changes are inevitable, however, despite the cues of differentness. "I was definitely sleepy and listless and began to feel some depression. I began to worry about when I would be released and became conscious of a slight dread that I might actually become psychotic and not be released. I began to feel a closer identification with the patients" (p. 64). A new identity struggled to emerge. "Miss L.'s friendly but nonfamiliar treatment of me disturbed me even though I understood it, and I began to feel a sense of resentment toward her which I quickly generalized to all staff members and 'paid help' in the hospital. This feeling did not abate during the week; if anything, it increased. . . . I felt confused and tired. I felt that it was an effort to move. I said to Jean, 'Look, I can't learn that. I feel lousy. I'm tired and sleepy. My head feels funny' " (p. 64). "The feeling of identity with the patients and social distance from the staff began to increase. However, I still continued to feel warm toward the ward attendants. I became noticeably more restless both in the laundry and on the ward. I paced the corridors from time to time, and once, in the laundry, I undertook a complete inspection tour of the place, looking intently at all the machines and gadgets but actually having no interest in any of it. I would take several long walks to the drinking fountain, although on none of these trips was I thirsty. I would speculate a good deal about the sociological implications of hospitalization, but frequently these ideas would be interrupted by lengthy indulgences in fantasy. Indeed, fantasying definitely increased as time wore on" (p. 66).

Deane seemed to be seeing his world from a new perspective, struggling to hold on to his identity as a sociologist or at least to withdraw from a social setting that was forcing him to adopt a new identity. Later, "I had a series of nightmares which seemed to be continuous. One I still recall very vividly. I was sitting at a table. My middle son, Gordon, aged eight, was sitting on my left, and Dr. Brooks was sitting directly across the table. I was much older and very tired. I kept dropping my food and spilling my milk. Gordon kept telling me about it and urging me to stop doing this, but I couldn't seem to prevent it. Gordon's face became indistinct, and he looked lumpy like clay. Then I wasn't sure whether he was Gordon or Thatcher, my three-year-old son. I put my hands over my face and, in some strange way, made a square out of them. I realized that I was undergoing an acute schizophrenic reaction. I started to cry in despair" (p. 67). The dream seems thematic of changing identities, role reversals, regression, and personality splits.

At the end of his hospital stay came the wrenching return to a former identity. "Once outside of the hospital, I actually broke into sobs for a few seconds. I walked across the street to my house. I almost cried again when I greeted my wife and children. All that day,

I was restless and tense. I drank innumerable cups of coffee and smoked endlessly. Sunday night I slept badly and was bothered by nightmares. In fact, at the time of this writing, which is now over two days after my return, I still feel considerable tension and a rather intense desire to move restlessly about and do exciting things. My sleep is still somewhat disturbed, and my dreams are of a nightmare quality. . . . I observed that familiar parts of the hospital which I had seen many times, such as the laundry, the tunnel, the OT departments, and 1 South, appeared different to me than they had before my stay (or have since). This is in no sense a perceptual distortion. It is rather a condition of seeing things through a 'different set of eyes,' which has the effect of making the familiar appear unfamiliar" (p. 67). During Deane's hospitalization even his speech pattern had changed. "It seemed to me that I developed a mode of speech which omitted many connecting words, that I tended to speak explosively and faster than usual, and yet in a lower and softer register" (p. 67). His mode of thought was different. "Fantasy and autistic thinking tended to grow during the week. My mind was flooded with an almost childish preoccupation with the sensory deprivation I was undergoing. There was a great concern and anxiety about cigarettes and a huge desire for coffee" (p. 68). Other familiar themes of patient life are present in Deane's article: lack of knowledge about the routine and the parallel need for orientation, humiliating and inadequate facilities, and the special adaptations of particular patients.

Deane concludes with an unsuccessful attempt to force his experience into traditional psychodiagnostic categories such as anxiety, depression, reaction formation, regression, and dissociative reaction, suggesting that these states were maladaptive responses to patienthood. On the contrary, we believe these to be normal, adaptive responses to the institutional pressures exerted on the mental patient. Perhaps that is what Deane had in mind when he suggested that "some of the symptomatology of mental patients may be due to the effects of hospitalization and not to the fact of mental illness per se" (p. 68). The tendency, however, is to label these responses with psychiatric terminology and subsequently dismiss them as typical pathological responses without exploring the possibility that they are adaptive responses to a pathological environment.

4. *Psychiatric resident* (Rockwell, 1971). — Don Rockwell arranged to spend three weeks in a 26-bed acute treatment ward at the

Langley Porter Neuropsychiatric Institute as part of his psychiatric residency. His alternate identity was known to patients and staff. Even though he spent some time each day in his office in the ward the impact of his experience as pseudo patient was, in his terminology, "startling." He considers such an experience to be valuable training for mental health professions, both in terms of what they learn about patient life and what they learn about themselves. He notes, as do most researchers who take this approach to learning, that the "reality of these concepts has for me become experiential rather than intellectual" (p. 216).

Rockwell experienced a change in time perception common to other live-in investigators. "Time is different here. . . . For the patients and for me today, this [Monday] morning is just the beginning of another long day, an extension of yesterday which will merge into tomorrow. Nine o'clock this morning has become no different from nine o'clock yesterday and only slightly different from nine o'clock tomorrow" (p. 217). The staff, however, perceived Monday morning as the beginning of a new workweek.

A change in one's sense of time is both a product of and a contributor to the experience of boredom. "Most of these 'crocky' complaints revolve around 'drowsiness,' 'apathy,' 'boredom,' and 'nothing to do here.' . . . these complaints are justified for most patients, most of the time. . . . The patients, even on an active ward, have more time on their hands than they can fill — unless they're manic, of course. As a result they find the ward dull and they become apathetic, they withdraw, and they further regress" (p. 220).

The usual discovery that one's values change, that previously minor events become major, is echoed in Rockwell's report. "Just as one learns of a new apartment's more subtle drawbacks after one has lived there awhile, so one only appreciates a ward's subtle deficiencies by experiencing everyday life on it. Little things in our physical milieu which we nonpatients cope with by actively doing something about them — for example, the dripping faucet or dirty floor — are not readily coped with in the hospital" (p. 217). Food is one of the elements in one's world which becomes increasingly important. Not only does it provide something to do in combating ennui, but it provides a time marker for dividing up the day and for distinguishing one day from the next. "After breakfast this morning I left the patients and attended the morning ward staff meeting" (p. 217).

The perceptual and cognitive changes that accompany identity change can be frightening to the experiential researcher. Rockwell noted: "As I lay in bed, I became aware of a muffled, distant sound, identified first as a baby's crying. As I made more of an effort to define the sound, I experienced two things. First, the thought that I had really gone off the deep end and was hallucinating struck me with more than a little associated anxiety; and then, to my great relief, came the realization that the sound, in fact, was the strange gurgling of pipes in the wall. At that point it became clear to me how easily someting like this could be elaborated into a great deal more by an anxious patient" (p. 217). The last sentence is an important one, suggesting as it does experiential researchers to emphasize the difference between themselves and real patients and thus to confirm their true identities.

Rockwell found some evidence of personal regression. "Also of great interest, from a self-understanding viewpoint, was the rearousal of my adolescent intrapsychic conflicts and even a particular nervous mannerism I had given up in early adolescence" (p. 221). The sense of rejection, paranoia, and resentment which accompanies this kind of identity shift appeared in Rockwell's experience. "Through my peripheral vision I noted that the nurses and the doctor on duty were in the nurses' station and were 'watching me.' I became self-conscious and anxious. They suddenly began to laugh — inaudibly, but visibly, through the glass of the nursing station. LAUGHING AT ME! was my immediate reaction, and my anxiety was immediately compounded with anger and a creeping concern over what they might be laughing about. I had no idea, but the suspense overwhelmed me and I got up and went to the nursing station. I was paranoid for a brief but vivid moment" (p. 221).

Rockwell also provides illustrations of the functioning of "the patient coalition." When a staff member became noticeably upset, the patients colluded with the staff to deny the existence of the upset by refraining from commenting upon it. Rockwell also discovered the existence of communication networks among patients and between patients and nurses which were largely unknown to him before.

The routinization of life, the enforced dependency, and the humiliations of daily existence are also noted by Rockwell: "Many times patients' complaints are 'put down' by such comments as, 'That's the way it's always done,' or 'The rules don't permit that,' or 'The administration wouldn't go for that.' Although such reasons imply that a particular aspect of ward life is unchangeable, most of them in fact do not hold up when actively challenged" (p. 220). "The patient's daily life is forced into a hospital schedule for himself. He is herded by the staff from place to place, his leisure and privacy are constantly intruded upon by the staff, and his objections to any of these intrusions are interpreted to him as evidence of his pathology" (p. 222). But it is not only the scheduled existence that undermines self-esteem. ". . . we tend to split off the patient, to give him a different status, to see him not as one of us but as one of them. On the ward this manifests itself most clearly in the degradation of the patient, as commented on so lucidly by Goffman and by others. . . . [the patient's] behavior is by and large interpreted in ways that confirm the label of deviant, rather than affirming his membership in the human race" (p. 222).

Finally, the realization that he was living alongside "crazy" people struck Rockwell most forcefully at night. "Prior to my 'living in' I considered myself 'objective,' 'understanding,' 'empathetic,' 'unprejudiced,' and so on, about the mentally ill. . . . Not long after I started 'living in' a new patient was admitted. I saw little of him the first day and knew only that he was withdrawn and perhaps suspicious. That night as I lay in my bed, all of the childish stereotypes about madmen and lunatics came back; all of my civilized, rational, educated veneer disappeared and I recognized how thin that veneer is in most of us" (p. 221).

5. *Student volunteers.* — Another source of information about the experiences of patienthood is found in the Wellmet Project Proposal (1969). As part of their preparation for residency in halfway houses, two student volunteers were placed in a Boston state hospital. Their accounts are more literary than those of the nurses, but the themes are remarkably similar.

The boredom and meaninglessness of patienthood come through clearly: "This is an utterly vegetable existence. The young and middle-aged men are more pitiable and wretched than the old men, who seem somehow to have mastered the grinding attrition of confinement and boredom — at least superficially." "We just sit . . . and sleep (the bedrooms aren't locked like they are upstairs) and shuffle around and sleep and eat and sleep." "All this shuffling going on. Up and down the hall. The television . . . There are no activities planned for any of the patients. They walk around the dayroom and pick fights with one another. . . . My God, what do these patients do with themselves — they don't even look out the windows." And the accompanying change in the patient's time sense appears in these accounts, too. "The clock over the television. Watching it all the time. Judge time by the passing of [TV] programs." "The monotony — the cramped constraint — crushes."

The regimentation irritated these young people. "It rankles me to be awakened by the callous attendant for a headcount at 3 A.M. as all the naked light bulbs hurl their dismal light against the cruddy yellow and green walls. I hope he did get away." "There is no choice involved. You sit and pretend to watch television. You go to dinner. You eat what's served you. Take your pill when you're ordered to — no choice. Nothing." "Everyone gets his drugs in the morning and the afternoon. They line up. Bed time is at 8:00. We get up at 6:00."

There is loneliness in being different, but there is camaraderie, as well. "What chance do these boys and men have? What opportunity does any of them — why didn't I say 'us' — have to receive any warmth or affirmation of the quintessential humanity, and goodness, of each person on C-3?" "There are no groups. Each person remains an exclusive entity except for rare moments in which two persons who have known each other for a long time, i.e., several months or years, communicate with each other. Each individual is left to his own isolation. This enforced aloneness in most instances intensifies the suffering of persons — why haven't I called them patients? — unable to deal with their divided selves and unable to fathom the source of their incompleteness. Enforced isolation, which numbs all sense of competence and confidence in individual identity, is the heart of the patient experience on a locked ward."

There is humor, too, in the state hospital. " 'I'm gonna write a book about this place,' said Charley, one of the precious few with a sense of humor. It was over Sunday dinner. 'What are you going to call it?' 'Metropolitan State Shithouse,' Charley enunciated as his solitary upper tooth began to dance in his guffawing mouth. Charley has resided in this place which he hates and from which he always used to escape (before a new ward nurse began to give just a little T.L.C.) for twenty years. 'You'll never get out of here, Charley, you're too old, you're 55, you're unemployed, you've got no trade; you'll never get out. You don't want to go home; you've got it too good here.' These were the words of another man, just turning 31 years, who sat at a table working on a color-by-number pencil set and who spoke without the slightest trace of feeling. It was as if he were stating a fact and there was not the slightest conceivable chance of argument." Humor is priceless in the ward, providing distance from the dreary existence, relief from tension, a new perspective on a monotonous existence, and, sometimes, a cutting down to size of the staff authority figures and the self-important.

These accounts reveal the same curious combination of feeling different from the other patients because the researchers are aware of their special purpose in being there and of recognizing a subtle new identification. "The attendants continually compel me to remember who I am and prevent me from functioning as a patient. Damnation but it's frustrating to have attendants and nurses seek me out, look at me knowingly, and begin to converse with me within earshot of my fellow patients on C-3. They unconsciously force me to differenti-ate." "We try to pass ourselves off as patients. But we look too clean, too knowledgeable (knowing we'll be out of here in another day)." "What right do I have to come in here, take notes, and leave — forgetting about all the shit?" Yet the students felt change, too. "I feel like a tropism — being pulled toward the depression all around me." "I have a different kind of feeling toward this place now. Yesterday and this morning it was treated as a kind of dull bore-dom — something to be lived through — but having no lasting effects. Tonight, I feel very strange. . . . I want to change but I don't quite know how. . . . Now that it's closer to the end, I'm afraid I'm going to be trapped here, people are going to forget about me — and I'll die. My life is nothing, I'll always be crazy."

There is the familiar lack of adequate facilities. "There are no doors on the bathrooms. The lowest point of degradation, I think. . . . There are no covers on the toilets either." "The ward has a feculent stench. It hits you as soon as you step into the drab green corridor." "I'm indignant now, yet there's no outlet or channel for my rage. So it's covered and I sleep close to twelve hours each day. That leaves only twelve hours of waking frustration."

6. *Two psychologists* (Goldman et al., 1970). — This report describes two live-in experiences: (1) a social psychologist posed as an acutely depressed patient for one week in an admissions ward; (2) a clinical research psychologist posed as a long-term psychotic in a chronic care ward. The experiences of these two researchers were similar enough to permit their being written up in a single article, emphasizing again the strong, consistent pressures of institutional life.

There was the usual boredom: "An immediate and overwhelming reaction in both observers to hospital life was boredom. . . . mental patients themselves were not at all oblivious to the barrenness and emptiness of their physical surroundings" (p. 430). With the boredom came the customary subjective change in the observers' time perspectives. Time was measured in relation to chronological landmarks: "You don't use the days of the week to tell time, but you say, 'Oh, that was the day we waited in the hall for the floor to dry after breakfast instead of going right into the dayroom.' Or, 'That was the day we had ice cream' " (p. 430).

The feelings of humiliation and powerlessness are common to patienthood. The authors argue that the nature of the attendants' job encourages them to keep patients in a dependent, powerless position so that attendants can exchange small favors for cooperation and assistance in ward maintenance. "Mental patients, who are characteristically restricted to such a degree that they are extremely dependent on others for even the most minor amenities of life, could 'win back' some of these apparently minor rights by assisting attendants" (p. 431).

The paranoia that some observers experienced reached its zenith in the report of these two investigators: "Both researchers experienced a fear that they had been betrayed by their colleagues. Each was remarkably concerned about whether he would be left in the hospital indefinitely, only to be forgotten by friends and relatives" (p. 429). One researcher had even worked out an escape route. There is evidence of the fear of identifying themselves with other "forgotten" patients in the style of the report, which strongly emphasizes the differences between themselves and the patients. Perhaps those most threatened by patienthood experiences make the strongest distinctions between themselves and patients in their writings. For example, "If a fear of betrayal can readily be evoked in 'normals,' it is likely that similar apprehensions and suspicions are aroused in mentally ill persons upon their initiation into a mental hospital" (p. 429). The authors also make a point similar to Rockwell's insight, that is, that situation-specific paranoias are not necessarily symptomatic evidence of mental dysfunction: "The personal experiences of the two observers suggest that many of the suspicions harbored by patients may be situationally induced and, therefore, not always classically paranoid reactions" (pp. 429-430). Perhaps if we knew the situational context of any paranoia it would "make sense," as others have argued.

These researchers also saw the need for "better orientation procedures for new admissions" so that patients' initial experiences could be interpreted more constructively. They noted the lack of equipment that would provide meaningful activity for patients during the long days. For example, "Patients did not have easy access to newspapers or calendars" (p. 430). Their research brought about specific changes in this latter area.

7. *Anthropologist* (Caudill et al., 1952). — Caudill, an anthropologist, stayed for two months in a psychodynamically oriented ward in a private psychiatric hospital. The hospital was affiliated with a psychiatric training center. His research identity was known only to two senior staff members. His presenting symptoms included excessive drinking and depression. Apparently he received medication, including paraldehyde. Most of his fellow patients (both male and female) in this open ward were young, white psychoneurotics.

Caudill's account focuses primarily on functions of the patient coalition. He does, however, note several other experiences shared by other participant-observers. For example, he mentions the time-sense change and the lack of activity associated with change in time perception: "One evening a group of eleven patients were discussing the lack of activities in the hospital, and they came to the conclusion that it was part of a conscious plan by the staff to increase the intensity of 'twenty-four-hour-a-day' therapy" (p. 320).

Value changes are noted by Caudill: "The patients felt that many of the ordinary conventions and social gestures of the outer world were made temporarily meaningless by hospital life" (p. 318). ". . . new physical objects on the ward assumed an importance all out of proportion to what they would have had in the outer world. A new couch placed in the men's living room became a focus of attention and topic of conversation for over a month" (p. 323). Often these changed values were not perceived by the ward staff. For example, after much effort and a long wait, the patients finally succeeded in having the ward phonograph repaired. "On the afternoon the phonograph was returned, a group of six patients were listening to music at the time the therapists made their rounds, but none of the doctors made a social remark about the pleasure of having the machine in working order" (p. 329). It is this inability to perceive ward existence from the patient's perspective which contributes to the extended waiting that patients must endure in order to obtain important objects and services. In this instance there was a lapse of six weeks between the time patients began agitating for phonograph repairs and the time the phonograph was fixed and returned.

In Caudill's ward the physical layout, clothing, and food service seemed to be adequate, but humiliation and demeaning ritual were present in attitudes and interaction habits of some ward staff members. "After . . . [a nurse] had left, Mr. Davis commented that she had 'treated us like seven-year-olds.' " "At another time the staff, without consulting the patients, decided to give them a valentine party. Many of the patients did not wish to go, but did so anyway as they felt that they should not hurt the feelings of the student nurses who had organized the party. The games introduced by the nurses were on a very childish level; many of the patients felt silly playing them and were glad when the party was over and they could go back to activities of their own choosing" (pp. 321-322). The control exerted by staff over the lives of their psychiatric patients is taken for granted in hospital life. Caudill himself was not permitted "going-out privileges to visit the library." He observes that from "the patient's viewpoint, the therapist was a benign omnipotent authority beyond whom the patient could not look" (p. 320n).

Caudill perceived the patient coalition as "a partly conscious resistance to those aspects of the hospital routine which were unduly 'infantilizing' " (p. 323). He also noted that shifts of mood within the patient group, especially feelings of depression and rebellion, were associated with the imposition of cycles of restrictive and permissive administrative control on the patients' existence. In his view, research in a broad range of settings with similar structural features (including naval vessels, orphanages, prisons, and so forth) has generally resulted in findings of "apathy and depersonalization, regression, denial of reality, attempts to maintain threatened self-esteem, increased wish-level and fantasy, and the formation of stereotypes concerning those who control the authority and power" (p. 332).

Caudill, along with several other observers, suggests that some activity usually classed as pathological behavior might be more appropriately interpreted as a response to the social setting in which the mental patient is immersed. "Nevertheless, such friction [with hospital routine] did occur, and the subsequent frustration led to behavior on the part of the patients which, although it overtly resembled neurotic behavior arising from personal emotional conflicts, was, in fact, to a considerable extent due to factors in the immediate situation" (p. 330). He calls for systematic study of the relative importance of immediate social setting variables on the one hand and personal historical variables on the other in seeking to understand the behavior of patients in psychiatric wards.

Caudill points out that other behavior patterns, involving dramatic social confrontations with staff members, might be related to the powerlessness of patienthood. For example, Mr. Davis created scenes when in the presence of his therapist and only then. Swearing and other verbal abuse may have been both a response to the frustration of impotence (directed at the concrete and symbolic authority figure in this setting) and an attempt to exert control over this omnipotent figure, that is, to force the therapist to respond to Mr. Davis. Another example concerned the "putting on" or kidding of student nurses who sat around in the living rooms listening to materials they could later incorporate in their reports. To perceive such figures as gullible and purposely to provide them with misinformation were symbolic efforts to bring them down from their position of omnipotence.

What specifically did the patient coalition provide in this hospital setting? First, the patients gave Caudill much-needed information when he first came to the ward. He writes of their orienting him to appropriate attitudes toward eating and letter writing. Group unity and social support were strongly emphasized within the patient coalition. "Although acquaintances among the patients would be made on the basis of similar backgrounds and interests, and much time was spent in gossiping about the social characteristics of others, these activities lacked the invidious overtones they would have carried in the outer world. Along with this went a muting of outerworld distinctions on the basis of race, ethnic group or social class — it was as if the patients had agreed that such categories had little meaning in a hospital" (p. 319). Probably the lack of importance of common social labels stemmed from the fact that patient status and world view, with their strong contrast to staff status and world view, overshadow other applicable categories in this setting. "However, one of the women shortly brought the group together again by saying, 'Well, what the hell, we are all in the same boat in this place, so don't worry about it, it's all right.' . . . It was almost as if whenever, within the hospital setting, a disagreeable episode took place, the unity of the group, and its tolerance, had of necessity to reassert itself" (p. 319). In addition, the patients illicitly bought stuffed animals from fellow patients as a gesture of support, sat up with one another during stressful periods, refused to inform on one another when results might be punitive, provided sociable competition for game playing, shared food and conversation, and generally provided one another with mutual understanding and support. Caudill says the patient coalition was further subdivided into cliques and dyads, which usually functioned to strengthen overall group unity.

Caudill was concerned that there might be setbacks in the progress of other patients because of his living in, although, to his knowledge, "no discernible harm was done." In addition, ethical considerations, personal strain on the researcher, and the bias caused by the researcher's identification with other patients were considerations that Caudill considered disadvantages in this kind of research. On the other hand, he felt his study generated "a rich body of data" incompletely recognized from other perspectives.

8. *Psychologist and pseudo patients.* — Rosenhan's (1973) study was different from the others in purpose. It was directed toward the issue of whether or not sanity is distinguishable apart from an individual's assigned label and the situational context in which he exists. In other words, the question he probed was: Would sane persons be discovered in places for the insane? He found, by and large, that they were not, except by some fellow patients.

The eight pseudo patients had varying occupations and backgrounds. They entered twelve hospitals (new and old, public and private) in five states on the East and West coasts of the United States. They claimed to hear voices in order to gain admission, and they falsified their names, and their occupational histories. Thereafter they behaved normally in every way, ceasing to show any symptoms of disturbance. They remained in the hospital from seven to fifty-two days, with an average stay of nineteen days.

The pseudo patients experienced initial nervousness as well as considerable psychological stress, which seemed to them appropriate to the hospital setting. Many of them were experiencing their first encounter with a psychiatrically disturbed population. Soon they learned that their fellow patients seemed sane for long periods of time and that they were perceptive enough to uncover the researchers' subterfuge, even though staff members did not. The researchers discovered (and concealed) the fact that other patients, too, were secretly disposing of medication in the toilets. They noticed the spatial segregation that placed staff members in glassed-in quarters ("the cage") much of the time. In sum, they began to identify with regular patients and to become members of the patient coalition.

The efforts of some researchers to escape from the identities their environment imposed on them reflected desperation and, on occasion, the absence of humor. "Some examples: a graduate student in psychology asked his wife to bring his textbooks to the hospital so he could 'catch up on his homework' — this despite the elaborate precautions taken to conceal his professional association. The same student, who had trained for quite some time to get into the hospital, and who had looked forward to the experience, 'remembered' some drag races that he had wanted to see on the weekend and insisted that he be discharged by that time. Another pseudo-patient attempted a romance with a nurse. Subsequently, he informed the staff that he was applying for admission to graduate school in psychology and was very likely to be admitted, since a graduate professor was one of his regular hospital visitors" (p. 256).

Rosenhan touches on the issues of boredom, of being ignored, of lack of privacy, and of restricted movement. One man's note-taking was interpreted by his physician as his adaptation to a poor memory. Verbal abuse and name-calling were common. Toilets without doors were found in some hospitals. Not only staff but volunteers had access to the intensely personal accounts and descriptions of patients in the clinical record files. Staff members checked on the patients' personal hygiene. Physical examinations were made in a semipublic room. Patients were talked about in their presence as if they were not there. A nurse unbuttoned her uniform and adjusted her brassiere as if male patients were not present or would not notice her action.

Rosenhan emphasizes the pervasive powerlessness and depersonalization of patienthood. "Powerlessness was evident everywhere. The patient is deprived of many of his legal rights by dint of his psychiatric commitment. He is shorn of credibility by virtue of his psychiatric label. His freedom of movement is restricted. He cannot initiate contact with the staff, but may only respond to such overtures as they make. Personal privacy is minimal. Patient quarters and possessions can be entered and examined by any staff member, for whatever reason" (p. 256). Rosenhan considers the two factors of powerlessness and depersonalization to be countertherapeutic products of destructive attitudes toward mental disorder, the staff hierarchy, financial difficulties in hospitals, and too much reliance on psychotropic drugs to effect cures.

9. *Journalist* (Barry, 1971). — Anne Barry, a journalist spent one week as a patient in a locked ward of Bellevue Hospital. After her initial difficulty in convincing authorities that she was sufficiently disturbed to warrant admission, she was taken by ambulance to the hospital and diagnosed as a paranoid schizophrenic. Only two friends knew of her plan. Her prescribed medication was sometimes taken, sometimes disposed of surreptitiously: "I took my medication obediently, but tucked the Thorazine tablet under my tongue when I drank the paper cup of water. It was easy enough to amble down the hall to the bathroom and drop it in the toilet" (p. 52).

Barry's experiences as a patient closely parallel those of the professional researcher-patients. Her highly readable account carries the ring of genuine empathy and sharp awareness of people and setting. She learned the key rules for getting out: "From staff I soon learned that I should try to be good, cooperative, respectful. I must appear serious about wanting to get well" (p. 64).

Boredom was a problem for Barry, as it was for the others. "I had steeled myself against fear and rage, but boredom like this I had been unable to foresee, I hadn't come close" (p. 54). Lack of privacy ("Like every other patient I was to be deprived of my privacy for the duration of my stay on N7" [p. 45]), loss of identifying personal possessions ("I had left my bathrobe on the end of the bed, and so it, too, was gone, with my change purse in the pocket, and my book. The last of my possessions, gone! Another terrific sense of loss" [p. 28]), and submission to institutional routine ("The staff set the routine. The times for sleeping, meals and recreation were determined by the staff, and were arbitrary" [p. 188]) were her lot, too.

The humiliations associated with stigmatized status and powerlessness are commonly described by all experiential researchers. Being ignored is one such humiliation. "How could she be touching my property, and paying so little attention to it, or to me? . . . She was for the first time aware that I had heard a conversation taking place three feet away from me" (p. 23). Waiting on a staff member to provide something simple, yet essential, is another source of humiliation. "For twenty minutes I was passed from one side to another, and on to the practical nurse, a clinician, the head nurse, and back to an aide with permission to use the telephone" (p. 41). "What was more painful than the headache was the dependence. Not to be able to take an aspirin on my own was to be treated like a child, and I reacted like a child" (p. 63).

Partly in response to the enforced dependency, patients banded together. Initial fears of fellow patients had to be overcome. "I was nervous here for unexpected reasons. I couldn't help wondering if some patient, or a sadistic aide, would attack me. . . . These ghosts, my wardmates, stumbling along the hall on the way to the bathroom, hawking and spitting into the basins, crouching over the toilets in their doorless stalls, seemed far from violent" (p. 27). Initial overtures of friendship were made. "From time to time some of the ladies would make tentative gestures to get to know me" (p. 38). " 'Listen, everybody, this here is a nice girl. She don't talk much because she's scared, she's new here, but she'll get a lot better soon. Everybody be nice to her' " (p. 31).

The result of frustrations and humiliations at Bellevue, as elsewhere, is the patient coalition. "The patients constantly reinforced 'good' behavior among the group. They were always teaching, supporting, counseling in small ways: The sense of shared captivity I believe was much more effective than the Thorazine in keeping the peace" (p. 190). "There seemed to be a special ambience in the ward, a gentleness between the patients based on concern for one another's feelings" (p. 32). ". . . to complain against another patient seemed a form of treachery" (p. 46).

Barry, too, noted the sensitivity of many patients to nonverbal communications of feelings and attitudes. "Each of us developed an uncanny sense of another's mood, and a feeling for the ability of others to respond" (p. 101). "Like the other patients I tended to disregard words. I picked up my cue from the supplication in her eyes" (p. 57).

With acceptance into the coalition and the sharing of institutional "mortification," as Goffman (1961a) puts it, came identification with the patient role. Identity began to blur. Journalist became patient. "I didn't know whether or not I was putting on an act" (Barry, 1971, p. 17). "I would catch myself working through fears not so very different from those of the real patients, and I would be brought up short by similarity" (p. 38). "As soon as the door was locked, I certainly *was* a patient, and the only question for me, as well as for the others, was what sort of patient I would be" (p. 187).

The interesting issues of how setting helps to determine identity and how behavior helps to determine feeling states are raised indirectly in most of the experiential accounts. Barry touches directly on these questions: "I was unaware of this attrition of my physical sensitivity until this night, and so also unaware just how much of my sense of my own being was determined by my responses to my immediate physical environment" (p. 152). "Because I was acting out paranoia, I began to feel somewhat paranoid" (p. 34). Barry also deals with the themes described above: value changes, the sense of being locked in, the fluctuating feelings of artificiality as a researcher who would leave the setting soon, various personal adjustments to patienthood including some self-enhancing activities, the need for orientation toward opportunities and routine, the emphasis on food, the intimidating newness of initial days on the ward, the lack of equipment for activity, cooperative arrangements between aides and patients, and the distorted presentations of self offered by patients to staff.

In sum, Barry offers her reader a sensitive, insightful account of patienthood as viewed through one journalist's eyes.

*Summary.* — In summarizing the findings of this diverse group of live-in researchers in various kinds of psychiatric hospital wards, let us examine what they had to say about patienthood, the ward environment, and their own experiences. There is agreement that one's sense of time changes as he exists within the stifling boredom of routinized and uneventful confinement. Time is measured by events, not by days. Weekends lose their meaning. Activities are few and often meaningless. Time is invested in waiting. In such an atmosphere values begin to change. Little occurrences and small lacks become disproportionately large. Food, in particular, takes on special significance, providing a topic of conversation and a chronological marker.

The patient feels ignored, abandoned, dependent, resentful, and powerless. He may be locked in with no sense of privacy yet he feels isolated and lonely. He has to use meager, sometimes humiliating, facilities. He may wear poorly fitting hospital uniforms which rob him of a sense of personal ownership and identity. His life is structured by regimentation which exists for the convenience of the ward staff. His choices are minimal and are often artificially resolved for him by others. His activities are frequently interrupted at the convenience of others.

As he enters the ward the patient often senses a need for orientation and instruction which is not satisfied in an organized way. Other patients are his chief source of information. They initiate contact and draw him into a patient coalition that provides a measure of collective defense against the powerlessness of patienthood. The coalition gives patients a sense of usefulness and esteem. Mutual support and exchanges of cigarettes, money, and food cement relationships among patients. Similar social exchanges form the basis for a working relationship between patients and aides. Within the patient coalition there is a hierarchy of status and privilege. There is also anxiety associated with living alongside and being dependent upon one's fellows who may be loud and violent and who are labeled "crazy." The patient, like his peers, is likely to be extremely sensitive to the feelings and attitudes, both positive and negative, of others. Social relationships may provoke excessive response or defensive withdrawal. Interestingly, when viewed by live-in researchers, patients seem to be more sensitive, knowledgeable, flexible, and competent than they are generally credited with being.

Patients may engage in positive, self-enhancing activities. Creative work opportunities are sometimes found. And some patients make specialized, personal adjustments toward existence. Hospital life, however, may not offer much in the way of developing skills useful outside the hospital setting.

The researchers themselves were sometimes bothered by a sense of artificiality. Aware of the temporary quality of their patient existence, they understood that their situation might give them a different perspective on the hospital. Some pseudo patients emphasized the differentness between themselves and their fellow patients, in part, we suspect, because of the following phenomenon.

Most researchers began to experience an incipient identity shift. They felt themselves becoming patients. The transformation was manifested by extreme mood swings, difficulty in concentration, sleep disruption, and paranoia centered in the delusion that they had been abandoned and would have to remain in the hospital for the rest of their lives. Dreams would often be marked by nightmarish fantasies of shifting identities, becoming schizophrenic, and so forth. Several reported a feeling of tremendous relief on being released from the setting and discussed their initial difficulties in reassuming former roles and self-images. Except for those who felt most threatened, all researchers admitted to a strong identification with fellow patients. With understandable qualifications, they found the experience useful in training and research.

Finally, on the basis both of their observations of other patients and of their own experiences, several experiential researchers began to see some behaviors no longer as merely symptomatic expressions of pathological personalities but as meaningful responses to a powerful, sometimes destructive, setting. When we have more information about situational pressures, we will, in all probability, be better able to appreciate the flexibility and adaptability of humans, even those who are labeled "mental patients."

## PREPARATIONS FOR THE EXPERIENTIAL STUDY

To give the reader knowledge of the background of DKR (the experiential researcher) we have included personal history relevant to the project. At the time the research was undertaken, DKR had had seven years' experience in suicide research. He also had a "significant other" who was periodically suicidal. In obtaining a doctorate in anthropology, he had specialized in cultural and psychological anthropology.

DKR had previously played the role of pseudo saboteur during US Navy war games. He had played the male lead in a UCLA Theatre Arts Department television production. And he had participated as patient, therapist, and outside observer in his dissertation research into a Zen-based form of psychotherapy in Japan.

Immediately after the experiential live-in research Dr. Reynolds noted some interesting parallels between the research and the pseudo sabotage he did for the navy in the early 1960s:

> At that time, my mission was to slip aboard a US Navy ship in port and plant fake explosives around the engine room. To accomplish the mission the necessary planning involved four stages of activity: (1) getting aboard, (2) locating the engine room, (3) planting the explosives, and (4) getting away.
>
> An identity had to be created. In this case I came aboard carrying films, appearing to be a projectionist with hands full so that the Officer of the Deck wouldn't require me to show an I.D. card. This

identity also permitted a bit of light banter about bringing on "a good one to show tonight," further distracting attention from my unauthorized boarding of the ship.

Once aboard I found myself relatively unprepared with regard to my knowledge of the ship's structural design. Fortunately, the strategy worked out beforehand involved my asking for a particular engine man supposedly in order to deliver a message from the radio room. We had reason to believe this engine man would be on duty in the engine room. Thus I would be directed to and have some reason for being in the vicinity of the engines. Small explosive packs were in my pockets and plastic explosives were strapped around my waist.

After planting most of my "explosives" I was fortunate enough to actually come across the engine man. A simple detail, the "wrong" name stencilled on my uniform shirt, made the engine crew suspicious of my identity. Eventually, I was "captured" and returned to my ship with all but the fourth and final stage of my mission accomplished.

In the neuropsychiatric ward research the establishment of a pseudo identity was equally crucial. Once in the ward it was necessary to have adequate understanding of what to look for and to keep at hand the proper equipment to execute the task (in this instance recording equipment by means of which he could preserve a record of his observations). The timing and the method of achieving discharge were also of importance.

Although we tried to anticipate problem areas in both settings and to devise counteractions for potential difficulties, it was clear that specific crises could not all be foreseen. The researcher had to depend on his own resourcefulness to carry out his role appropriately through predictable and unpredictable situations.

## Creating the Alternate Identity

Three major considerations were taken into account as we created the identity and history of David Kent. David Kent Reynolds is the full name of the anthropologist who became the experiential researcher. Throughout this report we refer to Kent in the third person. It is a literary convenience, but it also represents our recognition that he is within, yet somewhat alien (in time and behavior) to, Dr. Reynolds. He had to be sufficiently suicidal to be placed on suicide observation status; he had to be fairly typical of young male suicidal persons; and his history and character had to fit the researcher's as closely as possible (without being so close as to create psychological discomfort during the creation or reporting of the identity).

The resultant self was a shy, withdrawn, introspective, self-doubting young man. Kent was somewhat compulsive, dependent, tense, with flatness of affect, inappropriate smiling, and bodily complaints. He bore scars on his right palm from a suicide attempt. The personal history of David Randolph Kent was as follows: He was born in Dayton, Ohio, on September 28, 1940. He went to school in Ohio through the twelfth grade. His mother was very protective and he was very fond of her. His father was a tool- and diemaker who spent little time at home, preferring to devote his evenings to drinking at the corner bar. The father left the family when David was about six or seven, never to be heard from again. The boy and his one sister, a year and a half younger, fought a great deal in their early years.

Kent served in the navy from 1958 to 1961. During that period Kent had had one period of depression, treated on shipboard by pills, which was a reaction to his girl friend's leaving him. He was honorably discharged a radioman third class petty officer. He felt that his three years in the service were the best of his life. He made a few friends in the service, one of whom, Larry Evans, plays a part later in the story.

On discharge from the service Kent went to Saint Petersburg, Florida, where his mother was then living. From 1961 to 1963 he attended Saint Petersburg City College. His sister married during this period and moved to Atlanta, Georgia, where she now lives with her druggist husband and their three children. In 1963, when his mother died of cancer, Kent became extremely depressed. Dazed, he just sat around for weeks. He received no special treatment during that period, but he felt that a large part of his reason for living had been taken away from him.

From 1964 to 1966 he worked in a gas station, pumping gas. He did no mechanical work because he was not "good with his hands" and because he did not like to get dirty with the grease.

From 1966 to 1968 Kent worked as a sales clerk in a clothing store in Saint Petersburg (actually, it was a department store called Webb's City). There he met his future wife, who was working as a cashier. They were married in July 1968 and shortly thereafter Kent was fired because he was not aggressive enough in his efforts to sell. He began living on his wife's income. In 1968 and 1969 he was mostly unemployed although he did get a few clerk-typist jobs for short periods. The longer he remained unemployed the worse his domestic situation became. Kent admits that the problems were all his. He felt that his wife was wonderful, perfect. Her mother was equally fine, in Kent's opinion. He simply could not make a living.

In the spring of 1970 Kent's wife left him. He bothered her at times, trying to bring about a reconciliation. She called the police, and he was in some trouble with the law because of this episode. His wife apparently relented and allowed him to move in temporarily with her and her mother. But when his friend, Larry Evans, wrote inviting him to come out to California to get a job in the aerospace industry, Kent's wife encouraged him to accept the invitation. The plan was that she would follow as soon as Kent had established himself.

In August 1970 Kent came to Los Angeles by Greyhound bus from Saint Petersburg. He looked for a job at several places (notably Douglas Aircraft Company in Santa Monica). Nothing panned out. He earned a few dollars as a parking lot attendant, and his wife sent him a little money.

Kent made few contacts in California. His friend Evans was in Los Angeles, but he seemed to grow more distant as Kent's failure to get a job persisted. The young man met a few girls in a local Baptist church. But he had no money to take them out, nor did he have any desire for girls who, he felt, were interested in "you know what." So he led a fairly isolated life — sleeping, eating, looking for a job, and sitting around waiting. He was somewhat nervous and anxious and occasionally tearful in his sorrow over the folly of his life.

On Monday, July 5, 1971, their wedding anniversary, Kent called his wife collect to let her know how much he loved her. She told him she had met someone else and wanted a divorce. She was not going to meet him in California after all. Kent was crushed. He went home and swallowed twelve Seconal ("red") capsules in a suicide attempt. The Seconal had been prescribed for insomnia, tension, and head-aches a week or two before by a local physician. He was discovered rather by accident by his friend, Larry Evans, who promptly called the Suicide Prevention Center. Evans was advised to take Kent to the Los Angeles County General Hospital Emergency Receiving Unit. There Kent's stomach was pumped, and he was discharged the next morning with no treatment other than physical care for the emergency condition. Kent still more or less wanted to die, but he did not make plans for another attempt. Nevertheless, he knew life was not worth living as it was.

On July 6 and 7 the unkempt veteran wandered around depressed, confused, alone. Evans found him on the morning of July 8. Kent looked disheveled and had just missed being hit by a car when his friend found him. Evans called the Suicide Prevention Center again and was advised to take Kent to the local VA hospital. Kent went along voluntarily. He did not particularly care where he went or what he did.

Kent arrived at the VA hospital at 7 A.M. on July 8, 1971. His attitude was expressed in his own words: "I think I have a mental problem and I need to be in a hospital or something. I'm afraid I'm going crazy. That must be the reason I did what I did. I don't think I'm nuts, but no one in his right mind would try to do that."

Kent's history and identity had been created and refined at a meeting of staff members at the Los Angeles Suicide Prevention Center on June 18, 1971. Using a nine-item scale for predicting the suicide potential of younger males, Kent showed high potential in the following areas: he was married, Caucasian, had recently been markedly confused and disorganized, had been thinking of suicide nearly all the time, had had a problem with criminal behavior, and had zealously accepted traditional, culturally defined sex roles and goals. Two items were unclear: whether or not his wife was also suicidal and whether or not he was legally divorced. On one item of the high suicide potential scale he did not exhibit the characteristic associated with extreme risk: he had not recently been thinking of killing someone else.

Several other consultations proved of value. On June 22, 1971, the authors had met with a psychologist and a psychiatrist from the VA hospital in which the outsider perspective on suicide observation status had been obtained (Part I, above). They emphasized the need for role playing as a training device. They also believed that medication of some sort would have to be administered. They suggested cheeking the capsule or tablet in order to avoid its effects. On June 23 the researchers met with the building supervisor of the ward into which Kent was to be admitted. The ward had been selected as one fairly typical of those in that particular VA hospital. One ward had been rejected because the ward psychiatrist might recognize the researcher; another ward had been rejected because of a recent upheaval in its organization and staffing. It was decided at that time to bypass routine admissions procedures when Kent entered the hospital. Otherwise, there would be too many details to anticipate and cover. A normal-appearing patient file including current information and past history, as well as a VA identification plate, had been prepared beforehand for Kent (see Appendix B).

Prior to entry into the setting we anticipated a number of potential problem areas and prepared contingency plans for them. We decided to bypass admissions procedures, as noted above. We worked over Kent's personal history to provide high consistency but low "checkability." We created false addresses for relatives as well as a fake social security number, military service number, and other identification documents. Note-taking during hospitalization was to be done in a small notebook, or diary. Alternate possible means of getting information out of the setting and preserving data included telephone calls to a friend, visits by a friend, and private interviews with the building supervisor. We planned to have Kent avoid medication, if possible. Techniques for doing so included cheeking, putting the pill under the tongue, and using chewing gum to conceal the pill until it could be disposed of. Placebo medication was considered as a way of escaping the effects of antidepressants, but we rejected it as being too complicated. We discussed the probable consequences of being caught concealing medication. Our consultants advised that even if Kent's subterfuge was discovered and he was forced to take all his medication, the effects on his functioning would probably be minimal. DKR memorized the names, the appearance, and the possible side effects of the two antidepressants most likely to be prescribed for him, Elavil and Tofranil, so that even without ingesting them he could pretend to feel the effects. We planned at first to have Kent sign out AMA ("against medical advice") in order to forestall the routine follow-up procedures we believed accompanied regular discharge. Later on, however, we decided to try to manipulate Kent's presentation of suicidality so that he would spend one week in the locked ward on suicide observation status and one week in the open ward; then he would push for an approved discharge, MHB ("maximum hospital benefits").

We also had to anticipate various examinations. Kent's most recent suicide attempt method was selected so that there would be no residual signs that ought to show up in a physical examination. He was to take psychological tests and social service interviews naively, in his role as patient. We considered tactics for avoiding fights and homosexual advances in the ward. We made arrangements to gain access to all records of Kent's hospital stay.

Kent's appearance and the contents of his pockets were carefully planned. He was to wear a dirty, striped shirt, old, dirty, gray-green slacks that were too large for him, and dirty cotton underwear and socks. His shoes were to be old, unshined, and scuffed. He was to take no shower for the three days preceding admission, and his hair was to be uncombed.

When he was admitted, Kent carried in his pockets an old notebook with a few old entries in it, an old but usable ball-point pen, no wallet, a handkerchief, a picture of his "wife," and two dollars and eighteen cents. In his memory he carried the home phone numbers of the building supervisor and his co-researcher. In the event of trouble he hoped to gain access to a telephone and call for help.

Videotaped role playing proved most useful in developing the techniques used in creating David Kent, or, to put it another way, in immersing David Reynolds in a suicidal depression. With advice from a psychiatrist and a psychologist the researcher learned to slow his speech; he learned to be less articulate and helpful to a staff interviewer. During these extended preparatory sessions the experience still retained an artificial quality. The researcher learned some appropriate lines, such as "I don't know," "I don't feel like talking now," "Why don't you leave me alone?" He taught himself an appropriate gait and posture and lowered the volume of his voice. He began to accept the idea that there was no other place to go, that the hospital was the end of the line. He managed to squeeze out a few tears.

During the actual research experience the new identity emerged much more clearly. Reynolds developed a set of techniques, some cognitive (repetitions of "It's hopeless," "There's nothing I can do," etc.), some postural (slumped shoulders, eyes downcast, head forward and down), and some behavioral (shallow breathing interspersed by sighing, immobility, a slow, shuffling gait when walking), as well as situational cues (his ward dayroom) and social cues ( the social mirroring of the expectations of others) — all of which helped to create his alter identity. We have more to say below about multiple identities and the disadvantages inherent in the concept that each of us has only a single personality; here we simply wish to report that Kent became a very real person in this psychiatric setting. How real the reader may determine for himself as he reads the personal account of the researcher's in-hospital experience.

*Areas of Observation*

Because of the exploratory nature of the study and because of the suggestive influence (with the possibility of self-fulfillment) of pejoratively slanted hypotheses, we elected to assume an observational-empirical stance rather than one of testing hypotheses. In other words, we selected areas to look at, rather than emphasizing preconceptions of what to look for. The areas we chose indicate the specific focuses of interest as well as our general theoretical approach.

*Cultural values.* — Our culturally shared values include the positive valuing of privacy, independence, and personal space (Hall, 1959; Sommer, 1969). In a social setting where these aspects of living are perceived to be depleted or lacking altogether, what are the effects on the behavior, cognition, and emotions of the S-status patient.

*Stigmatization.* — The suicidal mental patient is stigmatized in two ways: he is both neuropsychiatric and suicidal. Is stigmatization present within the ward subculture? If so, how does it affect the patient's self-perception?

*Sensitivity to communications of others.* — While occupying a stigmatized status, a person is likely to be extremely sensitive to the communication of others' attitudes toward him (Goffman, 1963b). If the suicidal patient perceives a sense of stigmatization, what expressions from others are ego-satisfying? What expressions are personally disturbing? What acts are perceived as supportive and as showing interest and concern in the patient as a human being, and what acts are perceived as showing distance, professionalism, coldness, and disinterest?

*Institutional pressures.* — In psychiatric hospitals, the patient coalition is a main source of social pressure and support for the patient. How is the suicidal patient accepted by patient groups? How does patient-patient interaction (in contrast with patient-staff interaction) affect the suicidality of a patient?

*Patient-staff interaction.* — It is clear that patients usually see their relationships with staff members or the staff role functions differently from staff members. Decisions such as placing patients on or removing them from suicide observation status may be made without their understanding of the procedures and of the factors taken into consideration. How does the suicidal patient define the impact and role functioning of various staff members on him (such as ward physician, resident, nurse, aide, social worker, psychologist, and other ancillary therapists)? How does he perceive the decision-making process that determines his hospital fate?

*Patient identity and self-presentation.* — There is some evidence that the psychiatric patient is capable of presenting to the staff an identity that will be useful to him in some ways (Goffman, 1961a; Braginsky et al., 1969). How does the suicidal patient go about presenting a suicidal identity to the staff and to other patients? How is his identity documented? On the other hand, how does a patient communicate improvement? Once he has been defined as suicidal, is the task of presenting wellness within the hospital more difficult than that of presenting suicidality? Which cues are observed and recorded by staff members and which are ignored?


## THE JOURNAL

What follows is the introspective observer's account of his experience as a depressed, suicidal patient in a VA psychiatric hospital, only slightly edited. We have elected to leave the more general statements and the emerging hypotheses as they appeared so that the reader has some idea of their situational meaning, that is, the meaning in the context in which the ideas developed and made sense. The oscillating perspectives of David Kent and David Reynolds are apparent in the journal account. Sometimes quite personal and narrative in style, it becomes at other times more formal and analytic.

The journal is presented in its entirety. We feel that this descriptive account may well be the most important aspect of this book and that its usefulness may long outlive our theoretical and generalized statements by providing other researchers with meaningful raw data.

### July 22, 1971

This journal is essentially a chronological account of my experiences as a suicidal inpatient in B__ Hospital from July 8 to July 21, 1971. I am dictating on July 22 from my notes. I must begin by saying that the experience of becoming depressed was not entirely artificial. By drawing on and exaggerating certain natural tendencies and personality characteristics, I suspect that anyone with practice can put himself into a depression. The experience was very real to me. There were physiological changes within me, and the spontaneous thoughts and feelings that welled up within me were consistent with genuine depression. Yet even when I was feeling depression there was a part of me that was separated off, observing and noting for this report what was going on within me and outside me. The experience was very trying and very challenging, and it was unique; I will always treasure it as a benchmark in my life. It provides me with a base for empathy with depressed and suicidal patients which I would not otherwise have had. In other words, I feel it was worth investing two weeks of my life. Perhaps I should also confess that it afforded a fairly well-controlled, compulsive anthropologist an opportunity to behave in a strange, insensitive, self-indulging manner for a short period of time without threat of long-term consequences for that strange, loose freedom of behavior. With this introduction, let us begin with the morning of July 8, 1971.

*July 8, 1971, Thursday*

I got up early, dressed in the dirty old clothes I had planned to wear, went outside, and had my research assistant take a couple of photos of me with the dirt and the grease that one would expect to see on someone who had been wandering the streets for two days. I walked the two miles to the VA hospital, which gave me an opportunity to become a little tired, get into my role, get appropriately dirty, scuff my shoes, and spread a little more dust on my hair and body. As I began to feel David Kent emerge my world began to shrink. I think the problems of privacy and personal space are irrelevant for the severely depressed patient. My world was just slightly larger than the space my body occupied. It was as if I were living in a tunnel or had blinders on my eyes. My gaze was directed down and the people I passed were no more than trousers and shoes. And the ground that I walked on was blurred and dirty and unimportant. The feelings of "I don't care," "It's useless," "It's hopeless," grew naturally within me. I arrived at the hospital at 7 A.M. (the time I was told that the social worker would be there). As a matter of fact, the social worker didn't arrive till 7:30 and in that half hour I sat in the admissions office waiting room. As I sat and caused no trouble, people ignored me except when I was in their way. The workers who were sweeping and mopping asked me to move out of their way. Otherwise, there was no attempt at conversation, no move to find out why I was sitting there, and no attempt to see me as a human being. People looked through me. The depressed Kent interpreted that as more proof that the world didn't really care about him. He was sensitively picking up social cues that would validate his feelings of worthlessness and hopelessness. Finally, I asked the admissions secretary if the social worker had arrived and was told that she hadn't. Then I sat down in a chair and several times later the admissions secretary passed me, but as far as I could tell she showed no recognition of my presence. In fact, I had to ask her again whether the social worker had arrived. Only then I found out that, in fact, she had arrived a little while before. The social worker took me into her office and gave me a brief interview. Then she expedited the admissions procedure and called the ward directly. The ward sent someone over to pick me up and escort me there. At that time the staff knew I was on suicide status. I recall the escort saying, "Is this the one?"

I walked to the ward from the admissions building very slowly, head down. To be quite frank, I later couldn't recognize who the aide was who escorted me from the admissions building to ward 207B where I was to spend the next two weeks. I do remember his telling me that I was being cooperative and that this was a good sign, that I'd get out of the hospital soon. As we walked from the admissions building to the ward, he had already begun to tell me what was going to happen to me. I think it's a good idea to inform patients, in general, that such and such will occur and what it means. Not very much of what he was saying, however, sank through the layers of depression to a level of consciousness where it could be recorded and remembered for the future. But the emphasis on being a good, cooperative patient had begun even then. And the dimension of degree of cooperativeness is crucial in determining what one's patient experiences are like in the hospital.

I was ushered into what I suppose was the nurses' station. Again the recollections are fuzzy. It was, I recall, a fairly large room and there were several people in it; there was a phone, and it was a busy kind of room. The description corresponds to what I later learned was the nurses' room. At that time a number of people were introduced to me as ward personnel. They gave polite greetings, but later I didn't recall any of their faces or their names, either. The overall gestalt is useful to note here, however. Even though nothing was sinking in there were people trying to be helpful, being friendly, being concerned. And that filtered through the depression. The details of their offering their names and using mine and of the nurse who put her hand on my arm and then pulled it away when she felt that I was offended by it stuck with me. Another thing I recall is that people were continuously saying, "I know this distresses you but . . .," and then they would go ahead and carry out the procedures that they had planned; or, "Really I know how you feel, but I have to ask you these questions"; or, "It's important for me to get your weight." In some sense these apologies, while carrying out the procedures, supported the view that I was a useful person and my feelings counted for something. On the other hand, the fact that they carried out the procedures whether I desired them or not, whether I felt up to them or not, suggested that the procedures were more important than my feelings.

The ward on this particular day was in a state of disruption. The tiles were being taken up from the floor and being replaced, so there was a lot of noise. The source of the clatter and pounding was explained to me. Because the tiles were being replaced, there was a great deal of confusion and disruption of routine. I sensed the hassle that was going on. I was taken into a small room and was weighed, measured, and asked a few questions. In the room was a locked cabinet full of medicine. I spent a lot of time looking at the medicine and thinking about how I would like to get my hands on a bottle in order to kill myself. But I lacked the energy to act on these thoughts. Another part of me was wondering whether the aide would pick up my staring and my concern with the medication as cues to suicidal intent.

I was then taken to another room (it turned out later to be the conference room) where I sat at a table and several people asked me a seemingly endless series of questions about my past, why I had come in to the hospital, and so forth. I'd been in the ward only about half an hour, but by that time I was already beginning to learn about the limitations accompanying suicidal status and the advantages of getting off status. A doctor came in, asked me some questions, and suggested that psychodrama would be useful for me, but the aides told me that I couldn't go to psychodrama while I was on suicide status. The implication was that I couldn't participate in many activities while I was on suicide status. The aide also told the nurse that he was going to have to take my temperature rectally but that if I was going to be cooperative and not try to bite down on the thermometer, he would do it orally. I agreed to cooperate and he held the thermometer very carefully while the reading was made.

They asked me to empty my pockets and eventually to take off my clothes and put on the hospital pajamas, the "blues," as they are called. I was told that my pockets were being emptied so that anything of value could be put away for safekeeping and anything of danger could be taken away from me. I was also told that the blues were to make me readily identifiable as a special status patient and that as soon as I got off suicide status I would get my own clothes back.

The term, "special status," was described to me in two ways. It made me a kind of special patient who needed extra attention, but it was also called S-status or suicide status with the implication that I needed to be protected from myself.

The aide who brought me up to the ward got a little impatient with my slow speech and asked me to hurry up. He said that if I hurried up, we could get this business over with a lot faster. He was told gently but firmly by the head nurse who was doing most of the interviewing that it was all right, that depressed patients often can't speak any faster. I was very quick to pick up his critical attitude toward me and the defending, nurturant attitude of the nurse.

The doctor made a very good impression during our initial interview. He came to the conference room, and he seemed very concerned and very interested in what I had to say. He asked what I thought the hospital could do for me. I told him that the best thing they could do was to give me a handful of pills all at once and let me die. He responded that he had hoped I wouldn't say that. During the interview, there were more people dropping in and out, more names, all of which slipped completely through my mind without catching in my memory at all. I was tearful and spent a good part of my time either looking down or looking at the windows (again hoping, as a researcher, that they would pick up a cue that I was checking the possibility of attempting suicide by that route). They asked me if I had eaten breakfast. I told them that I hadn't, that I wasn't hungry, and that I didn't want anything. Nevertheless, they said they were going to order a tray for me, and one was brought in. When I refused to eat from it, they brought the juice up to my lips and tried to get me to drink at least the juice. I said I didn't want any, I wouldn't drink it, I wanted them to leave me alone, to get off my back. At this time I was feeling a bit of anger. It wasn't really as strong as anger; it was a sort of feeling a person gets when he is tired and people are nagging him. I wanted to be left alone, but I was powerless to stop them.

After these interviews — the questions asked are still very vague in my mind although I apparently answered appropriately, using the personal history that had been prepared earlier — I was taken to a shower room where I was asked to change my clothes and get into the blues. I didn't feel any sense of degradation in being asked to take off my personal clothes. I was very much relieved to get out of the questioning phase. The blues were clean although I was still dirty and they were comfortable but very sloppy. The aide pointed out to me that he didn't want me to feel as if I were a convict but that I was wearing blues so that they could watch me better. I was given some privacy in which to change clothes. This was the beginning of what I found consistently during my hospitalization — the black male aides are careful not to press the patient who is on suicide status. He is given a great deal of privacy and personal freedom. The aides go to great lengths in order to avoid having the patient feel as if he's constantly being watched or pressured.

I was then taken to the dayroom and for most of that first day someone sat beside me. The aide or nurse would ask if I wanted to talk, and I would wearily shake my head. I would stare at the floor and they would simply sit there. It was a good feeling to be close to someone as long as they weren't pushing me.

In a very touching gesture, one patient came up to me and mutely offered a cigarette. I shook my head in refusal, and he went away. Both patients and staff learn that another patient's refusal to accept a gift or an overture of kindness is not to be taken as an affront but rather to be interpreted in the light of the patient's illness status. I sat this way throughout the morning, my thoughts drifting, looking occasionally at the windows, noting that they were screened, tears occasionally coming to my eyes. At lunch I ate a small amount. I was watched fairly closely, although I was allowed the regular stainless utensils with which to eat. Back in the dayroom I was told that I hadn't eaten very much and that if I refused to eat, there were other ways to make me get the proper amount of nourishment. This was a veiled threat. The "other ways" were not spelled out.

Time passed very slowly in the afternoon. I could hear the television even though I didn't feel up to watching it. I could hear things that were going on even though I was looking down at the floor. It was interesting that although my senses of smell, taste, vision, and touch were depressed, my hearing was still alert to pick up things that were going on around me.

In the afternoon the ward was marched off to a recreation area in the patio behind building 210. I walked very slowly, unable to keep up with the pace of the other patients. I didn't try very hard and, anyway, I simply couldn't. An aide fell back and walked along beside me. I spent almost all of the recreation period lying on the grass. When I headed toward the bathroom in the patio no one asked my destination. I went inside and was allowed to use the toilet in private. There was an aide standing outside. Apparently he had been listening to the sounds that I was making. He poked in his head just as I was drying my hands. When he saw me he pulled his head back out and walked away. When I emerged from the bathroom, he was several yards off walking away. Thus I didn't feel that I was under constant observation. Perhaps he didn't want me to get the idea that they expected me to kill myself.

We returned to the ward and again I sat submerged in my depressed thoughts. I had the feeling then that my depression was coloring the atmosphere of the whole ward. I learned later that the patients and the staff were very much aware of my despondency and of their inability to get through to me at that particular time. It was during this afternoon that I experienced the first research crisis. It made me think very carefully about whether the study should be continued or not. The crisis was the attempted suicide of another patient in the ward. For if I was influencing the ward as I believed, then it might have been that my depression contributed to this other person's suicide potential. I had to think very carefully of the value of the research for suicidal patients in the long run. What good was it to learn how to prevent some suicides if, in the process, lives were lost?

On that afternoon the first hint of the suicide attempt came when a patient told the aide sitting beside me that there was a patient lying in the bathroom. The aide said he couldn't leave me. The patient responded that the man looked half dead. The aide rushed out of the room. When he returned, I asked the aide if the patient had died. He said that the patient hadn't died, that he had only wanted to die. I asked if he had tried to kill himself. He said, "No." Later I discovered that the aide had told me a lie. Mr. W. had attempted suicide by hanging.

Shortly afterward I thought I overheard two young nursing aides joking with slight bitterness that they had so many special patients that they wondered if the administration was trying to make a special ward out of 207B. I don't think they realized I overheard them. Their comment added to my feeling that I was a burden to the staff.

The nurse in charge reacted to Mr. W.'s attempted suicide by locking the door to the ward porch saying to the aide that there were too many dangerous objects out there. It was true that the ward porch at that time was cluttered with a miscellany of potentially dangerous objects. When a patient asked why the ward porch had been locked, however, the aide told him that it was because it was too cluttered; no mention was made of danger. Patients are to be protected, deceived, maneuvered.

I received my first medication at 4:30 P.M. on that first day. The patients on 207B were given medication in the following way. They lined up in front of a medication room and the nurse handed out the medication in small paper cups; the patient put the medication in his mouth and used the same paper cup to hold water which he drank in the presence of an aide; he then threw the cup into a wastebasket. I actually took the medication the first time to get a feel for its effects on me. On my relatively empty stomach (and keeping in mind my general sensitivity to medication) it made me somewhat dizzy, blurred my vision, and left a terrible taste in the back of my mouth. I suspected that it might interfere with my keeping up a good cover story so from that time on I was able to conceal the medication under my tongue, drink the water, and later spit the medication out into a piece of toilet paper or directly into a flushing toilet.

We went to dinner. Again, I didn't eat very much. After dinner I dozed a bit and was awakened by a nurse on the evening shift who interviewed me. She asked me essentially the same questions that I had been asked earlier, and I became suspicious that they were double-checking my story. Later I found that it was necessary to repeat my story for a number of aides who either hadn't read the records or preferred to get the story firsthand from the patient (or, possibly, they had read the records and had forgotten them). This particular nurse asked her questions in a kind of skeptical way. She probed and prodded in such a way that I had the impression she didn't believe what I was saying. She would ask questions like "And you've *never* been in the hospital before?" or "And you haven't done *anything* for the last two days?" as if she didn't believe that it was possible for one to wander around for a day or two in such depression. I felt anxiety during the interview not only because I felt the nurse was sharp enough to uncover loopholes in my story but also because I felt (as I think any patient might) that she was attacking my honesty or my credibility. I didn't like her at the start but later I came to see that her type of questioning was her way of expressing interest in a patient's history.

Before receiving evening medication the patients were lined up at the door of the hallway and searched for matches. I took the handkerchief, the wallet, the rolls of toilet paper (on which I blew my nose), the notebook, and the pen out of my pocket and held them up. Then the aides checked my other pockets for matches. After this procedure we got our medication. Then we went to bed. On that first night Mr. K., an aide, came in and gently tucked me into bed. It was comforting and soothing to have this kind of nurturant person put me to bed. Hospitals would do well to pick carefully the aides patients see when they go to bed and when they wake up in the early morning. These are very important temporal landmarks, especially for the depressed patient who may have difficulty in sleeping.

As I lay in bed reflecting on my first day in the hospital, I recalled the contrasting attitudes of sarcasm, criticism, hurry-you're-causing-waves on the one hand versus the patience, the understanding, and the attempts (even though they were sometimes blundering) to make me feel better. The attitudes I picked up from the people around me were my outstanding memories of that day. The other feature that stood out later as I thought back to that first day was that I didn't know much of what was going on. Lots of things were happening to me. I didn't know what was routine and what was special in my case. What could I reasonably expect from my day in this place? I had been given some written information (see Appendix C). It gave me a comforting sense of control, but I was in no condition to read it at first. Even after laboriously getting through the contents once or twice I was unable to recall a couple of minutes later what I had read.

## July 9, 1971, Friday

On July 9 I awakened to discover that the best time for killing myself in the hospital ward was early morning. Razors were lying about on the hall table. Aides, busy with their various routine tasks, were out of sight. There weren't enough night-shift aides on duty to keep individual watch on the special patients. I started to get a drink from the hall fountain, but an aide appeared and shouted "Stop!" Thus I discovered that I was not to take anything orally until some lab tests had been done that morning. I was handed a cup and told to urinate into it. I was escorted to the lab.

In the lab I first noted the particular privilege-granting authority invested in the aides. A female patient who possessed a privilege card was supposed to have her lab work done after us closed-ward patients. After chatting in a friendly manner with the aide, however, she was told by him to go to the head of the line. The lab technician drew a blood sample. I was struck by the professional, friendly, yet impersonal attitude of most of the laboratory technicians in the hospital. I was treated as a normal person in the labs and in the auxiliary therapy units, in contrast with the interactions in my home ward. After the bloodletting I was taken to breakfast. It was the custom in this ward for suicide-status patients to march at the front of the line when the patients were herded to chow, particularly when the number of aides available for escort was limited.

After breakfast I sank into my chair in the dayroom, head hanging. The chief nurse went around to each patient asking him how he was feeling. I learned then that it was Mr. W. who had tried to commit suicide, for the nurse asked him if his throat hurt. He very tearfully told her (and anyone else who asked him) that he wanted to die.

It was on this second day that my team leader began to make an impact on my life. Mr. D. was the nursing assistant who had been assigned as my team leader. He got me a toothbrush, a comb, and some mouthwash. The last was in response to my complaint about the bad taste in my mouth. I began to learn that rewards and requests would be funneled through Mr. D. He also brought me a tube of hair cream for brushing my teeth(!?). Was he checking on my alertness? Apparently not. At any rate I ignored it, using only mouthwash on the toothbrush. No favorites here; every patient got mouthwash that morning, the only morning it was given out while I was hospitalized.

Later that morning I was taken for X rays. On the way I noticed that passing staff members said "Hello" to the nursing assistant who was escorting me but ignored me. Of course, they didn't know me yet, but I picked that up, too, as a kind of rejection; it was another increment of evidence in my case that no one really cared about me. On the way to the X ray lab I had two chances to jump out in front of oncoming cars. They were going fast enough to be unable to stop or swerve had I actually wanted to kill myself. I mentally filed away that piece of potentially useful information.

Back in the ward, an aide gave instructions to the new aide who was to keep an eye on me. I thought they were talking about my concern with the windows. It was tempting to think that every private conversation among the aides concerned me. Again, there was a confused mix of grandiosity and worthlessness. Later that morning I took a shower. I was told that I would have to wash my own underwear since I had brought only one set with me. I should get in touch with my friend to bring more underwear.

I went to admissions staff that morning. I don't remember much about it. I recall that I cried. Perhaps that was when the doctor probed into my suicide attempt. Did I expect to die? Did I make provisions for rescue? He again invited me to psychodrama. There were a few minor errors in the personal history that one of the nurses read to the group, but I didn't bother to correct them.

At admissions staffing, the patient is brought from his "home turf," the dayroom, into a meeting room filled with authority figures who will decide his future. They ask him personal questions. He must give public answers. They discuss his case before he enters, during his interrogation, and after he leaves. Officially the meeting is an effort to coordinate treatment plans. But perhaps it is also a ritual to display staff power and confirm the necessity of hospitalization for an anxious, helpless person. Judging from my treatment, the display and confirmation functions were at least as successful as the coordination of treatment.

I talked with Miss J., the chief nurse, that day. I had asked her the day before why they couldn't just let me die. She brought the subject up and asked if I remembered what she'd said. I replied that she'd said it was "her job." She said that it's the job of medical personnel to keep me alive, that society allows us certain rights but it doesn't allow us the right to kill ourselves. I had the impression that she really was concerned with me as a patient and as a person. She was trying her best to respond to a very deep and morally charged question to which we both needed a good answer. In other words, her rationale seemed shaky but her concern was sturdy and helpful. She told me about Mr. X., a patient who had come into the hospital and had been placed on special status. He was later discharged with what she called a "hot line" to the hospital. He came in every day for his detail, but he could call any time that he felt blue. It happened that Mr. X., who was on escort detail, was in the ward at that moment. The nurse introduced us. She asked him if he would drop in to see me on Monday. She noted that it's often good for a patient to be able to share his feelings with other people who know how he feels. Mr. X., nondescript, leaning toward the homely, was not an attractive fellow. Yet apparently he could claim (daily?) a kiss from this nurse, and he didn't hesitate to do so. I was a bit embarrassed to watch the kissing. I stand in awe of this woman's self-sacrifice; she really gave of herself to help her patients.

At lunch I observed the pressure an aide can exert on a patient who is giving him trouble. A certain hostile patient was asked repeated questions, embarrassed publicly, forced to sit in a particular chair in the cafeteria, required to put his tray in a particular slot in the rack at a particular time, and so forth. The aide demonstrated his power to strangle the patient's sense of autonomy and freedom. We patients were well aware of this power. Later I discuss the methods of passive resistance a patient can use to check an aide from over-extending himself.

After lunch we were again taken to the patio area behind building 210. No one played ball. There was no ball. I couldn't have played ball even if I had wanted to because my pajamas would have fallen down; they were too large for me. Furthermore, my robe covered the snapless fly of my pajamas, hiding the fact that I wore no underwear. These clothing problems went unnoticed by the aides who assumed that I didn't participate in athletic activities because of my depression. While resting in the patio I talked briefly with Mr. W. He told me he wanted to die. He couldn't sleep; the medication didn't work. He felt that his was a hopeless case. I slept briefly on the grass. I was watched as I entered the bathroom, but again the aide was walking away as I exited.

Later on that day I was given a medical examination by some young residents. There was no problem with the thermometer; they didn't even consider that I might bite it. I'm not sure that they knew that I was on suicide status. I was treated pretty much as any patient might be treated.

The ward porch had been cleaned of assorted debris during the day while we were out of the ward. As I wandered out to the porch, however, I found a hanger. I slipped it through the screen on the window, checking to see that I could have strangled myself with it if no one caught me in time. I then took the hanger to one of the aides who accepted it without comment. The reader will share my relief that this incident was duly reported in my records (see Appendix B).

The Catholic chaplain arrived and talked with a patient in the ward. I asked him if suicide was a sin and he said, "Yes, it is, because only God has the right to take life since only God has given life." He asked what religion I was. I said I guessed I was Baptist. He supposed that Baptists felt the same way about suicides. He said that suicide really isn't a solution to life's problems. I said, "Thank you." He asked, "Did my talking help?" I said, "I have to think about it." He told me to ask him any time if I had any questions. He asked if I was on suicide status and I said, "Yes." He got my name and left.

The evening shift came on and a female aide came down and sat down next to me. She told me she had been assigned to watch me. I did some pacing on the second day. Walking, like sleeping, is a fairly effective way of avoiding social contact. It's hard to come up to someone, face him, and engage him in conversation if he is continuously on the move. Thus I walked and feigned sleep (as I'm sure other patients do) to avoid social contact.

Contact with other patients, however, had begun to become important to me by the afternoon of my second day (July 9). It was not the patient's job to be friendly and to be approachable; therefore contact with fellow patients was, at times, more meaningful than contact with aides. Patients had relatively little power. Contact that communicated friendly concern was the primary resource we had at our disposal to offer in a social exchange. One patient stood beside me silently for a while. Later he touched my arm several times as he walked by my chair. These hesitant forms of contact were helpful to me in pulling out of my depression. It may well be that this primitive form of social contact — the closeness, the touching — may be the kind the depressed patient can best appreciate. Such gestures don't imply a contrast between someone else's wellness and the depressed person's melancholy. When I first saw the gentle aide on the evening shift that day I said slowly, "Good evening, Mr. K." He seemed genuinely pleased that I had remembered his name. Later he remarked on that greeting.

After dinner we again went to the recreation area behind building 210, where the aides played volleyball. One patient who was not very good tried to play, but the aides covered his position so that, in fact, he wasn't able to play much at all. I couldn't walk around during that recreation period because the aides were involved in the game, and they wanted me to stay where they could keep an eye on me. I began to feel some resentment toward the athletic aides on the evening shift. What was the hospital for? Was it a place for them to have recreation or was it a place for them to help the patient? The high standards of play in the volleyball game and the competitive atmosphere were such that the patients really didn't feel comfortable taking part in the game. After all, we had spent much of our day sitting around. We weren't likely to be as coordinated or as energetic as persons who customarily led a more active life.

After we returned I played some chess with Mr. K. and watched television and went to bed. The patients in the locked ward all seemed relatively eager for bed at night. Sleep, television, and drugs offered escape from a drab existence. The doors of the sleeping area were kept locked during the day. Patients weren't permitted to lie in their beds until after evening medication. Stray thoughts drifted through my mind as I lay in bed that night.

I reflected that cigarettes and coffee were very important socially in the ward. Coffee was brought to the locked ward in the morning and in the afternoon. It gave the patients an opportunity to buy a cup and to converse. It broke the monotony of the long stretches of dayroom sitting. Cigarettes were exchanged to gain esteem and to initiate interaction. Asking for a light and bumming a cigarette were common encounters in ward life. The interaction that revolved around the television set was noteworthy, as well. Because there was only one colored TV in the ward dayroom, and because patients had differing tastes, one might wonder how particular shows were selected. Some shows were consensual favorites, such as cartoons or baseball games on Saturday mornings. For more specialized programs some patients would rush back from a meal or another activity so that they could be there first to turn to a particular program they wanted to see. A few times during my stay one patient asked if he could give a "channel check." Then he would flip the channels until he found a program that everyone seemed to like. Another approach was simply to ask the patients watching if it was all right to watch another program. Often no one really cared what was on TV. Later on I discuss the systematic reinforcement of uninvolvement and detachment throughout patient life which accounts for the patients' lack of concern with the program on television at a particular time.

I gazed into the darkness and recalled another instance of my mixed feelings of paranoia and grandeur. Earlier I had overheard a nurse talking with an aide just as she was coming on duty. She told her that she felt good until she got to the ward that day. I immediately interpreted her complaint to mean that she had felt fine until she arrived at the ward where my depression caused everyone to slow down and feel despondent. I feared that I had lowered her spirits. In fact, as the conversation continued I discovered that she felt bad because the ward was disorganized owing to the replacement of the floor tiles and the consequent disturbance of routine. I also overheard a couple of aides discussing their perception that the Elavil had "lit a fire" under me. They said that I used to be very slow but that I had begun to pick up some energy and activity. It is amazing what patients hear! Staff seemed to assume that we turned off our hearing unless spoken to directly. Inability to overhear conversations is a quality commonly attributed to nonpersons.

## July 10, 1971, Saturday

On the morning of July 10 I shaved unsupervised. Again razors were strewn about on the hall table. As patients got up the aides had the task of telling some of them about lab tests, filling out reports, and so forth, so there was no chance for them to supervise a special patient. I also discovered that during the morning's confusion I could go into the dayroom unwatched and write my notes. It became my routine to do so each morning. After breakfast we were again taken to the patio behind building 210. I was beginning to feel somewhat more sociable then. I sat and listened to other people converse. One schizophrenic patient, Mr. H., was speaking meaningfully, but in symbolic form. For example, he was telling a nurse that we have to scratch through the bark in order to discover whether or not a tree is alive underneath. I think that he was saying that we had to wade through some of his meaningless speech in order to see that there was a live, sensitive human being underneath. The symbolism seemed to escape the nurse. Perhaps she wasn't looking for it. She wanted to discuss my problems. The structure of the conversation was built on relatively short questions from her followed by long pauses and short responses from me. The long pauses in the conversation and the lack of any remark as I stood up and left to walk around the area were social cues that my problems were sufficiently annoying that I couldn't maintain the proper social niceties.

This nurse was fairly popular. She was transferred the next day to another building. I appreciated her interest in us on her last day. I saw her twice in the hospital grounds after that. Once she smiled her recognition and the second time she looked past me. I had been dropped from her familiar world. We ask a lot from staff members of psychiatric wards: to become involved with a succession of short-term patients, and to show genuine, individual concern about hundreds of different people and problems that are always the same. That anyone should succeed at such an undertaking is remarkable.

About this time my world was becoming larger. I was discovering new parts of the patio area that I honestly hadn't noticed before — huge grassy areas and tennis courts and a badminton court. I had been there several times but I simply hadn't realized they existed. It took more than a week of visits before I had a fairly complete picture of this circumscribed area.

We were then taken as a group to the canteen. I bought a Coke for Mr. W. The jukebox was playing. The canteen was a phony place, a place where one pretended to be on the "outside." It was a welcome change from sitting in the ward, though. We returned to the dayroom and watched the ball game on television. An aide was poking good-humored fun at an old gentleman patient who had used the word "funky." That was when I first realized that both aides and patients used some of the other patients for their own entertainment. For the most part the teasing was not ill intended and the patient who was doing the entertaining reveled in the attention that he got. Sometimes the joking was destructive because it reinforced "crazy" speech and behavior.

Earlier I wrote of the aides' power to subdue and manipulate patients. I don't want to leave the reader with the mistaken impression that patients were completely at the staff's mercy. There are certain modes of behavior which made the aides' work a great deal more difficult. These were passive forms of resistance: making the aides wait until the slower patients finished their meals; pretending that we didn't understand, thus forcing the aides to repeat; acting as if we didn't hear the aide until he had to give his command several times; or making the aide move to pick up something or hand something to us. These were subtle but real symbolic methods by which the patient could express his small share of power and autonomy in this system.

After lunch we were taken to the dayroom of the open ward

because new tile was being laid on our dayroom floor at the time. There I read a magazine. "I read a magazine." Thus I described the passing of an entire afternoon! Four words cannot offer any meaningful description of the crawling clock, the studied placing of page on page, the innumerable shifts of body, the gradually tiring eyes, the lack of sane alternatives. We went to dinner. After dinner I went into the bathroom of the dayroom of the open ward where I saw several razors lying around. I took the head off one of the razors at 5:40 P.M. and hid it in an old piano out on the porch of the open ward. One patient wandered out and found the razor head lying in the mechanism of the piano, but he said nothing. Another patient who seemed to be keeping an eye on me (although he was fairly disturbed himself) rummaged around apparently searching for the razor. I became worried that a patient might pick it up and use it on himself, so at 6:10 P.M. I slipped it onto the nurse's table. I did not mention what I was doing and no one saw me do it. Mr. G., a patient who had been sitting near the nurse's table, was called out a few minutes later and talked with the nurse. I suspect she was asking him where the razor head came from. It was medication time. Some time after I had lined up in the medication queue the nurse told me that I wasn't supposed to receive my medication then. No one told me what medication I was receiving or what schedule I was to follow. Another unknown. Another symbol of lack of control over my life. Later the chief nurse did tell me my medication and dosage on the two occasions when medication changes were being considered.

By this time it was clear that the patients' assertions that there were "hundreds of ways" and numerous opportunities to commit suicide while on S-status were not fantasies at all, particularly if the patient is alert and sets up staff complacency with cooperative behavior. There were plastic bags, there were hangers, there was broken glass along the edges of a window in the dayroom, there were razors readily available, and there were opportunities to jump in front of a car. In terms of timing one had to watch especially for changes of routine. For example, when we were temporarily using the open-ward dayroom there were a number of extra opportunities for suicide. The determined patient must watch for "loose" periods, that is, periods when we had just returned from a movie or from a meal or from medication, or when we first got up in the early morning. The suicidal patient has almost endless time to discover methods and to implement his plans. Even in the most careful of wards, I suspect there are several ways to effect a serious suicide attempt. Some aides and many patients recognize this fact. (Nevertheless, we later argue that suicide observation status is probably very useful in preventing suicides, but not because it effectively removes all opportunities for suicide.)

## July 11, 1971, Sunday

I remarked to aides that I had slept well the night before. I had decided to forget about my wife. I was emphasizing the improbable solution that I had to keep active, that I didn't want to think about her. An aide told me that I was looking better.

On that particular morning the razors were watched more closely than usual. I wondered if the aides had picked up my razor activity from the afternoon before.

From a patient's perspective, it is easy to criticize the aides for not properly caring for the suicidal patient. But much of the aides' and nurses' work is invisible to the patient. Some patients are unaware of the tasks that are performed in the ward offices when the aide isn't actually present in the dayroom. Only what directly affects the patient's life is noted or understood by the patient. Then, as the patient progresses to the unlocked ward and begins seeing what else the aide does, his direct contact with the aide is cut to a bare minimum by assignment to a detail, by receiving day passes, and so forth.

As I started coming out of my depression I began to be bothered by the thoughts, "What am I doing here?" "These guys around me are crazy." "I'm not like them . . . or maybe I am." The militarylike restrictions began to bother me more and more. The lack of privacy, the lack of personal space, began to be annoying. My world was no longer private and narrow. I needed more breathing room. The limitations imposed on me by my special status began to become onerous. For the most part, as the depression lifted and I looked for freedom, I found niches of privacy eating, in the toilet, on the ward porch.

After breakfast I had difficulty in the bathroom because of extreme constipation. This condition is nonexistent in my normal adult life. The inactivity of my depressed life may have contributed to this change. Perhaps the psychological holding back and holding in of depression contributed, too. I certainly couldn't explain the physiological turnabout in terms of medication because I hadn't been taking the Elavil since the first evening.

I stayed in the dayroom for awhile before taking a shower. I accidentally left my watch in the shower. When it was returned to me, I felt an exaggerated sense of my own incompetence and failure. Even small failures may be exaggerated by the depressed person. Another concern contributed to the magnification of my inadequacy. It was the worry that the role was becoming reality.

I pondered that morning the difficulty for staff in handling suicidal patients. In order to determine suicidality staff members had to depend largely on the patient's statements of his intents and feelings about self-destruction. The suicidal, depressed patient may give an outward appearance of normalcy. Without the reminders of hallucinations or other crazy behavior, it must be difficult for the staff to keep in mind that there is something very wrong with the depressed patient and that he is in need of constant protection from himself.

I talked with the nursing assistant who had accompanied me from the admissions building to the ward. I honestly didn't remember him from our first encounter. He told me that his job is not to help me die but to keep me alive. He said there are too many sad sacks in the world. He didn't want to run my affairs, he said, but I was fairly intelligent and perhaps I should go to school and become a teacher. He asked if I had written a letter to my wife yet, and I told him that I hadn't. He said that if she lived close, he would telephone her for me; but since she lived in Florida, it was too far. I was crying softly as I paced on the dayroom porch trying to conceal my tears. My pacing was interrupted by an aide with a newspaper. He handed it to me with the question, "Do you want to read the sports page?" This gross attempt at distraction turned out to be relatively effective at that moment.

At lunch there were tablecloths on the tables because it was Sunday. I wasn't sure what tablecloths were supposed to do for us. One other patient said that there were always tablecloths on the tables. (This is not true.) I suspected that the patients didn't notice the change and didn't care.

I felt myself naturally drawn to Mr. W. who was the only other seriously suicidal patient at the time. He told me that he would kill himself when he got the chance, that he wanted to die, that he had nothing to live for, and that he had tried to kill himself. He asked,

"Did you know?" I told him I knew. He wanted to know how I had tried to kill myself. He wanted to know if I had been admitted for a suicide attempt and whether or not I had been committed to the hospital or had come in voluntarily.

That afternoon while I sat reading on the ward porch an aide brought Mr. W. out there for a session. I overheard his peculiar technique for handling this suicidal patient. I suspect that I was meant to overhear it, the message being that I might be like Mr. W. twenty years later if I didn't shape up. The aide was telling Mr. W. that he had to talk about his problems to the staff, that they weren't capable of opening up his head and seeing inside. There had to be a reason why he came back to the hospital, and there had to be a reason why he tried to kill himself. Mr. W. countered with his typical response. He had nothing to live for, his problems began long ago in 1945, he was simply unstable, and there was nothing that could be done for him. The aide responded that, in his own case, if things weren't going well for him, he'd do some soul-searching to find out why life was so hard. The aide's tone was aggressive. I can well understand his frustration and anger at Mr. W. for failing to respond to a gentler approach.

During dinner I began to see that patients become an audience in front of whom the aides perform. The daily hospital world is a circumscribed realm in which the aide is top man most of the time. Out in the larger society the young, black aide is seldom in a position of authority or prestige. The hospital world may take up much of the aide's time even after his shift is over. He can hang around socializing with the other aides. He can play basketball and volleyball with his peers. Thus conditions in the hospital favor the natural development of a kind of aide clique. The structuring of the ward society provides the aide with a great deal of gratification, prestige, and authority with accompanying responsibility. By this, my fourth hospital day, the depression had begun to lift and people seemed to care about my staying alive; I began to hope. We were taken to a recreation area in the afternoon. I was free to mingle with patients from several wards. The sun was warm, the grass inviting, the faded lawn chairs . . . But where was the aide who was supposed to be watching me? He, like the others, was off playing basketball. He didn't care that I was on suicide observation status. His game was more important than my life. It dawned on me that the staff had been making a fool of me. How simpleminded I'd been to believe that these strangers could ever really care about my life. I was just another increment of nuisance and work for them.

I wandered around the area testing garden hoses for flexibility and fit as a way of hanging myself. No one paid any attention to the small fellow in baggy hospital blues. The others were all engrossed in their own worlds, and I really didn't exist for them then. The hoses weren't going to suit my purpose, I'd decided. Then, as I headed for a chair, I stumbled upon a piece of worn and weathered rope lying in the grass.

Joy! Fear! And the beginnings of a consuming anger that could emerge now that a mode of expressing it had been found. I would show them! I sat in the chair in plain sight of my fellow patients and tied a hangman's knot in the rope. No one asked what I was doing, no one tried to restrain me, no one told an aide, no one seemed to notice at all. My stomach felt empty, hollow, and hot. I couldn't share my anger at the uncaring staff even with my patient peers now because they were indifferent to my death, too. It was all decided now. No other alternative presented itself nor did I seek one. The only way I could punish them and avenge myself and disturb their holy routine and show them I meant business and escape any punishment they might wish to visit on me and mock and hate and spit on them all — the *only way* — was to hang myself.

I carried my rope (how precious it had become, my conspirator now) to the tree hidden behind the barbecue pit. I threw the rope up over the limb . . . At the time I was genuinely frightened that I might actually do myself harm, so the rational, observing aspect of my personality made arrangements that would prevent me from being carried away by the flood of feelings that threatened to overwhelm me. I pulled on the rope until it broke. Only then did I put the noose around my neck and rub it back and forth until I suspected there were red, angry marks on my skin. My story was to be that I had attempted to kill myself but that the rope broke.

I took the broken rope to the aide at the basketball court and told him that the damn rope broke, that the ropes that they left lying around here weren't strong enough. He didn't understand at first but then he asked if I had tried to use it. I told him that it was too damn weak and I walked away and lay on the grass. There was a tremendous sense of frustration that no one genuinely cared whether I lived or died.

The aide's first response was to come over to where I was lying and tell me that I'd better stay right where I was on that hill so that they could keep an eye on me. (Such administrative restrictions are commonly the first response of nursing personnel in time of crisis.) A few minutes later another aide came up and asked if I'd tried to kill myself. I said "Yes." He asked where I'd found the rope. He said, "What are you trying to tell us? That we're not taking good care of you?"

He checked my neck. He, too, told me to stay on that grassy hill. He asked if I played volleyball. I told him that I didn't play volleyball, that I felt better, and that I was glad that the rope had broken. I talked briefly with Mr. W. (a fellow patient on S-status). He was then lying on the same bank. He knew I'd attempted suicide. I told him I wouldn't do it again. A nurse came over and asked me questions about why I'd tried to kill myself. She asked if I'd participate in the volleyball game that had just started. I told her I'd shoot some baskets. I did while she watched. I was kept under constant supervised observation during the rest of that period in the patio.

After we returned to the dayroom a nearby patient got the worst chewing-out that I heard throughout my hospital stay. My interpretation was that the aide was very angry at me, but he exploded in the direction of a more aggressive patient sitting close to me. I was watched more closely in the dayroom that evening.

The next morning one aide said to another to be careful and watch the (it sounded like) "RES" patients. I thought back over the first few days of treatment. Now I had begun to develop a general picture of what ward life would be like. The morning shift was focused on therapy, the afternoon shift specialized in leisure activities, and the night shift maintained the status quo until morning. Weekdays were therapy days. Saturdays and Sundays were slow days of boredom. The cycle of activities was determined by routine schedules. And schedules were made to fit the staff's time preferences and interests. Going to activities could be thought of as a progression out from, and back along, the spokes of a wheel whose hub was the dayroom. Activities began and ended in the dayroom, whether the activity was breakfast or testing, lunch or sleep. The dayroom was the center of patient life. Although this account may appear to paint days filled with activity and meaningful events, that is far from the truth. The days were long and mostly uneventful. Boredom was the rule, not the exception. But boredom must be devoured mouthful by gagging mouthful like tasteless air-filled cream pies. Boredom is not something to be written about.

## July 12, 1971, Monday

I noticed fewer razors out this morning, and there was a closer watch on those that were to be seen. I went into the bathroom and shortly afterward I heard someone call in through the door, "You OK, Mr. Kent?" The cloak of supervision had been pulled a snap or two tighter.

Mr. X., the outpatient, came to visit me. He began our conversation with the question, "How was your weekend?" I learned that this opening gambit was pretty standard throughout the ward. It had different meanings, though, depending on whether it was asked by a patient or a staff person. For staff the day was divided into hours on the ward and free hours, the week into a workweek and a weekend. The weekend was for recreation, for getting away, for trying on new roles, seeing new sights. For the patient the weekend was an attenuated extension of the week — more time in which to do even less.

Mr. X. was a rather nervous but friendly fellow. He sat with his right leg crossed over his left, his foot constantly bouncing. The conversation was pitifully forced but helpful on a primitive level. I felt the need to end it appropriately but didn't really know how. Mr. X. had a date that weekend and was proud of what had been a big step for him. A patient came in and offered the two of us candy. I didn't feel up to accepting it but Mr. W. did. The chief nurse came in and talked with me while sitting on the arm of Mr. W.'s chair. She explained that I was to be considered at a staff meeting the next day; it was the next step in my hospital progress. As we chatted she asked if I still had self-destructive thoughts, and how my weekend had been. I told her my medication was too strong, that my eyes weren't focusing. She said that she would try to get the medication reduced. She mentioned that we should begin planning for discharge. Vocational testing, when I felt better, was anticipated in their plans for me. How long did I expect to stay in the hospital? she pressed gently.

There was a kind of group meeting that morning. Patients made verbal slips such as calling the aides "doctor" or "sir." We sat in a circle. I listened without contributing. It was in the group meeting that I first "learned" about the possibility of going AMA (i.e., being discharged against medical advice). Before then Kent had naively believed that he could leave only when the staff gave permission. The nursing assistant in charge of the group meeting kept a close eye on the clock. Precisely at 9:15 A.M. the meeting ended, on schedule. I had the feeling that the meeting was almost a formality, and the usefulness of it simply wasn't understood very well by either patients or staff. Perhaps the person in charge felt that private informal discussions with team leaders were more effective. To the patients the meeting served as a break in routine sanctioned as part of therapy. It was a formal, ritualized chance to complain, ask questions, and learn by listening.

After the group meeting I showered and washed my underclothes out by hand. I felt that the aides were particularly kind and sympathetic that morning. At lunch I learned another of the (illegal) privileges of aides as I overheard one patient offer to get a sandwich for an aide. He refused the offer this time.

The afternoon was slow. I recall a nurse telling me that my eyes were pretty. Even such gross flattery was appreciated by a nondescript person emerging from depression. I played chess with a Filipino nurse. Even minor victories were filling me with elation. The danger of elation brought on by success was that I felt the pressure to try to succeed at other things. I knew that if I tried enough things, I would fail and get slapped down. It's the sudden plunge from cotton-candy success to rock-bottom failure which hurts sufficiently, I suspect, to precipitate suicidal activity. Mr. W. offered me some of his chocolate bar that afternoon. I was pleased at the gesture and accepted his offer. I read a lot, but I got tired of reading. Then I paced. The television fare was insipid. It was difficult to sit still for it.

After dinner we went again to the patio area behind building 210. There I shot baskets and played catch with the softball. I quickly became physically tired because I had become accustomed to the sitting existence of patient life. I couldn't join in the basketball game that was being played later because of fatigue; anyway, my pajama bottoms would have fallen off, they were so baggy. Furthermore, I didn't have any tennis shoes (there were no extra "public" shoes left in the large cardboard box). I explained my reasons for not participating to one of the aides when he asked, and he accepted them as excuses commonly given.

I played chess later in the evening. That evening I found that several patients' beds were being rearranged. Mr. W. had been having trouble sleeping. Since he was on suicide status, his bed was prominently in front of the door to the sleeping area. When the door opened, the light from the hallway shone directly in his face. That morning I had suggested to my team leader, Mr. D., that I would be happy to switch beds with Mr. W. so that he could sleep better. My bed was just inside the door, but to one side in the shadows. What was finally decided was to place Mr. W., a somewhat aggressive patient, and me in the three-bed seclusion room across from the toilet. The fact that there was no locker for any of us in the seclusion room seemed unimportant to the aide who made the switch, but it mattered a great deal to us. We had been deprived of more than our lockers by this change. Though lacking locks the metal cupboards represented something of the personal and private aspects of life. Like our beds they symbolized space that was ours, but it was space that could be invaded, manipulated, even withdrawn at the whim of the staff.

When we got into bed after medication I tried to close the door in order to shut out the light, but I was told, "You can't close the door. You're on suicide status." I felt there was mixed sarcasm and sadism in the aide's voice. The light flowed into the room until Mr. K., my friend, came by and closed the door so that the light wouldn't bother us. We didn't forget our benefactor. This may seem like a minor incident, but there are few events in a patient's ward life of any greater consequence. I lay in bed thinking that patient life is best described as a series of forty-five-minute waits punctuated by interruptions. An attitude of detachment and noninvolvement was consistently fostered in us. We might be watching a television program, but when the time came for us to go to an activity or to a meal, the television was abruptly turned off. If the patient was reading or conversing, these pastimes were also interrupted for a scheduled activity. Similarly, involvement with other patients was sometimes disrupted by a sudden lack of response as they turned inward to listen to voices or blot out a painful sequence of thoughts. Involvement with the aides was cut short when their shift ended.

I also thought of the growing attachment I had to the nursing assistant, Mr. K. His was the first name I had learned in the ward. A few hours after he had been introduced to me, he asked me what his name was, and I couldn't remember it. So he told me very gently and kindly again, and I remembered after that. He seemed to care that I learn his name. He was very quiet and nurturant, yet masculine in his way. He was effective with dependent, depressed patients. He pressed the withdrawn, reluctant patient just enough without splintery pressuring. He would let me know that he trusted me by disdaining the required search during the nightly pocket check for matches.

*July 13, 1971, Tuesday*

I was up at 4:30 A.M., unable to go back to sleep. Partly I was nervous about going to staff that morning. I tried to go into the dayroom, but I was told that patients couldn't go into the dayroom yet. I learned that there was a lights-on signal that informed patients when the dayroom was on limits again in the morning.

At 5:15 I wandered back into the hallway to the nursing table and told the aides that I couldn't sleep very well this morning. They told me that it was almost time for me to get up anyway. I don't know how often bed checks were made in that ward. I do know that there was no check between 4:30 and 5:15 that morning. I told the aides that a noise had bothered me through the night. They listened and said it was the radiator. In fact, it was a forgotten sprinkler running outside the window all through the night.

As I looked into the bathroom that morning, I saw Mr. W. shaving. He complained that he slept only on rare occasions, but I doubted it. At night he lay very still, and he was hard to arouse during the day as well as during the night. He said he had no opportunity to kill himself but would do so as soon as he had a chance, yet each morning he shaved himself unsupervised. The razors were out again this morning. I was reminded that the morning was an opportune time to commit suicide.

My thoughts strayed from topic to topic as I sat writing notes that morning in the dayroom. (1) The semi-interest that the staff showed in the patient was probably very realistic. Staff members did seem concerned and interested, but it was probably hazardous to fake more interest than was genuinely felt. Sometimes the bland semi-interest was frustrating for the patient who was longing for rich expressions of love and concern. This problem is also found outside hospitals; it pervades our society. (2) How distracting and entertaining the hallucinatory ramblings of some patients were! One man hallucinated in English and Spanish. Some patients longed for attention. Attention seeking became almost a game for them. They didn't go for medication; they failed to make their beds or carry out other routine tasks; and they waited to be asked (or yelled at) personally before they attended to any of these simple duties. In contrast, the good patient, the cooperative patient, in addition to doing his assigned work regularly, was never really involved in watching television, reading, or whatever. That was because his name might be called out at any time over the intercom system and he had to be ready to respond immediately. Thus the good patient was always expecting interruption. (3) I speculated about what a ward for non-cigarette-smoking patients might be like. It would be remarkably different from this ward. There would have to be very few ashtrays, probably a minimal amount of morning and evening sweeping and mopping, and no pocket checks in the evening for matches. The social interaction pattern would be severely disrupted without cigarettes; patients would have more spending money. A different life setting would emerge from the single factor of removal of cigarettes.

As usual, morning cigarettes were distributed, with free GI cigarettes going to patients without funds. Medication was passed out. At 6:25 the coffee came in. Mr. D., the aide, arrived early. I told him I was nervous about "staff," but he said not to worry, that I wouldn't be in there alone; he would be there, too.

I talked informally with two warm, kind Filipino nurses. They had a language problem and lacked deep understanding of American ways. They were looked down on by some of the nursing assistants who saw them as having better pay and higher prestige yet being less capable of understanding the patients. One of these nurses emphasized that because I was an honest and principled man my attempts at working in sales were not successful. She remarked that we all suffer when we lose someone we love. I asked her if she had ever broken up over anything. She said she'd had sorrow in her life too, but not enough to cause depression to the same degree as mine.

That morning there was a patient meeting run by patients. It began with a moment of prayer and meditation followed by the pledge of allegiance, reading of the minutes, and some minor business. On that particular morning Dr. L., the new psychiatrist for the ward, was introduced formally to the patients. We had heard of the change several days before. Since our contacts with the psychiatrist were minimal the change made little difference to most of us. The introduction was followed by polite applause from the patients. I expected many whispered remarks in that Dr. L. was a woman —

attractive, blond, and well built. My expectations were unfulfilled, perhaps because of the generally nonsexual atmosphere in the wards. For most of us the nurses, too, were gendered females, but they were not "women" in the sense of socially desirable or attainable cross-sex companions. The professional role permeated their personae. Perhaps the medication was a factor, as well as the minimal amount of sexually oriented stimulation coming into the ward. After the introduction of the new psychiatrist, several patients' names were drawn out of a hat. They were awarded twenty-five-cent canteen coupon booklets. Then the meeting was adjourned. During the meeting some patients were sleeping and one patient was disruptive.

Mr. X. visited me in the ward that morning. He said that I was scheduled for an 11 A.M. dental appointment. This kind of information was very valuable to me. It gave me some sense of control over my day. Usually the locked-ward patient had no idea that he had been scheduled for an appointment until he was called by his escort. He was also able to tell me that the "staff" to which I was to be presented started at 9:30 and not just "this morning." Waiting for that important event was upsetting. I was too nervous to be even temporarily distracted by reading or television.

I was able to write a letter to my pseudo wife, Sharon, telling her that I wouldn't dispute the divorce, that I didn't blame her for finding someone else, and that I hoped she had good luck in the future. There was a lot of feeling invested in this letter even though it was directed to an imaginary person. I realized that my nervousness came not only from anticipation of going before the staff but also from the decision to write this liberating letter. And perhaps I was fearful of coming off suicide status.

It was about this time that I began to perceive myself as a burden on other people. Before then I hadn't cared much what trouble I was causing others. But as the depression lifted day by day, I began to see that I was utilizing (exhausting?) the resources of many people in getting myself well. I talked about these feelings with Mr. D. He reassured me that the staff didn't mind, that they were there to meet my needs, and that it was their job. Nevertheless, my feelings remained the same. I began to make plans to leave as soon as possible so that I wouldn't put more of a strain on the staff than necessary. A low self-image could emerge only when I recognized again that other people inhabited my world, and when I compared myself with them.

The disposition staff meeting proceeded smoothly. The tears that puddled out as I talked about the letter to Sharon were natural and genuine. The doctor asked about the contents of the letter. I told him briefly. The letter had been sealed and mailed by Mr. D. My attention drifted as I wondered if a staff member had read it and if there was anything in the record about it. From the staff discussion it seemed likely that I would come off suicide status in a couple of days. During this staff meeting Dr. S. probed into the issue of my expectations for rescue during the recent suicide attempt. He said, "This is very important. I want you to think very carefully about this. Did you really want to die?" I hesitated — I guessed so. I was dismissed rather abruptly. It was as if a consensus decision concerning my case had been made so I could go. The staff had asked what I would like to do. But, in the end, I was told what they would do about me. This resolution was both intimidating and reassuring. There was no question that they made the final decision and that they assumed responsibility for the decision.

I was escorted to my dental appointment by an aide. The X-ray series took fifteen minutes and I was back in the ward. As we walked the aide asked about my history. He apparently hadn't read it. He told me that having a history of mental hospitalization makes it harder to get a job. Was he chiding me? Was he criticizing my weakness? I said, "Yes, but I didn't know any place else to go." He concurred that I had done right, that I had to get myself straightened out first before I could get a job.

Although Mr. D. had been reminded during the staff meeting and again shortly after the staff meeting that I was to go to psychodrama that day at 1:30, nevertheless at that time we patients were marched down to the patio area. So I reminded him yet again. He admitted that he'd forgotten about it, and then he accompanied me personally back to the open ward where the psychodrama was to take place.

I had very strong feelings about the practice of psychodrama in that ward. On the whole, I resented it. It forced classical analytic interpretations of childhood and personal history on the patient. It was a method of teaching proper emotions toward specific situations, with "proper" meaning "what the therapist considered appropriate." The key actor-therapist (who called psychodrama an action therapy, not a verbalizing therapy) verbalized a great deal. Selected patients acted out key scenes based on events in their pasts. Then the professional people were asked to comment on and interpret the drama. There were more professionals than patients in this group!

The patients' views were disvalued, often ignored or omitted. There was a great deal of ego-tripping and mutual backslapping for "insightful" (that word meant "boldly phrased yet acceptable") comments from in-group members. The word "shit!" brought smiles and nods from listeners. I abhor the game playing that may hide under the guise of sincerity and frankness in T-group, group therapy, and psychodrama. The psychiatrist and most of the members tended to give simple interpretations of the patients' complex experiences. They categorized one person's childhood as "deprived" and felt they understood him completely on the basis of that label. One patient's problem seemed to center on his guilt at sending his mother to a nursing home and his dissatisfaction with their subsequent relationship. I wondered why he didn't try to make amends and straighten out the relationship with her rather than trying to learn, in the group, how to handle his guilt more constructively.

The three people who enacted scenes for the group in that particular session might be called a kindergartner (his first time at doing a scene), a third grader, and a high school graduate of psychodrama. I was sufficiently aroused to risk exposure of my role by giving a toned-down interpretation of what I had seen. Eighteen people were trying to teach a young black patient in the middle of the group the proper attitude toward his mother, toward emotional expression, toward verbalizing his feelings, and so forth. I was ignored and passed over, and I wasn't encouraged to respond after that. I hadn't made an appropriate comment. The conditional encouragement and support for the acceptable comment which were offered to the patient soon became distasteful to me. Encouragement and support were very useful for me when I was deeply depressed; but as I clawed toward the surface of depression and gasped breaths of reality, the artificiality of such support became stifling, not invigorating. A couple of people later asked me how I felt about psychodrama. I told them that it took a little getting used to. I pointed out, for example, that it was hard to know all about the sources of love in one patient's family of twelve children since only the relationships with the father and mother had been examined.

By the afternoon I had begun to manage a hesitating but genuine smile. It felt good. It was hard, though, to keep from becoming hyperactive and hypereuphoric. There was a tendency to go overboard a bit after holding myself in check for so long.

I asked an aide in the early afternoon for scissors to trim my mustache but apparently he forgot. I asked Mr. W. again in the evening, and he, too, forgot. But when I reminded him before bedtime he got the scissors and watched unobtrusively while I used them. They were sharp-pointed scissors, but we had established so strong a sense of mutual trust that I think he could feel confident in letting me use them.

That evening my notes read as follows: "Mr. W. is really a good guy. I wouldn't attempt suicide on his shift even if I felt like it." It may be that the most effective way of keeping a suicidal patient alive is for at least one member of each shift to establish a good relationship with him so that he feels a personal reluctance to commit suicide. Certainly my anger at some aides contributed to my pseudo suicide attempt.

As I sat in the dayroom that evening, I overheard a patient telling a nurse that in order to get back into the hospital, he had lied when he said he was thinking of killing himself. He said that he had no more notion of killing himself than anything but he feared they wouldn't have taken him into the hospital otherwise.

After dinner I became engrossed in the all-star baseball game on television, but it was interrupted by movie call. Since we were scheduled to go to the movie, everyone had to get up and go. We went to building 210 (the women's building) to watch the movie, *On a Clear Day You Can See Forever*. After the drabness of ward life, there was a tendency to overinvolve oneself in the engrossing fantasy of the movie. I was chilled, thrilled, and near tears in response to melodrama that would have little impact on me in other circumstances.

By this time I had begun to learn some of the survival tactics of patienthood. When I showered and selected new pajamas I checked to see that all the buttons were attached and that the snaps weren't mangled and unusable. I began to hurry slightly so I could be the first one back from a meal in order to turn to the television channel of my choice. I learned to conceal bread in my pockets to feed the birds in the shrub outside the ward porch. I had learned to roll up toilet paper and use it for tissue (to blow my nose and to hide and accumulate medication). I learned to get up early to ensure there was hot water for shaving.

I found myself gazing through the windows at the outside for long periods of time. I was still sensitive to the reactions of other people around me, and I was quick to interpret them as rejections.

Acts that were certainly not intended to relate to me in any way I took quite personally. For example, Mr. K. came back from the movie that evening and began playing dominoes with another patient without sitting down to what I had come to think of as our "usual" game of chess. I felt rejected because he hadn't offered to play.

I found the hospital routine very much like duty in the armed forces. There was much waiting, the frequent use of a person's last name as the term of address for patients and for aides, a lot of ordering around, a dullness in the interaction and stimulation. It was a sense of guys-being-together, much like the camaraderie that enlisted men feel in the service. Intercom announcements were repeated; they sounded very much like the word passed over a ship's intercom in the navy. We were called at various times by various people "guys," "fellows," "men," "OK, let's go," "gentlemen," "locked-ward patients," "207B patients," and so forth. None of these was delivered in a tone of voice which was demeaning. In fact, when in the cafeteria the aide called, "OK, 207B, let's go," there was a feeling of esprit, a kind of in-group identification that was warmly rewarding.

## July 14, 1971, Wednesday

I got up at 5:30, shaved, brushed my teeth, and wrote my notes. During medication that morning the patient in front of me tried to conceal his pills in his pocket. The aide easily caught him, saying, "What do you think I'm up here for?" But, as usual, I had no trouble concealing the medication and spitting it out later. The difference was primarily because I had built up an identity as a cooperative patient.

After breakfast the scheduled morning meetings were called off. I was told personally that the meeting I had been assigned to attend wouldn't be held that day because there was not enough staff. Shortly afterward, a group announcement to this effect was made. Dr. L. and the chief nurse made the rounds. The doctor remembered that we'd met in psychodrama and in staff. I told her I was about ready to go off suicide status. I told Mr. D. the same thing and he replied, "When you're ready, come and tell me." Mr. W. was crying as they made their rounds. He told them that he was going to kill himself. "They" had taken everything away from him, he said, but he'd do it. The staff couldn't seem to get him interested in anything.

I read that day. I played some chess and then I taught a nurse how to play chess. I found that teaching emerged inevitably and spontaneously in my behavior. I couldn't escape it. I played billiards and read a magazine. I showered and changed clothes. I felt quite well. In this simple style of life distractions such as eating or showering or sleeping become important and pleasurable. The aide who had forgot the scissors the day before brought them to me that day. Ah, well . . .

I was beginning to socialize more. I found myself naturally conversing with the younger and clearer-thinking patients. New faces kept appearing and disappearing in the ward. As I got better and started interacting with the staff there was a period in which the older, sicker patients began to avoid me, to walk away as I approached, and to fail to respond to my efforts at conversation. It was as if they were communicating to me, "We don't need each other anymore."

I decided that morning, during one of the long periods of waiting, that it would be useful to have psychiatrists, social workers, and psychologists work on a 1 P.M. to 9 P.M. shift now and then or even regularly. A late shift would be useful because patients have very little to do in the afternoon and evening; it would utilize office space more efficiently; it would make use of the patient's "dead time" instead of having therapy personnel competing with one another for appointments in the morning.

Mr. D. and I discussed psychodrama. He said that I had to want to go to it, that I shouldn't go just because someone told me to attend. I told him I felt ready to come off status. He arranged for an interview with the building chief, Dr. C., in a private office. Dr. C. was the only person in the building who knew my other identity. I passed him my notes. I learned then that an account of my suicide attempt hadn't found its way into the nursing notes. Dr. C. removed me from suicide status. As planned, I had been on S-status in the locked ward for seven days.

I had the feeling that Mr. D. was proud that I was doing so well. The chief nurse talked briefly with me about continuing psychodrama. When the evening shift came on in the locked ward, one aide knew that I was off suicide status, but a second aide didn't know it. I was somewhat disappointed that this step wasn't public knowledge. But the incident revealed the unimportance of suicide status in the aide's perception of me as an improved patient. In fact, it didn't make much difference (except legalistically) whether I was on or off suicide status. The aides considered me no longer suicidal.

No one had explained to me the privileges associated with coming off suicide status and getting a privilege card. So I asked about it. I was told that with the card I would be in the quieter open ward, that I would be able to stay up till 10 P.M., that I would be able to attend more activities, and that I would have more freedom. By this time I was highly motivated to change wards. The day seemed to grow longer and longer in the locked ward. All the books had been read, all the games played, all the magazines leafed through. I found myself more and more out of the dayroom and in the short hall of the locked ward. Aides tried to keep patients out of the doorway in this hall so that they wouldn't bother the staff. The aides also wanted to have a clear view of the length of the long hall between the locked and unlocked wards. But since the patients were kept out of the line of sight of what was going on outside the locked ward, they had no perspective of what was happening in the second-floor unit as a whole.

That afternoon Mr. W. said that the staff had tried to kick him out of the hospital even though he didn't want to go. He said that he wouldn't be accepted by his family in New York or by the VA hospital in New York so he had attempted suicide in order to stay in this hospital.

At dinner I sat near Mr. H. who occasionally did strange things, such as putting a teaspoonful of hot coffee in his shirt pocket. He also kept cigarette butts in his ears. One new young patient at the table, on seeing the coffee gambit, seemed personally offended and told Mr. H. he was acting "crazy." I responded, "It's a small price to pay." The old-timers around the table nodded, though the young man seemed to think my speech was crazy, too. What I meant was that crazy behavior hurt no one yet it ensured Mr. H.'s right to stay in the hospital where he was comfortable. Mr. A., another patient seated next to me at dinner, had told me earlier that he could shift his mental view of things when he became bored in the ward so that everything looked new again. I told him that I envied him; I couldn't do that. He replied, "You can't be expected to do it. It took me sixteen years to learn how. You can't learn overnight." I turned to the young patient, "We have a lot to learn from these two, Mr. H. and Mr. A." The four of us agreed that it was true. Our elders had learned to adapt in a nondestructive way to the hospital environment. They were relatively satisfied with their existence as it was. They had come to terms with patienthood.

After dinner several of us were called out to the conference room. The aide explained that we were to attend an admissions group meeting whose purpose was to orient us to the ward. He admitted that an orientation was overdue for some of us, but "other things" had come up. I'd been in the hospital a week by the time of the orientation. I had been alert for three or four days. I was already familiar with everything that he mentioned. Members of the group brought up a few questions that the aide himself wasn't able to answer. When that happened he wisely sought the necessary information from an experienced old-timer patient. The aide expressed surprise that I was off S-status and that I hadn't received a privilege card immediately. Apparently, my card was withheld because I lacked the opportunity that afternoon to pick up my civilian clothes from another building.

We were given a choice that evening of going to a movie or to a party. The party was sponsored by a Jewish war veterans' group. It might have been aptly titled, "Bedlam Bingo." It was run prominently by elderly ladies who came across as stereotype Jewish mothers: "You poor thing. Are you sure you've eaten enough? There are lots of doughnuts and coffee." We played bingo; there were good prizes and refreshments; finally there was piano playing with sing-along tunes. Whenever a volunteer won she gave her card to one of the patients, usually an obviously disturbed patient or someone who loudly requested her patronage. The male volunteer who called the bingo showed his detachment from the whole affair by going off to a corner and reading a book after he'd finished his task.

The bingo parties provided two kinds of resources: canteen coupon books that were offered as prizes, and other prizes that could be kept, traded, or sold for cash. Also, the refreshments were a welcome distraction even if only coffee and doughnuts were served. I felt a sense of hostility toward the volunteers in this activity which I hadn't felt before and didn't feel later. Perhaps the source was the volunteers' somewhat condescending "you-poor-thing" attitude which emphasized the sickness of the patients. The patients showed detachment and ingratitude by talking, wandering around, and generally causing confusion and disorder during the bingo session. Whether their activities were purposive or not, carried out with awareness or not, the effect was bedlam. This bingo party contrasted with two others that I attended later, in which different attitudes from volunteers elicited different responses from patients.

### July 15, 1971, Thursday

I made my bed, then learned that my effort had been wasted because today was sheet-changing day in the ward. We had changed our sheets the Thursday before, but I had no way of knowing whether this routine occurred daily, weekly, or sporadically. As I sat in the dayroom, one of the most entertaining of patients, Mr. S., began talking with me. He used his hallucinatory conversation in an artistic, creative manner. "I am the great Billy Goat of the universe. . . . I am a medicine man of samurai blood. Isn't it beautiful?" And he looked at me and smiled. He said he wasn't afraid of death or life. Mr. S. smoked a lot. He was very thin and very old. He would die soon of emphysema. Mr. A. brought him a cigarette. Later, Mr. A. offered me a yellow tag he had picked up off the floor. These gifts were signs of good faith and comradeship.

The freedom of Zen may be, in a sense, close to the freedom of the so-called insane. Some of these patients seemed to have elected the life of insanity with its freedom from social responses and responsibilities. They became a kind of despised priesthood in our hospitals. Mr. A., Mr. H., and Mr. S. embodied this kind of twisted freedom.

At breakfast we were directed to sit together in one section of the cafeteria. No one explained why. Then we all had to go directly back to the ward. Those of us in the locked ward were then herded to the open ward. Even the aides didn't know why we were all staying in the ward that morning. It turned out that psychology service had arranged to question us about our use of narcotics.

I was given a privilege card and a snack pass that allowed me to have coffee or ice cream at the American Legion Auxiliary canteen once each day between 1 P.M. and 3:30 P.M. I picked up my clothes at the clothing and personal effects office. They were returned to me unwashed and smelling of dirt and oil from the morning of my admission. There were a number of holes in the back of the shirt where the stamping of my name and hospital ID number had caused the synthetic fibers to melt.

At the OT clinic where I was given vocational testing, the therapy trainees had an impersonal, professional attitude. After several testing sessions they warmed up a bit, however. After vocational testing I was free for the rest of the morning provided I kept my appointment to talk with Mr. D. According to the daily pattern in the open ward, I was to check in around 11 A.M. for consultation with my team leader. When I returned to the ward, I was told that my friend, Larry, had visited and was on his way out. I managed to catch him on the stairs. It was very good to see a friend, to talk. My spirits rose. I asked him to bring me a change of clothing. Larry was, in reality, a doctoral student briefed and sent in to offer an outside contact halfway through my hospital stay.

I had some free time after lunch and so I walked down to the patio and wrote notes. I felt physically tired from testing and walking that day. I sat and reflected that on moving to the open ward the patients that I had grown to know in the locked unit seemed like old friends, not merely acquaintances of a bizarre week. Especially I thought of Mr. W. When the two of us were thrown together by suicide status, we had reinforced each other's behavior to some extent. Now I had progressed faster than he. Would it provoke another setback for my friend? Would his lack of progress stand out as another failure, making him feel even worse? Now I had graduated to privilege-card status. I could lose myself in the larger society once out of the ward. My dress was the same as that of staff personnel. I could walk off the hospital grounds, and no one would know that I was a patient provided my behavior was appropriate. I speculated that it might be useful to have a kind of ceremonial rite of passage demonstrating progress in the transition from locked to unlocked ward — an introduction of the graduated patients to a gathering of patients and staff, perhaps. Some personal history, spoken by a fellow patient, could play a part in the ceremony.

I spent some time sitting in the open ward, getting adjusted to my new surroundings. I asked the nursing assistant, Miss B., if she was nervous. She turned her head quickly whenever anybody walked behind or beside her. She said she had to watch everything on the closed ward, and since she spent most of her time there she developed the habit of turning quickly.

I found out that the readiest source of information in the open ward was, again, the patient group. The open ward was a more homelike place, with drapes at the windows and more normal conversation among the patients. I still found myself with nothing to do, but I had more space in which to do it. A second cafeteria line which had puzzled me earlier turned out to be for the privilege-card patients. Interestingly, some of the PC patients continued to eat with the closed-ward patients. Some did it because they were on a special diet. But some simply rejoined their familiars and would continue this practice until told not to do so. Whether or not a patient from the open ward was permitted to visit in the closed ward depended on which staff members were watching the door of the locked ward, which patient wished to visit, whom he was visiting, and what was his purpose. Patients were not supposed to visit in other buildings without special persmission, but this rule was sometimes relaxed. Patients from other buildings would show up to chat with old friends from time to time.

Staff and patients frequently asked me if I had been in the hospital before. They seemed to expect that I had been. Perhaps I had adapted too readily to the open ward. Perhaps patients are expected to return. I felt myself seeking, appreciating, savoring my new freedom, yet at the same time awed by it and feeling nostalgia toward the old and the familiar. It takes a certain amount of courage to go out into what had become a big world after a week in the locked ward. An aide said, "Pardon me," when he stepped in front of me. This minor courtesy was meaningful to me in communicating that I was still worth the polite niceties of interaction.

Back to vocational testing. The testing was simple. It included putting nuts on bolts, fitting pipes together, putting marbles in holes, and putting together puzzles evaluating perception. After the testing, at about 3:20 P.M., I went to the American Legion Auxiliary canteen, just barely making it in time to get my free ice cream. Then I slipped off without incident to my office for a few moments in a more rewarding identity. It provides noteworthy illumination on facelessness in our culture that after working six years in a building some 300 yards away from my ward, no one had recognized me. Back in the ward, I took a shower. The open ward had a variety of government-issue socks, washrags, and shampoo. These small luxuries may offer some incentive, to patients who know about them, for leaving the locked ward. As I prepared to shower, a patient volunteered a great deal of information about the ward, its resources, and how to obtain them. Information passing permeates the patient subculture. There is little else at hand to offer.

While I was visiting the locked ward, a female aide told me that I was looking much better. A nurse held my hand as we tried together to cheer up Mr. W. I was informed that I was supposed to stay away from the locked ward during the day, although arrangements hadn't yet been made for me to sleep in the open ward. I asked for a locker somewhere because I would have some clothes shortly. An aide said that he'd see about it.

I ate supper on the privilege card side of the cafeteria for the first time. The line was slower, the selection of food was smaller, and the serving was more slapdash. I was confronted with a new problem: With whom do I eat? Loneliness accompanies freedom.

After supper I played basketball and catch in the patio behind building 210. I loaned a dime to Mr. W. on our way to a dance at the theater. The young girls at the dance hadn't been briefed about the do's and don'ts of handling patients, so they treated us pretty openly. Their USO organization visited various service clubs and hospitals in the southern California area. The primary dimension of interaction with these girls was not sick-well but rather male-female. The emphasis is probably less destructive than some others.

I turned to a ward wrapped in its usual clubby enlisted-men's-barracks atmosphere. I played chess with an aide and told him how helpful he'd been to me. Suddenly, I found that I had been assigned a bed in the open ward. A fellow patient showed me where the linens were. Circumstances forced me to keep asking questions of those around me because no one seemed to appreciate how little I knew, and people usually didn't volunteer information unless they were asked. The ward situation pulled from us forthright, aggressive, assertive behavior in order to get maximum privileges and benefits from our environment.

During that day I was hyperactive, almost euphoric. It was a rebirth experience, a reawakening to society and people I had known in another context. But I saw them with new eyes. I was struck by the size of the hospital and the complexities of the eddies and pools of humanity within it. I began to recognize the importance of time in scheduling and routine in the wards. The clocks were all in very good repair, and I found myself frequently consulting them. Without a wristwatch the ward wall clocks would have been even more important to me. I pondered the fact that no one ever told me that nursing notes existed. I suppose patients had some sense that people were writing notes about them, but they never saw them and no one mentioned them. I saw the doctor only during staff meetings, during general rounds, and in the special circumstance of the interview leading to my coming off suicide status. I began to formulate the Reynolds Rule of Contact and Effect: "The amount of contact the patient has with a staff member and the direct effect the staff member has on the patient's daily life are inversely proportional to the staff member's salary."

*July 17, 1971, Friday*

I woke up at five this morning and wasn't able to go back to sleep until the lights went on at 5:40 because the patient in the bed next to me snored so loudly. Losing even a small amount of sleep made me feel tired and depressed that morning so I decided to exaggerate the feelings to see what would happen. Perhaps the staff would pick up the possibility that my sleep disturbance was related to my assignment to a work detail that morning. I ate breakfast on the locked-ward side of the cafeteria. It was almost like going home.

Later I sat in the dayroom with my head in my hands until someone asked how I was feeling. I told him that I wasn't feeling very well, that I hadn't gotten much sleep last night, and that I was worried because when other people lost sleep, they didn't get so depressed and low as I was. At 8:30 my group leader, Mr. D., asked me to see him at eleven so we could talk about it.

Then the chief nurse came in and made her rounds. She sat down and wanted to talk further with me about my sleep loss. Miss J. was a conscientious nurse, insightful and experienced. She asked the right questions. She asked why I felt low. She immediately recognized the possibility that my depression was precipitated by my being assigned to begin my work detail that morning. She said that sometimes trying to push oneself too fast is just as bad as going too slow and that maybe I should wait awhile. There was, however, a veiled threat that I'd have to go back to the locked ward and lose my privilege card if I didn't continue with my detail. The chief nurse told me that, of course, lack of sleep affects all of us differently. She agreed with me that it wasn't normal to be so upset and depressed over one night's lack of sleep. She said that she herself had a migraine that day, but she still had to carry on. She confided that her migraines were often caused by tension and that there was a connection between tension and anxiety and body upset. She seemed to be communicating that she was like me in a way, and that she understood how I felt.

I asked her what was wrong with my mind and wondered if the X rays of my brain had shown anything abnormal. She suggested we go in and check and said she'd also check the possibility of giving me bedtime medication to help me sleep better. Then she asked me to follow her into the nursing station office. She checked through my records and found that I was already receiving sleeping medication. She said that I'd probably heard that they gave us medication to pep us up and then they gave us more medication to put us to sleep. She didn't want to increase my medication at bedtime. She didn't want to decrease my Elavil. So in the end she decided it was best to change the timing of the Elavil, giving it in the morning and at noon rather than in the morning and in the evening. We would make that change this very day, she assured me. She looked at the brain X ray report and reassured me that there was nothing abnormal.

Miss J. remarked that when my visitor had been there the day before, she had tried to set up a meeting with him, but he was on his lunch break and couldn't stay. He'd probably call in later and set up something with the social worker. She pointed out that I did have a resource on the outside and that even if I were to leave the next week I would have this resource available to me. She pointed out that there must be a kind of contract between her and me, that she would try to fulfill her responsibility as part of her job, and that I had a responsibility to inform her if I ever had any feelings of wanting to kill myself. She said, "This is more than just a nurse-patient relationship. This is a kind of person-to-person relationship. We have to be able to trust one another." Beautiful!

She called Dr. L. over, and Dr. L. again remembered who I was. Miss J. told the doctor what she'd been telling me, and the doctor seemed to concur. I pushed a little, requesting psychological testing. Would that tell me what was wrong with my mind? Nurse J. couldn't understand why they hadn't already tested me because the request had been in for more than a week. The doctor then added that she didn't think there was anything wrong with my "functional capabilities" (whatever that might mean to a novice patient), but that sometimes emotions overwhelm us.

Dr. L. reassured me that I had behaved in a very gentlemanly manner in allowing my wife to get a divorce without any argument. She suggested that I tended to hold in emotions, particularly anger. She advised that if I started to express some of these emotions, maybe my "breadbasket wouldn't feel so empty." The flavor of the conversation with these two professionals was that they understood and cared, that they weren't trying to press me to go too fast. The nurse then remarked that what we can do is learn to function in spite of the way we feel and that each time we're hospitalized we know a little better how to control the way we behave and what to do about our feelings. And with plans for me to continue to my dental appointment, to continue in the open ward, to move to a bed away from the snorer, to change the timing of my medication, and generally just to carry on, I was dismissed.

I think the interaction was, realistically speaking, about the best possible response to my relapse the nurse and the doctor could have made under the circumstances. It was very creditable and very meaningful to me. I felt their sincere concern. I left that meeting in the nursing station with just the right balance of knowing that getting better was my responsibility but that I had some educated, professional backup help when I needed it.

I slumped, fretting in the waiting room of the dentist's office. Early that morning I had been handed a card informing me of this appointment. According to the instructions given out in advance of my work-detail assignment, I was supposed to know one day prior to any appointments so that I could inform the OT clinnic that I wouldn't be showing up for my detail. But I had learned of the conflicting appointment only that morning. When I told the chief nurse about the problem she had phoned a message to the clinic, even though I had been specifically instructed that there was no one there to take such messages over the phone. Did they realize these breaches weren't my fault? Well, it was better than failing to show up with no annoucement at all.

I suddenly realized I had lost track of the date and the day of the week. If someone had assessed my contact with reality by asking me the day and date they would have arrived at an inaccurate conclusion. Day and date may be essentially meaningless in an institution. I heard a patient saying there was a little dead kitten outside on the grass, and he could see it through the barred windows. The word "dead," like the word "suicide," caught my attention immediately. Were they talking about me?

At eleven o'clock I complained to my team leader about feeling bad because of lack of sleep. He too suggested that I change my bed. The patient sleeping next to me had a reputation for keeping patients awake at night. I didn't want to cause trouble, but he again reassured me that it was no trouble, that any patient should be able to sleep at night. He promised to write an order allowing me to sleep in the seclusion room of the locked ward if I were having trouble sleeping in the same room with Mr. S. He also advised me to remind the evening shift to change my bed although he would write a note to that effect.

At 11:30 A.M. I reported for medication, but I was told that there was no "card" for me yet. I didn't know what this information meant. The nurse who was passing out the prescription cups didn't seem to care about the matter, and so I didn't care either. I left the ward, wandered outside the building, and lay on the grass, not caring whether or not they found a card for me later that hour. After a while I felt better.

At lunch I was told by a patient and later by a nurse that the chief nurse was looking for me. So after lunch I went back to the ward and found Miss J. She told me that my friend had brought some clothing and left. I asked her if she had filled out the activities schedule for my detail planning. The activities schedule informed the detail when the patient was to be excused for other activities. She hunted for it and found it, interrupting a telephone conversation to do so. I was almost late to occupational therapy at 12:30 P.M. There, more testing awaited me rather than assignment to a work detail as expected. At the end of each test the response was always the same noncommittal "good." No results were explained or interpreted to me. The tests went on and on. I was given short breaks between tests, but I grew increasingly tired and made more and more errors. The OT trainee was kind, chatting about her job in a normal manner. I pointed out a few errors in the test instructions and in the punctuation and spelling of the typing test. I couldn't resist doing that. I did as well as I could on some of the clerical tests, wondering all along how the OT personnel would be able to handle a fairly bright patient. There was a kind of professional cheerfulness pervading the room in which I took the OT tests, and the attractive young women provided a welcome change of pace. It was easy to be sane during the occupational therapy testing. It paid off to be well in this setting (for me and for others), and I was fairly certain that information about how well I was capable of behaving wouldn't get back to my home ward. The ward, you see, is a place where it pays to appear sick.

After the testing I hurried over to the American Legion Auxiliary canteen for an anticipated ice cream. I arrived at 3:15 but found it closed and the three old ladies leaving. I was dismissed very abruptly by them and felt genuine resentment toward them for closing up early. The importance of that simple reward wasn't perceived by the volunteers. And I had come to see it as due me — one might say, my "just dessert."

I picked up my clothing from the ward and had the clothes marked. The markers in the clothing room were efficient and kind. Although they showed more interest in a pretty girl who had brought another patient's clothing over for marking than they showed in me, I felt no resentment because, in a sense, such behavior is culturally normal for males. I did not take it as a role-related personal insult.

Testing limits, I showered at 3:45 P.M. not waiting until the scheduled shower time of four o'clock, but no one said anything. Apparently showering was freely accomplished outside scheduled times in the open ward. At 4:10 I asked an aide to unlock the door to the sleeping quarters so I could get to my locker. The sign over the door said it was supposed to be open between 4 P.M. and 5 P.M. The aide said she was supposed to open it at 4:15, but she would do it early for me. And she did.

After washing some clothes in the shower I asked an aide where to hang them up. He told me there was a dryer on the floor below ours, and he directed a patient to show me where it was. Again I had obtained necessary information only when I discovered that I needed to know it and asked specifically about it. Some information came rather late. For example, one patient made private arrangements with the morning-shift aides to get my government-issue cigarettes when he learned that I didn't smoke. But on the last three or four days the aides gave the cigarettes directly to me so that I could give them to him or to whomever else I chose.

I watched an aide play pool with Mr. W. It was good to see my S-status friend out of his chair and active. The aide never tried to let Mr. W. win. Good! When I won a chess game from this aide, I sometimes kidded him that he had allowed me to win because victory was therapeutic for me. This was an effective, good-natured dig because he obviously tried very hard to win the games.

When medication was passed out in the evening, I told the nurse that I didn't get my medication at noon because there had been no card. Accepting my word in the matter, she gave me my regular medication then.

I dried my clothes and went to dinner. Meals are very important to a person in any institution. The meals in the hospital dining hall were varied, tasty, and filling. Second helpings were available. That evening I had two desserts.

After dinner I played chess with Mr. K. Then the locked-ward patients were lined up to go to play bingo at the theater. I decided to go along with them. As we stood outside our building waiting for the stragglers to complete our lineup, I overheard a couple of aides badgering one patient who was feeling sorry for himself because of his disability from the Korean war. The patient had been staggering about. He seemed out of contact. The aide told him he was either drunk or under the influence of a drug. Another aide joined in, "What if everybody did what you're doing, what if everybody gave up because he got a disability. I was in the service, too, and I got hurt, too." The first aide said, "This is 'reality therapy.' I got no sympathy for you."

During bingo I sat by the side of an old lady who was rather handsome and withdrawn. I had begun to identify with the staff as my depression lightened. I wanted to help her but couldn't draw her out. I had been doing my own kind of therapy with Mr. W. and some others. My therapy involved sympathetic listening and reality-oriented responses.

I won a handkerchief at bingo and gave it to a friend. There was much giving and offering of prizes by patients to patients and by aides to patients. The prizes were a scarce resource, a wonderful opportunity to have something to give away. It was heartwarming to see this kind of exchange.

The atmosphere at this bingo party was much different from the one at the earlier party. There was perhaps the same number of patients, but there was much more space for them. And there were many more volunteers. The volunteers were men, for the most part, and the atmosphere was much more one of equals having good fun and relaxation. I noticed that when gifts were refused or when patients failed to respond to friendly overtures from other people, no one seemed to feel put out. In a sense, there was more freedom to be different within the hospital than on the outside. Patients were more accepting and tolerant of the asocial, withdrawn behavior of fellow patients. As I walked back to the ward, a light sprinkle began to fall. The clouds were silver and gray. I felt uninhibited. I held up my arms and gazed at the clouds. I even stopped in the middle of the sidewalk and looked up for several minutes into the misting rain. The patient

role, along with the accompanying acceptance of unusual, idiosyn-
cratic behavior within the hospital, gave me the freedom to behave in
that spontaneous, open way. It was good.

After ward cleanup I read, took my medication, and went to bed
with a pillow over my head because they hadn't reassigned me out of
the bed next to the snorer.

## July 17, 1971, Saturday

The door to the aides' closet was open this morning. I went inside to
look for razors. While I was there I took a deck of cards and some
hair oil. Previously I hadn't known that these resources were available to patients. Exploration continued to pay off. An aide told me
to remind the afternoon shift to give me another bed. They had
forgotten to reassign me, though there were plenty of beds on the
other side of the room.

After medication I went into the dayroom to write notes. I
noticed that the ward was predominately a nonsexual living space.
There were no pictures of nude girls and no erotic magazines. Except
for the pretty female aides, a minimum of erotically oriented talk,
and the bland erotica viewed on television, there was no input of
sexually oriented stimuli.

The open ward had a small room designated as the coffee room.
A sign on the wall informed the newcomer that the room was for
drinking coffee and polite conversation, not for loafing or for sleeping. Particularly in the early morning, patients in good contact
gathered in this room to kill time before breakfast. A patient wandered into the coffee room calling himself the "ward doctor."
Occasionally Mr. S. and other schizophrenic patients came in to
"perform" for the patients there. Mr. S. called most people, "Noble
Friend of Honor." As I entered the room he bowed and said, "Japan
respects you." He was wearing a Japanese *happi* coat, slacks so short
that they barely covered his calves, two socks of different colors, and
sandals. He often wandered around with a necktie tied about his
head and a kerchief around his neck. That morning he engaged in a
kind of game with another disturbed patient in which they made free
associations to each other's word salads. They were smiling and
laughing during the course of the game. It was as if they were aware,
as was everyone else, that a game was in progress. The other patient
ended it by saying, "I like you, S." This kind of conversation is

entertaining to the better patients. But when it went too far, or lasted too long, they became upset because they wanted normalcy as well as entertainment. Most of the time they smiled and shrugged off Mr. S.'s creative but far-out conversations.

After breakfast I played solitaire and pool and taught an aide how to play baker's dozen solitaire. I heard that the locked-ward patients had gone to the canteen so I went over and sat at the table with three of them. Mr. S. was entertaining them with his ramblings. He called me "Tiny Tim of Infinity." He told us that planets run automatically by remote control, and when the astronauts land on them, they will find they are all worn out. He said that evil-frozen-hard will fail because he has conquered it. Mr. S. exerted some control over the young schizoid patient sitting opposite him. He used the pressure of his demand to force the young man to clean a canteen ashtray. But later, when the young patient refused to obey Mr. S., there was no conflict. Mr. S. simply ordered, with resignation, "All right, *don't* do it."

On returning from the canteen we watched baseball on television. The game took precedence over the movie that Mr. P. had been watching. He yielded gracefully to social pressure. After lunch I took a nap on a couch in the coffee room until I was awakened at 1:05 P.M. for bingo. The bingo program was carried out in the locked ward and was sponsored by an organization called Negro American War Mothers. Along with the patients, aides and some volunteers participated in the games. The television set was turned off. Coupon books were given as prizes. There were fewer patients participating, just those from the locked ward and a few of us who had been rounded up from the open ward. There were three kinds of cake and coffee. The whole setting was less professional and more easy.

After the bingo game I went golfing on the station with Mr. H. He took me on a circuitous route to the golfing area. It was unimportant that we went far out of our way. This route was the comfortable one for him, and we had plenty of time.

The open-ward patient's concept of time is important in understanding his life-style. The patient was rarely in a hurry. In contrast with the sometimes harried, hurried staff member, the patient could savor his meals and his conversations. He had time to invest in simple sitting and watching life slowly flow around him. He was usually free to sleep when he felt like it and to fill his hours with well-spaced activities. Within the institutional limits he was free to develop himself in many directions or to fall into a routine existence that could be slow paced because it was only minimally time bound. I combated boredom by bland routine spiced with special activities. The degree to which routine defined one's day was determined primarily by the patient's initiative and imagination (or lack of them).

The man who ran the well-maintained nine-hole golf course was very popular on the station. The course provided a nonhospital atmosphere and mild exercise, in contrast with the predominantly vegetable quality of ward life. The manager was aware that his facility was therapeutic in a sense that was rare within the hospital.

I showered and went across to the locked ward to visit Mr. W. I asked him if he wanted to play pool. He was pacing back and forth in agitated anxiety. He asked me, "Stick around, will you?" I paced alongside him. He told me I was a nice guy and wondered how old I was (again). He was worried that "they" would kick him out to New York where no one would take him. He asked if I would write a letter to his wife. He asked me to stay with him because he worried that he couldn't sit through the movie coming up that evening. I sat beside him at the movie, and he seemed all right. Using a formerly suicidal patient as an agent of therapy seemed to work out well in this instance. It gave me a perspective on my own difficulties. I had a great deal of time to offer my suicidal friend. I felt useful. Perhaps most important, I understood Mr. W. in a way few others could. The formerly suicidal patient as an agent of cure . . . Interesting possibilities . . . .

While I was talking with Mr. W. in the locked ward a nursing assistant came in and said, "You just can't stay away from here, can you?" I responded that Mr. W. had asked me to stick around. As I was talking another patient shouted at me to stop staring at him. I said I was just wondering what he was drinking directly out of the pitcher he held, but I looked away, careful not to antagonize him further. Later he said he was sorry and that he was very high-strung. He asked me if I liked him. "Yes," I said. "Why?" he asked. "Oh, I don't know," I replied. He asked me if I liked him even if he had killed a lot of "Chinks." I said, "Yes, I like you." I asked him if he liked himself. He was in Korea as a medic. There were many wounded soldiers he couldn't save because he hadn't been properly trained. A number of them had died in his arms. I told him every doctor saves some and loses some and that those whom he had saved must be very proud of him. He sobbed, "Don't say that." But he settled down and he slept. After that, we had a good relationship although it remained relatively casual. I feel that the timing of that interaction was crucial if there was any benefit at all. The only role-group members a patient can count on having around when he needs them are other patients. By this stage of my hospitalization more and more of the nondisturbed aspects of my personality were beginning to show through. These patients were pulling from me a strong need to give of myself.

At medication time that evening I told the nurse that I had received my medication at noon. She said "OK" and put the Elavil away. Her response was characteristic of the trusting relationship that can develop between nursing personnel and the cooperative patient.

That night there was again no reassignment of my bed. As I lay in bed, I considered how easy it was to justify the waiting and the inactivity in the ward, given the kind of world view that exists there. Time heals wounds; time helps us get over strong depression or anger; time gives the staff the opportunity to adjust the medication dosage properly; crises diminish in importance. Time and medicines are plentiful in psychiatric wards.

### July 18, 1971, Sunday

I got up at 5:40, shaved, brushed my teeth, and wrote notes in the small notebook that seemed to interest no one. On my way to the cafeteria a man stopped me and asked if I would deliver a stack of newspapers to the library. He gave them to me and I walked to the library and delivered them. I wondered if there was an implicit understanding that I would take one free for my services. When I asked him later, he just said, "You're a good man." I suppose it's easy to take advantage of patients in this way. A self-possessed outsider's voice rings with authority. The delivery man seemed to be an ex-patient himself.

After breakfast I encountered a patient who had been to psychodrama the Tuesday before. He said he had attended for three weeks. He had been in the middle (i.e., on stage) and he had played their game, but he thought it was "bullshit." Group therapy was much to be preferred, he confided. He said he'd been in the hospital a few months, he'd come in on a "hold," and he could walk out anytime. At this point he felt the staff couldn't help him, only hurt him.

"After a certain period of time you can only go down." He was planning to go to Israel and start a new life. He said he was hit in the face by an aide and that he "hates those niggers." "They may talk nice but they hate you, too." Everything is done for their convenience, he felt.

Again and again I heard from patients who had had broad experience in mental hospitals that the ward was structured for the convenience of the aides. Although the aides did make an effort to explain why rules existed or why a decision was made, there were many aspects of hospitalization which patients didn't understand and therefore resented. For example, one patient had been setting pins at the patient bowling alley for a long period of time. When he wanted to bowl a game or two himself, he was told that he couldn't until he got a doctor's clearance that he was physically fit to bowl. This was absurd! Setting pins was certainly more of a physical strain than bowling.

I went over to the locked ward to help move chairs back and forth for the cleanup crew. Mr. W. and some of the other disturbed patients didn't help move the chairs. Unless there was very little help available, such patients were not pressured to lend a hand.

I sat sunning myself in a chair in the patio near the canteen. Mr. S. performed for me his "sustaining shit soliloquy." He told me that energy was all around; that there was "sustaining shit" in the area all around us; that my listening to him pulled out of him the "sustaining shit" that had been accumulating inside. Cigarettes burned it up, so he had to keep smoking. His monologue lasted fifteen or twenty minutes altogether. Most entertaining.

Back visiting on the locked ward, I listened to an aide remind a patient that there was someone around when he took his overdose of pills, so the aide insisted that the patient didn't really want to die. Then he focused on a practical concrete problem, the patient's financial difficulty. The aide offered practical comments and interpretations and suggestions to the patient. This tactic was a common approach employed by the aides. They focused on practical, immediate problems and solutions to that kind of problem. Later on I contrast this policy with the attitude of the psychiatrist and others whose concern was not with practical reality but rather with early experiences and long-term emotional orientations.

I talked with the aide about Mr. W. He was well aware of the manipulative motivation underlying Mr. W.'s recent suicide attempt.

He said that Mr. W. was afraid, not depressed, and that he was using his talk about wanting to die to keep himself in the hospital. He said that a patient could not consistently and repeatedly put on tearful performances for anyone who would listen if he was genuinely suicidal. He went on to tell me of another patient who was continuously telling the staff that he was going to kill himself. The aide told me that he had said to the patient, "We can't keep you alive. If you want to stay in the hospital, talk to the doctor and discuss your problems with him." After that the patient went on a detail, accumulated some money, and left the hospital. I was fascinated as I listened to the suicidal success story.

In our conversation I casually dropped the information that I had attempted suicide on Sunday the week before. I spoke about it as though I assumed that he knew about it already. He listened to my life story of abandonment and depression. He advised me not to invest myself in one woman. "How can you love someone that much that you want to die when she's gone?" We talked about jobs and I asked him about the job of the aide. He said you have to be careful not to bring your problems from home and take them out on the patients. You've got to keep your private life and your work in the hospital separate, he felt.

At 9:40 that morning I was watching a baseball game on television and writing my notes. It was very quiet in the open ward. There were only three people in the dayroom.

At 10:30 I went to the Protestant service. The suits of the chaplain, the vocal soloist, and the chaplain's assistant somehow seemed out of place in the hospital theater. They seemed artificial and overly formal in contrast with the casual attire of the patients who attended. At 10:30 there were thirteen patients in the theater. (The seating allowed for 400 plus another 210 in back seats that were roped off.) By 10:45 twenty-three patients had arrived and the service had begun. The service was similar to any you might find on a small military base. A few odd behaviors were exhibited by members of the congregation. For example, one patient stood up for a short while during a song even though the rest of the congregation remained seated. After a rather good vocal solo we applauded. One patient left during the sermon, and another changed his seat during the sermon from the back of the theater to the front. Otherwise, nothing unusual happened.

When I returned to the ward, about ten patients were in the

dayroom watching baseball on television. After lunch I watched baseball on television and went golfing again. I read a magazine and watched more television. Mr. S. came in and invited me to the locked ward. He had somehow obtained a watermelon and was sharing it with his favorite patients. I then took a shower and talked with an aide. I asked if she thought that I was different from other suicidal patients or if there were many patients like me. She said that I came out of my depression pretty fast because I had a good attitude. Medicine could only do so much, she felt, but a lot depended on the willingness of the patient to get well. She made sense to me.

At 4 P.M. there was a picnic in the patio behind building 210. We had no choice but to attend because we weren't permitted to eat in the cafeteria that evening. That little restriction ensured a rather exceptional turnout. The recreation therapist and the music therapist were there to help dish out the food. I heard that the music therapist was very popular among the patients. In addition to her regular duties it was fondly related that she showed up weekends and evenings for special events and generally took an active part in patient life. At the picnic I met a couple of young black visitors who had come to see a recently admitted friend. They were telling me that it was difficult sometimes to tell who was a patient and who was not, but if you "talk to 'em" you can readily tell who's a patient.

At the picnic I spent about half an hour or forty-five minutes talking with Mr. W. He was still afraid that he was going to be kicked out of the hospital. He had "screwed up" things with his brother, his wife, his hometown hospital, and all other conceivable resources so that he didn't feel welcome anywhere. He said he drank about sixteen thousand dollars away. He believed his diagnosis to be "constitutional psychopath" (with emphasis on the constitutional aspect). He religiously believed that his early childhood had forced him into a particular adult pattern of adaptation. He apparently had seen his service record. He claimed that it included a statement that he was "permanently and completely disabled." In his conversation he freely threw around such technical diagnostic terms as "hysteria," "acute anxiety," and "schizoid personality." At one time or another all these labels had been applied to him. He said that the nurses and aides pushed him into a chair and threatened to put him on a plane back to his hometown if he didn't straighten up and become more active in the ward. He said that he would pay anything if I could get him pills so that he could commit suicide.

I frankly felt some sympathy for his request. He had made a mess of his life, and picking up the pieces at the age of about fifty-five would be very difficult for him. I believed that he genuinely wanted to die. I questioned him about his preferences for various methods of suicide, asking, for example, "Suppose I couldn't get the pills, how about a rope?" "No," he said; he had tried that. "Well, then, how about a gun? Or cutting?" Again he said, "No." He felt that these methods would be too messy. What he wanted was pills so that he could go to sleep and never wake up.

A patient from another ward who was attending the picnic joined in our conversation. He had recently become religiously oriented and was talking about "His [i.e., God's] plan for our lives." He talked of what he'd lost because of his alcoholism. At the end of our talk he thanked us for listening. He told us that at last he had begun to take responsibility for his own life. After he was gone Mr. W. said that he had heard all this before; that he'd gone to Alcoholics Anonymous but nothing had helped. When we went back to the ward, I changed into my pajamas and went to bed at 7 P.M. Of course, the aides woke me up to give me sleeping medication at 9:15.

### July 19, 1971, Monday

I decided that this was the day that I would start informing people that I planned to be discharged on Wednesday or Thursday. In general, the staff members I talked with consistently directed me to talk with my group leader about it. I tended to confuse the terms "group leader" and "team leader" because they sounded so much alike to me, but I was sure they meant Mr. D. He coached me about what to say when I went before the disposition staff. They would ask me what resources I had on the outside, and my response was to be that I would be getting a job, that I had a friend and an apartment.

I sat in the coffee room listening to eddies of conversation again. Mr. S. was playing the clown, entertaining his ready audience. He was singing an Indian chant and calling himself "El Diablo de Oro" ("The Devil of Gold"). Someone offered him a Chesterfield cigarette and he sonorously responded, "I don't need a Chesterfield, sir. My chest is clear." And then he barked, "The jig is up." He played a word-salad game with another patient, as was their custom. Another patient was complaining about the staff's accusing attitude. He had been complaining of diarrhea and an aide had asked him suspiciously, "If you have diarrhea, why don't you get up at night?" Another patient was complaining that because of a sunburn he had not been able to go to his detail. After about a week the people in his detail had called over to the ward wondering why he hadn't shown up. He said of the aides who had come to ask him why: "Why bother to ask? They could see my sunburn every day." They had seen him walking painfully around the ward every day with an obvious sunburn. There followed some perfectly normal conversation about traveling and tours and passports which could have taken place in any coffee shop or at any office water cooler.

Then we went to breakfast and after the meal watched television for a while. I went over to the locked ward and learned that Mr. W. wanted me to buy cigarettes for him. He didn't mention the letter I had helped him write to his wife, and he avoided my question about it. I got him to help me move a table during ward cleanup. Mr. W. didn't want to take part in any endeavor at this point. It was as if he had put part of his self-esteem in reserve. If he tried and failed, all was lost. But if he didn't risk himself, he preserved a minor advantage and had retained the flickering bit of self-esteem that he had left. What he needed, as I saw it, was to risk that last bit of self-esteem and to succeed.

Mr. D. took me to the ward porch to talk about my depression. Apparently he had picked up from the preceding evening's nursing notes that I had attempted suicide in the hospital. I told him that the account was true; I had attempted suicide, but I was glad the rope broke. I told him that I'd learned then and there that if I was going to stay alive, I was going to have to keep myself alive. No one could do it for me. He agreed that this was true. He asked me which aides were on duty, but I told him that I couldn't recall. Although he knew I had told an aide of my attempt at the time, Mr. D.'s parting words were: "You should've told someone. We could've given you more medication or something."

I went over to buy cigarettes for Mr. W. I waited for half an hour because the sign on the door said the canteen opened at 8:30 A.M. A professional person, perhaps a social worker, smiled and said "Good morning" as he went up the steps. It was directed at no one in particular and yet at everyone, and it was a much appreciated sort of greeting. Being treated as an equal by a normal person meant a lot. A patient was selling a pair of sunglasses for fifty cents. Having no luck he brought the price down to forty cents. Still he had no takers. Perhaps the glasses had been stolen. The usual cigarette bumming went on. When 8:30 came and the doors were opened, we were told that the part of the canteen in which cigarettes are sold didn't open till 9 o'clock. Since my detail was scheduled to start at that time, I had to return to the ward without the cigarettes.

I felt more sick and nervous in the morning than in the afternoon. Perhaps there was more pressure to perform properly in the morning. Perhaps I associated depression with certain staff members on the morning shift and a kind of relaxed sense of well-being with other staff members on the afternoon shift. As I paced back and forth on the ward porch, the habit made me more agitated than when I began. It might be better to keep an agitated, depressed patient still because the walking, the turning back and forth within a restricted space, exaggerated my feelings of panic, of having much energy but limited space in which to dissolve it. Did I pick up the pacing from watching Mr. W.?

I approached each task, each job, as if it were a crisis. Failing would be seriously destructive, and succeeding would simply make me face another crisis later on. I applied the term "stairstep phenomenon" to the feeling that each success set me up for a potentially bigger failure later. Back in the ward the chief nurse approached me with the regular Monday morning gambit, "How was the weekend?" I told her it was much better than last weekend but that I was a little nervous about starting my detail.

I sat in on the group meeting that morning. Various topics were discussed, such as clothing, showers, the Dodger game, and the meaninglessness of patient council representatives now that most of the council was composed of outpatients anyway. We talked of work details and the picnic. The picnic on Sunday was a big event, breaking up the humdrum ward routine. Yet some of the aides didn't even know it had taken place. We were reminded of the discrepancy between our view of the ward world and the aides' view, although we lived side by side for eight hours a day. I'm not sure that the aides appreciated the usefulness of these meetings for the patients, who found in them a formal opportunity to air grievances and learn about the ward. A couple of comments made during the meeting by our discussion leader, Mr. D., were particularly noteworthy. After one patient complained about Mr. S.'s stealing clothes at night, the aide responded that Mr. S. was one of our sicker patients, and we had to be tolerant of patients when they were disturbed like that. He also mentioned that in the kind of community in which we were living, everyone had to look out for everybody else. We had to have mutual concern and cooperation. As usual, the meeting ended promptly at 9:15 A.M. I couldn't help but feel that many of the aides considered it something of a mildly inconvenient formality. The seemed almost relieved when it was over.

I was late to occupational therapy because of the ward meeting. I arrived at about 9:20. The supervisor at the OT clinic said that I shouldn't have been late, that I should talk with my chief nurse about getting out early from my group meetings since it wasn't on my activities slip to be late that particular morning. I took the initiative to ask about the results of my vocational testing and got only a very brief summary. The testers suggested that I get a job in the clerical field since I could type approximately fifty-one words per minute with only three errors. They believed I should work in a sheltered setting at first. I discovered that only the summary of the testing went into my record, but the details of the testing were kept on file in the occupational therapy clinic. The therapist also gave me some advice of a general nature, suggesting I might to to City College or to night school. I felt somewhat let down that nearly nine hours of testing should result in this minimal, sketchy knowledge about my work potential. The OT trainees again talked freely with me and more or less as equals. Our conversation was like any conversation engaged in by three young people.

I suspect there may be some confusion between the occupational therapy vocational testing and the vocational counseling offered by psychology service. I'm not sure that the people in the ward know the distinction between them. Certainly the distinction was not pointed out to me. I learned about psychology service's vocational counseling that morning in the OT clinic. It was decided that I wouldn't get a work assignment after all, since my discharge date was coming up so soon. This information was verified by a phone call to the ward.

After leaving the clinic with instructions to report the test results verbally to my ward and staff, I went to the canteen and ate a piece of pie. I was struck by the general kindness and courtesy with which I was treated by salespeople (and secretarial personnel) throughout the hospital. The jukebox was playing its loud rock music, as usual. By this time I had become acquainted with an expanded variety of resources patients had at their disposal to offer other patients. They included running errands, loaning money and giving money, prizes won, offering lights for cigarettes, cigarettes, and information. As I ate I mused that within very broad limits it was difficult for the staff to discern what a patient knew and what he didn't know about hospital life and hospital procedures. It seemed to me that they assumed that the newly admitted patient had much more knowledge than he actually did.

I returned to the ward and talked with Mr. D. at 10:45 A.M. I told him that at the occupational therapy clinic they'd decided not to give me a detail or an assignment in the sheltered workshop setting since I was going to be in the hospital only one or two more days. I asked him about psychological testing or vocational counseling. He suggested that I not start anything, that it would be no use since I was going to be leaving the hospital so soon. He pointed out that I would be going to staff the next day and then I'd be getting out Wednesday. I felt a beginning of the disengagement from personal commitment which protected the psyches of Mr. D. and other staff members. Patients came and patients went and, near discharge, they had to begin to detach themselves from involvement in the lives of other patients so that by the time they left they would not suffer too deep a sense of loss. It was a kind of anticipatory mourning process. Repeatedly, we ask the staff member to involve himself in the life of a person and then that person is pulled away from him at discharge.

Back in the dayroom of the open ward there were twenty-four patients sitting around expressing various degrees of patience. They included day hospital patients and outpatients. I sat on the porch of the open ward. There I observed an interaction that reminded me how hard it is to determine by his demeanor whether or not a quiet person will respond normally to a simple question. One patient approached another who was seated quietly. He asked, "I saw them giving you a shot the other day. Do you get more than one a day?" The other patient just stared at him. He did not respond verbally at all, and after a minute the first patient wandered away. Again, the patient in good contact, the patient who knew the customs of the ward, did not interpret this inaction as a personal rejection. The lack of response was seen in terms of the sickness of the nonresponsive patient.

I talked with another nursing assistant about my suicide attempt the weekend before last. He laughed and said, "See, we can't stop anyone from killing himself. The patient can jump through a window or butt his head against the wall. We can't stand guard over him twenty-four hours a day. Anyway, people might make a big fuss and 'show' if you killed yourself, but no one really cares if you commit suicide. Someone would come in the next week and say, 'Where's Kent?' They'd tell him, and he'd say, 'Oh,' and that would be it. He'd forget about you." He told me I didn't really want to kill myself in the first place. As he interpreted my behavior, I was "heading for cover in the storm" by coming to the hospital. His argument seemed to be that the locus of my problem was in my wife, that I had built her up beyond reality. He was convinced that she had been playing around for a long time, that she had had nothing to gain by telling me (1) that she wasn't going to join me in California and (2) that she's found somebody else. So, clearly, she really had gotten herself involved with someone. And it was obvious to him that she'd been involved for quite a while. She was a grown woman, and she couldn't claim innocence as a young girl might. As he continued to denigrate her, I began to see that his approach aimed at the following sequence: She was less than I thought she was; therefore, she was less valuable to me as a person; therefore, the loss was not so serious as I initially considered it to be; therefore, I shouldn't feel so depressed. His orientation was essentially of a problem-solving nature. My problem was my wife and the solution was to forget her and find another one. The suicidal ideation was an irrelevant overlay, and it would disappear when the problem was taken care of.

He went on to discuss Mr. W. with me. Mr. W. the aide said, was talking "a lot of shit." "He has had five years to kill himself in, and he hasn't done it yet." The aide continued that he could "go research" and see the cause of W.'s problem, but it wouldn't be any good for helping him face the reality of the present. That is what he felt W. had to do — face reality. He was trying to get away from his problems, but we all have problems at one time or another. Mr. W. had to learn to face reality, to face his problems, and to deal with them effectively.

After lunch I went over to psychology service to see if I could get some psychological testing before I left the hospital. It wasn't open. I sat in a chair in the sun by the canteen reading and watching the girls go by. I reflected again that hospital life was best described as a series of forty-five-minute waits, punctuated by interruptions for half-hour activities. I learned in psychology service that Dr. C. was the psychologist in charge of testing for my ward. I vaguely remembered a name on a door and a face coming out of that door. Thus I learned that Dr. C. was a psychologist. By chance, as I got back to the ward, I discovered that a psychology trainee was to administer psychological testing that afternoon. Although testing had been ordered for me long ago according to the chief nurse, I was still not on the list for the testing that afternoon. Nevertheless, I was given the tests.

As I waited in the dayroom for the testing to begin, I introduced myself to a girl who was training to be a dietician. She was there to watch psychological testing being done and had no real sense of why she was supposed to do so — "To get to know the patients," she guessed. I'm not sure that the psychology trainee had much idea of how to go about testing anyway. It was a tragicomedy of people doing as they were told.

A female patient had been brought over to take the psychological tests during the same afternoon. She tried to get out of it but was gently pressured to stay. I responded to a short questionnaire, a sentence completion test, the Shipley-Hartford, and the MMPI test. (See Appendix D and the results of a blind analysis of the protocols below, pp. 153-154.) I was told by the trainee that he had never seen anyone score so high on the Shipley-Hartford. In keeping with my role I answered the MMPI questions so that I would appear depressed and somewhat neurasthenic. I wondered what the staff could do about discharge if a patient who said he was feeling all right tested out as severely depressed. No problem; the tests weren't scored before I was discharged.

I went to the Auxiliary canteen for ice cream and conversation. There I met a patient from the ward who told me that within the hospital you got what you looked for. If you were violent, then the aides sometimes had to use violence to control you. But he held a generally positive opinion of this hospital, certainly in comparison with the low quality and the high expense of some other hospitals he knew about.

At 3:10 P.M. as I passed through the dayroom on my return from the canteen, I noticed the female patient still testing. The psychological trainee looked at me strangely as though he had read through my MMPI responses. Or was this impression a paranoid projection after having exposed myself to his magical psychoscope? At 3:30, when the shift changed, there was a special meeting for the aides. I suspect there was a great deal of trouble for the aides who had been on duty the Sunday I attempted suicide because they hadn't reported it. There was a more officious atmosphere in the ward that evening. People became very concerned with regulations for a while. Someone asked me for the first time whether I was a 7 A.M.-6 P.M. or a 7 A.M.-10 P.M. privilege-card patient. I played chess as usual with my aide-friend, and that seemed to ease some of the tension. After supper I played chess again, this time with another patient. Perhaps the aides felt that I hadn't gotten them in trouble maliciously. Possibly they had been warned not to cause trouble for me as a reaction to their being disciplined. Nevertheless, I decided that it might be a good idea to spend some of the evening away from the ward to let things cool down. Or was all this my delusion? Certainly the ward atmosphere had stiffened. So at 6:30 I went to the theater where the drama group was scheduled to make a presentation. By a few minutes after seven the show still hadn't begun, so I left. I went to building 256 where there was to be a variety show beginning at 7 P.M. It hadn't started by 7:15 when I arrived. No wonder that patients were detached and uninvolved and apathetic. I learned that the drama group presentation finally started an hour late, at 7:30, and that at least one of the performers had been selected from the audience. The variety show did start at 7:20, and it was terrific. It was in the old Jewish show-biz tradition. It was a pro show "for the boys." We were treated as an audience. Obviously the performers sought our applause and devoured it when it came. It was a meaningful offering of talent and heart to a group of veteran patients. Cigarettes and bags of candy were passed out. At the end rolls and coffee were served. I felt much freer and more "together" attending an activity in another ward. If a staff member wanted to know how sick a patient really was, he would do well to observe the patient's behavior in another ward, at chow, at the theater, on his detail activity, at the dental clinic, and so forth. The ward seemed to pull "crazy" behavior from the patients.

Back in the open ward, the aide announced that we had to clean the floor in order to get medication and we had to get the medication before he would unlock our door so we could go to bed. In this way he structured reinforcements so that we were working toward getting to bed, to sleep — the poor man's escape from tedium.

As I lay in bed I remembered that one of the nursing assistants had told me how she had lost her husband by death not too long ago, and it had taken her about a year to fully get over it. "Time is the great healer," she said.

*July 20, 1971, Tuesday*

I got up, shaved, and received my antidepressant as usual. In the coffee room Mr. S. was again something of a mascot. He was reaping free cigarettes (he was not supposed to smoke because of his advanced emphysema) and coffee from his fellow patients. There was some general conversation about staffing and about a patient having gone AWOL and so forth. Mr. S. reassured us all, "Hitler is alive; he's with me! Hitler will live forever!" When a patient told the group that he had gone to the clinic that morning and they had drawn some blood, Mr. S. replied, "Magnificent! I like my coffee black — in respect to you, sir. [He was speaking to a young man in a black shirt.] Black for all eternity." When Mr. S. set his cup on the floor, the coffee room monitor reminded him to be careful not to spill it. Then another patient came in and brought Mr. S. a cup of coffee without knowing he already had one. When his friend discovered Mr. S.'s first cup of coffee, Mr. S. replied, "It's put here for a purpose. It'll sit there; it'll never be spilled — forever and forever. Those that want it won't be able to drink it, now and forever." And thus he joked his way out of possible bad feelings. Some patients were comparing watches and Mr. S. commented, "Those two watches will last forever. They'll never run down. A machine is a machine and it'll last forever." He talked for awhile about "thinking metal." He told us the Chinese had invented it with all their prayers. They were using chopsticks when the rest of the people in the world were eating with their fingers. "In the other galaxy I'll meet my Daddy Raymond. He'll walk right off my ship of life." Such conversation was highly unpredictable and quite entertaining. But I suspect the reader has noted already the obsessive concern with death in this dying man.

A patient wandered into the coffee room. He gave gum and cigarettes to anybody and everybody who would accept them from him. In fact, he had to wheedle some people into taking them. He was rather ridiculed and looked down on by other patients. Mr. H. came in and wanted my pack of cigarettes. I told him that I'd give him a few but that I was saving most of them for Mr. W. He refused my offering, "That's OK." He wanted the whole pack or nothing. And thus he preserved some of his pride.

I slipped off to the Central Research Unit for a short period of dictation. On the way back to the ward I stopped off at the domiciliary patio. The sad music from the jukebox ("Make the World Go Away") reinfored my feelings of sadness. The atmosphere of the domiciliary patio was very similar to that of the neuropsychiatric hospital's patio except that one didn't have to assume a crazy identity in order to stay in the domiciliary. In both places there was unfilled time. I returned to the ward and played pool. I was told to report to the waiting room in order to "go before the board." All seven patients who were to report for disposition staffing that morning had received identical slips informing us that our appointment was at 9:30 A.M. Of course, all but one of us had to wait. The atmosphere within the waiting room was moderately tense, mostly quiet. Staff members kept walking by the doorway and looking in. We didn't know who they were looking for or why — another reminder that the hospital was run for the convenience of the staff. At last I found out who the social workers were. As I waited in the room outside their office I read their names and titles on the door. The toilet opening off the waiting room was locked by the social worker after he had used it.

I waited and considered the variations in the value of cigarettes during the hospital day. Cigarettes generally increase in value in the afternoons, that is, when one's morning pack has been used up, when they are restricted, when a patient's funds are low, when a patient has a strong desire for a cigarette, and so forth. I've seen patients forced to beg and engage in other demeaning behaviors before another patient would hand over a cigarette. I've heard ordinarily smart-alecky patients humbly ask "please" for a cigarette when they needed one badly enough.

I was called into staff about 9:50 A.M. Staff members asked how I was feeling. "OK." They asked about my resources and probed a bit on this topic. There was no question about suicide, no mention of attempted suicide. I kept my plans and resources vague. The chief nurse seemed worried that I was being discharged so fast. She gave me the phone number of the ward in the event I might need it. A social worker asked if it would be acceptable for me to stay in the hospital and go out on a pass to look for a job. I responded that I would go out against medical advice before I could accept such a plan. There seemed to be a consensus that I had a work-habit problem and that a job in a sheltered setting would be best for me. They were willing, however, to give me the opportunity to go out on my own. I was dismissed with the hopeful words, "Good luck." As I left, a woman whom I took to be the ward secretary (but who later turned out to be a nurse) asked me when and where I was going. She wished me good luck if she didn't see me again. "Thanks."

I went to the locked ward to give the news to Mr. W. He had stayed in, missing the ward's beach trip that day. I told him I was getting out the next day. He gave me his usual story that he was still a "kid," having acute anxiety, being kicked out of the hospital, being kicked out by his family, having nowhere to go, feeling panic, and so on. This kind of story gets very tiresome after several repetitions. I can understand the feelings of frustration the aides must have felt listening to it every day. Mr. W. rejected all positive ideas. He seemed to care only about himself.

I strolled around outside and then returned to the open-ward dayroom. Many patients there I didn't recognize. One was an out-patient who slept in his own apartment and came to the ward each day. He had the clothing-room detail. The conversation in the day-room was of girls, shopping, clothes, and the like. I sat thinking and keeping up the notes.

The attitude of the aides toward suicidality and toward most of the other illnesses present was problem-oriented. The patients suffered from the same problems that everybody else had. It was the problems that needed to be dealt with. Thus, the specific symptomatology of mental illness was minimized while something understandable and capable of being dealt with was handled. It reminded me that not so long ago the concept of "personality" was used by psychologists in the same way the concept of "problem" was being used by the aides. One could deal ad nauseam with the same familiar Oedipus complexes, the same familiar passive-aggressive personality, or schizoid personality, or dependent-satisfied type. Thus one could deal with the same familiar problems — financial problems, woman problems, adjusting to one's disability, running away instead of facing difficulties, and so forth. This tactic of grouping behavior disorders and life circumstances into categories simplifies the task of the therapist. The price, however, lies in minimizing the individuality of experience.

While eating lunch on the privilege-card side of the cafeteria I joined in a conversation with two other patients. They spoke of the big changes in mental hospitals since the late forties. One of the patients had seen an aide get killed in the early fifties. They were aware that, in large part, the era of tranquilizers should be credited with bringing about these changes. One of the patients remarked that he thought it was too soon for me to go home, too. He had noticed that I was looking somewhat despondent in our group meeting the day before. The message was coming through on several levels. My move was premature. There was plenty of time should I decide to stay.

The patient was paid two dollars each Monday and Thursday for making the coffee. He felt (and I agree) that the job involved many hours and much responsibility for this minimal amount of pay. But he had grown rather attached to it. His major complaint of the moment centered on a pony-tailed hippie who owed about a dollar and a half to the coffee fund, and, furthermore, the lad wouldn't help clean up the ward room. The other patient said that he didn't get the discharge that he had wanted from the disposition staff, but, instead, had been transferred to another building that ran an alcoholics program. He appreciated the fact that he could sign out of the hospital any time he wanted.

Again I wrote notes in the interim between lunch and psychodrama. I considered the problems the staff members had in obtaining and storing information. It seems that one obvious strategy was to avoid accumulating useless knowledge about patients, that is, knowledge that would have to be forgotten shortly when the patient left and wouldn't be of much value in helping the patient in the present. Names, of course, had to be learned by staff and also perhaps some facets of the patients' problems, but detailed histories of the patients weren't necessarily read and memorized. A number of staff members weren't familiar with my case. Perhaps there was some division of labor involved. At any rate, getting a patient to talk about himself was a good ploy for assessing his current state and establishing a relationship.

An incident in psychodrama that afternoon revealed the contrasting orientations of the psychiatrist and the aides. One patient had been badgered by his ex-wife to provide extra funds for her to buy living room furniture. After the patient had reenacted the telephone conversation in which his wife had asked for the money and people had discussed the experience, a young black patient asked, "Does he have the money to buy the furniture?" The psychiatrist responded in a somewhat deprecating manner that the question raised "a reality problem." "We aren't concerned with that here but with emotional problems that usually have their roots in early childhood." What would have been a perfectly appropriate question had the patient been talking with an aide was inappropriate in this setting. Thus the patient learned that the problem-oriented approach of the aides was not acceptable to a particular psychiatrist at a particular time. I was struck again and again by the cartoon caricatures of, for example, the "bad wife," the "bad mother," the "rejecting father," and so forth, which pervaded the psychodrama session. These cardboard characters interacted in stilted, stereotypical scenes under Freudian direction to produce some mystical "therapeutic benefit" for the patient.

I was asked to perform that day in psychodrama. Circles within circles within circles. I told Dr. S. that I didn't think I should do it. He encouraged me, however, and I recounted a history in which my father was often drinking but not a drunkard, my mother was very protective, and my father had left when I was approximately five years old. My earliest (semifictional) memory involved a scene in which my mother and father were arguing. My father was telling my mother that I "wasn't worth a dime" and she was defending me. I spoke up and told them to "shut up" and "stop arguing." My father had hit me, and both parents had turned on me for speaking so rudely to my elders. The episode gave me a tremendous sense of martydom, a feeling of satisfaction that I had stopped them from arguing at such heavy cost to myself. The group seemed to feel that this fictionalized early experience had molded my life so strongly that my present behavior was understandable in terms of it. With this outcome in mind we reenacted the scene in front of the group. I played the tearful, depressed patient. A young therapist was particularly rough in the role of my father. He shoved me, pushing me over a chair. Apparently he wanted to provoke an angry response, but I took it passively, waiting.

When we reversed roles, however, my strict self-control relaxed for one brief but infinitely pleasurable moment. As my son, the therapist taunted and reviled me, "You shouldn't do that." I responded meekly. He pressed, shouting and cursing. At last, after a dramatic pause, I pulled back and let fly a hard right blow to his shoulder. A burst of applause from the audience! My anger had broken through! They couldn't know that the blow carried the force of all the frustration and exploitation and manipulation I had felt as a patient these two weeks. There was a lot behind that punch. In the critique that followed, I was praised for responding with appropriate anger. Afterward I felt some self-consciousness and then an acceptance from the group and an inward acceptance of my publicly expressed anger and violence. But the spotlight turned to another patient quickly, and I felt a sense of having been "dismissed."

Mr. W. had been observing my performance. Apparently some of the elements in my pseudo history reminded him of his own past. When he spoke of the resemblance the group's attention turned to him. He was eventually drawn out to play through some of his childhood experiences with a drunken, violent father. Perhaps psychodrama as it was practiced in this setting did have a genuinely cathartic effect for some patients. And it may have been helpful in that it provided them with a sheltered setting in which they could try out seemingly unacceptable behavior. But the intelligent patients with whom I talked were so attuned to the artificiality and image-presenting aspects of the psychodrama group that I doubt it was of much use to them. I wondered what all those professionals got out of sitting through it time after time. Was it some sort of training group?

After the psychodrama I began walking back to my office to dictate notes. A nurse from the ward happened to be walking in the same direction. In a friendly manner she took my arm, and we chatted as we walked along. She told me she hoped things went well for me. She considered me a "good man." She felt that a sales position wasn't the right kind of occupation for me. She believed I would be happier as a clerk or a typist. She said that she loved everyone in a way and in a way she loved me. She learned something from me just as she learned something from everybody, and she hoped that I had learned something from the ward, too. She told me that she would see me the next day but that she wanted to wish me good luck. These Filipino nurses had something of a language problem, but emotions of kindness and mothering nurturance came through clearly. This completely fortuitous encounter was a memorable experience.

After dictating some notes at the Central Research Unit, I found it was easily possible for me to slip off the hospital grounds, so I returned to my nearby apartment for about four hours that evening. I returned to the ward about 8:50. There I ran into a couple of the patients who had attended psychodrama earlier that day. They seemed reserved but rather protective of me and defensive for me as if I'd allowed myself to be conned. One of them remarked that he still thinks psychodrama is "bullshit."

An aide asked me where I was at 4:30 P.M. and I told him that I didn't get medication then. He said that they'd called my name over the intercom system. When I assured him that I got medication only in the morning, at noon, and at night he was satisfied.

At medication time I had a similar exchange with a nurse. I told her that I'd received my medication that morning at 11:30. She wondered how I could have because there was a card in the paper cup containing my medication and the medication was still there. I explained to her that I had been a little late for medication in the morning but that I had received it and that I was willing to take medication again if she thought I should. With a bit of reluctance, however, she took my word for it.

After medication I said good-bye to my favorite aide and went to bed. I did tell one patient that I had slipped off to prepare my apartment for the next day, but I was sure that he wouldn't tell anyone. There was a conspiracy of sorts among patients just as there was a conspiracy among staff.

### July 21, 1971, Wednesday

On my last day in the hospital I got up, shaved, and received my Elavil. I went into the coffee room where the conversation centered on people who don't pay their debts, people who regularly borrow, and, particularly, people who have the funds to pay their debts and yet don't. Several patients asked if I was going home that day, and a few of them gave me advice about how to get along on the outside. No staff member on the night shift said anything about my leaving the hospital, probably because I had never established much of a relationship with any of them. Mr. W. asked me to write a couple of letters for him. One was to his sister asking for her help in getting him home, and one was to his wife asking for news. Both letters were full of "I'm sorry," "Forgive me," "Help me," "I am desperate," and so forth. Mr. K. insisted that I post the letters in an outside mailbox. I paced a bit that morning, feeling somewhat nervous, wondering if I was really ready for discharge.

For the meeting scheduled for that morning, I was reassigned to the open-discussion group. Previously I had been assigned to the remotivation group which hadn't met the week before. It was explained to me that the remotivation group was for patients who didn't talk very much and needed to be drawn out. The open-discussion group seemed much the same at first with no one wishing to contribute. Although the meeting offically started at 8:45 A.M., no one began talking until around nine o'clock. Then there was some discussion about the distinction between nurses and nursing assistants. One patient pointed out that certain questions could be asked only of a nurse. One nursing assistant in attendance reacted by emphasizing the equally true opposite position that many problems can be handled either by nurses or by nursing assistants. It was obvious that both nurses and aides had very strong feelings about the distinctions and the similarities between their roles.

We discussed the wearing of uniforms by staff members. Some patients felt the uniforms were useful as a means of identifying the people in authority. I suspected they were concerned also with being able to identify staff quickly in order to modify and monitor their own behavior. The other side of the picture — that staff and patients could relate more on a human level when personnel were in street clothes — was also brought out. I suggested that name tags might be very useful, particularly for shy patients and for people who didn't remember names well. A nurse responded that a name tag was an authority symbol as well. We compromised, agreeing that if only the name of a person was given on the tag, and not his title, the system might be useful.

After the group meeting I went to the ward secretary's door in order to pick up my discharge papers. The hall was very busy, and I waited unnoticed by the door for several minutes. Dr. S. passed through the hallway and gave me some of his typical "you did fine in psychodrama" support. A nurse came by, reassured me, and told me to keep up the progress and wished me good luck on the outside. Mr. D., my group leader, noticed me standing by the door, asked what I was doing, and took over. He asked if I felt ready to leave and if I felt no depression. I apparently gave him satisfactory answers because he expedited the paperwork for me. I simply followed him around while he took care of getting signatures in the ward. He told me to call the ward if I had any problems, and said he would be there from Monday to Friday. He also invited me to drop a postcard and let the staff know how I was doing. At the end, he shook my hand. A fine man.

As I walked out to begin getting the off-ward signatures for my checkout list, a social worker happened by in the hall. If I couldn't get a job and the bottom began falling out, she invited me to call social service because she might be able to help me with temporary housing.

I returned a book to the library, and a young male librarian was very pleasant and kind. Similarly, in the clothing and effects room the staff was efficient and polite with "Yes, sir" and "Hi, brother" in greeting. I bought a thank-you card and cigarettes in the canteen. The saleslady, as usual, offered a kind "Thank you, sir." Throughout my hospital stay I found the sales and staff personnel to be very polite, as if they were taking seriously the letters and bulletins encouraging employees of the VA system to be pleasant to the patient because without him there would be no need for the employees.

While I was in the canteen I observed Mr. S. being caught in the act of shoplifting. The salespeople were saying that he had been caught so many times that he wasn't supposed to be in that area of the canteen at all. They were debating whether or not to call the ward. When caught, Mr. S. quietly walked back, put the pair of slippers he had lifted back on the shelf, and left.

As I checked out of the dental clinic, the secretary there said, "Good luck, Mr. Kent." The only exception to the general attitude of kindness I found in the pharmacy, where I was given no greeting. The pharmacist simply took my prescription without comment. There was an attitude of cold businesslike professionalism and little in the way of human warmth from either of the two pharmacists who filled my prescription. In contrast with the customary politeness that I had come to expect, mild rejection and self-limitation were expressed by the pharmacists. Perhaps I caught them on an off day. The last signature on the checkout slip was that of the discharge clerk. The clerk checked to see that each discharged patient had enough travel funds to get to his destination. Excellent idea.

Back in the ward I gave the cigarettes to Mr. W. and the thank-you card to Mr. D. As I started to walk back to clear my clothes out of the locker, a nurse told me that Mr. F. wanted to see me. Who was Mr. F.? I wondered. Ah, a social worker. I'm not sure that I would have learned of the appointment if I hadn't accidentally encountered the nurse. Perhaps the informal means by which patients were told about appointments or proposed meetings might be supplemented in the open ward by a message board or some other formal device (in lieu of appointment slips when the patient cannot be found immediately).

When I went into the social workers' office there seemed to be some mix-up. I wasn't sure that Mr. F. actually wanted to see me. He told me that Miss C. was my social worker. She was sitting at one of the two desks in the office. Together they began to talk with me. I felt rather uncomfortable because I had the impression that no one actually needed to talk with me, but since I was there they'd talk to me anyway. They soon put me at ease, however. They reminded me that the ten days remaining before my rent was due wasn't much time in which to get a job. They asked specifically whether or not I had entertained suicidal thoughts recently, and they checked to see that I had the proper prescriptions for a month's supply of medication. Mr. F. said that even in this short time I had made an impact on many people, and that many people were concerned about me. They asked me to keep in touch, and they gave me the address of a vocational rehabilitation center. They suggested that they might be able to help me with food and shelter if I was unable to find work within the next few days. I thanked them for their interest and concern. I left, cleaned out my locker, and slipped quietly away at 10:30 that morning.

No matter what sort of hospital experience one has had, I suspect he leaves (as I did) with a certain amount of loneliness and apprehension about the outside. I left what had rapidly become familiar and entered a world in which I was already no longer comfortable. I left people I had grown to know, and I faced acquaintances who had already changed. In only two weeks! At such a time it was good to have specific plans and specific goals and a specific destination. These I needed much as one needs stepping-stones across an unfamiliar stream until the outside world, the misty opposite bank, becomes visible and until it appears safe and predictable.

Sitting in my familiar yet now unfamiliar office in the Central Research Unit I look back on the two weeks of hospitalization, and several things still puzzle me. What happened to the contact man I talked with briefly on the second or third day? He said he was going to try to get some money for me. I asked him to come back a week or so later to talk to me, but I didn't see him again. What happened with social service? When I entered the ward I was given a list of names of people who were specifically assigned to my case. In the space where the social worker's name was to be written, there was only a question mark. In the first few days of my hospitalization, a social worker did come to interview me. She, too, said that she was going to see about getting me some money. On my last hospital day I learned that Miss C., a person whose face I recalled only from the staff meetings I had attended, had been assigned as my social worker. My direct contact with her was confined to that last day, and then almost by accident. Had I been administratively shuffled from worker to worker?

Another puzzle concerned my eligibility for outpatient treatment. It was never clear to me whether or not I was eligible or where I had to go to receive such treatment. On the other hand, I did have the sense that I could return to the hospital; I could call back; I could find in my home ward immediate practical help should I need it. Along with this knowledge came the impression that the people were concerned enough about me so that they were bending the rules somewhat. I sensed that the Veterans Administration might not condone the giving out of phone numbers to patients who were leaving, or the issuing of an invitation to call on the resources of the social worker when one was no longer a patient. And I very much appreciated the implication that I was more important to these people than VA regulations were.

Looking back over the whole experience of depression, I see that my world was very private and constricted at first, so attempts to get at the roots of my feelings (especially interactional forays aimed at solving my interpersonal problems) were doomed to failure because I frankly didn't register them. On the other hand, as my depression began to lift, I began to feel an increasing need to understand why I had attempted suicide, how I was different from and like other people, and what was wrong with me. I had a sense that I was seeking the answers to these latter questions at a time when the staff had already solved them for themselves, insofar as their understanding of my case was concerned. That is, the timing of my questioning was somewhat later than the period in which the staff had offered explanations. I did find, however, that when I asked directly the staff members were willing to talk with me about my depression in terms of their interpretations of its roots and its sequelae. Luckily, I was aggressive enough to ask.

And now it is over — or so I thought on July 21, 1971.

## POSTOPERATIONS AND DEBRIEFING

Within a week of Kent's discharge we had obtained the hospital records of his stay. Not only were they invaluable accounts of the perceptions of significant others in a psychiatric setting, but they were also documents that needed to be cleared from VA record files. They included an admission summary, nursing notes, doctor's progress notes, aides' reports, occupational therapy results, psychological testing results, and reports of physical examinations. Only two documents were missing; the discharge summary had been lost between dictation and typing and the letter Kent sent to his "wife" had been returned to the hospital mail room and then had disappeared. The pertinent records, which are presented in Appendix B, in general support the notion that staff members saw Kent as depressed (though not severely depressed) and suicidal.

## Psychological Testing

Psychological testing materials are presented in Appendix D. After Kent's discharge the ward psychologist was contacted. She offered to have the test results analyzed in blind fashion by a respected VA psychologist who consulted with and trained others in psychological testing. The consultant's analysis was monitored on tape. Here follow some excerpts from that tape:

> Right away the first thing that's most noticeable is that he only missed one word on the vocabulary test and if you do something you're not supposed to do and you took the vocabulary score and you look at the IQ, the vocabulary score is 20.6 equal to an IQ of 144 and he came out with an IQ of 139. So he's not very far off. His CQ indicates that . . .
>
> Well, he is a person with a D and a Pt up (on the MMPI), he is very obsessional, and ruminating, and anxious. The Si is so high, he's quite withdrawn and quite inactivated by his depression and his rumination because the Ma is so little. So I would see him as someone who is in considerable distress with a lot of compulsive preoccupation. . . .
>
> I would imagine that he is not at all good at pushing himself and consequently tempts other people to get into the position of pushing him. And what he does about that is a good question. What does he do about that? He puts people in the position of pushing him around and then he gets angry about it, of course. But how does he handle it? What does he do? Withdraw, sulk? Probably. . . .
>
> He said he came in because of depression and attempted suicide. We go back to this, the attempted suicide. . . . Getting this profile, with the Ma so far down, may be and often is, I think, the kind of thing we get following a suicide attempt. Did he make the suicide

attempt just before he came in? . . . Another time the Ma will go over very low is when they're so immobilized by their anxiety that they just sit in a funk. Then the Ma will be 'way down.' So he could be either one. . . .

"I'm scared by ropes." Did he try to hang himself? Is he afraid? Scared by ropes. That's a sure way to do it. . . .

Well, I would call this one a very severe depressive reaction. (Neurotic? Psychotic?)

Well, I think it's still on the neurotic side. I don't think he's psychotic yet because the Sc is too much lower than the Pt. . . .

[Is there any possibility that he could have been malingering on some aspects?]

No, I don't think so. I really don't think he'd malinger. It hangs together too well. With a malingering person, one feels more signs of inconsistency. I don't think, unless he's awfully clever, and has had a course in clinical psychology, and knows the admissions battery better than most of our trainees know the admissions battery, I don't see how he could have written such a beautiful sentence completion to go with this. They go together so beautifully. I don't think he could match them up. . . .

If you're concerned whether or not he is making himself look *less* sick than he is, rather then malingering sickness, whether he's holding back anything. He may be sophisticated enough. . . .

[What about this guy? Do you have any feelings about his prognosis?]

Well, I would think it ought to be reasonably good except for the social withdrawal. I would like to know what he has going for him to draw him out. . . .

Ma is too low, much too low. Particularly for a young man. . . . This could mean that he's trying awfully hard not to slip over into this grandiose schizophrenic state where he relieves all of his symptoms by suddenly feeling he's got everything worked out, he's got everything solved and he's got it solved in some unrealistic way. He may be trying not to do that and that would be why I would suggest giving him a Rorschach. If he takes the Rorschach and doesn't just give one safe response to a card, if he really takes it and gets involved, he might come up with something that looks a little bit serious and a little bit disturbing. . . .

I think that in the light of the fact that there is some possibility that he's covering up being more disturbed than he really shows on the MMPI, I'd ask him about the fear of losing his mind.

It is clear, according to this interpretation of the psychological test results, that Kent was severely depressed and possibly had recently attempted suicide by hanging. Since the testing was completed only a few days after Kent's near suicide attempt in the hospital by hanging, the psychologist's analysis is consistent with the events and with Kent's psychological state.

## Initial Staff Meeting

On August 3, 1971, the building chief and Dr. Farberow met with the ward staff responsible for Kent's treatment. They explained briefly the nature of the research. The staff had been notified the preceding fall that within the next year this sort of research would be carried out. They were asked if they wanted to venture guesses as to the researcher's patient identity. There was some success: one psychiatrist had recognized the anthropologist from a guest lecture he had given at UCLA. She had, however, noticed nothing unusual in his behavior as a patient, and so she had attributed the resemblance to misremembering. The chief nurse had observed some unusual behavior for a depressed person and supported the psychiatrist's guess. The other three nursing personnel and the psychologist were not sure. The important point here is that no one suspected the true identity of the researcher until they were told the research had been completed and were asked to guess who the researcher might have been.

Dr. Reynolds then entered. The atmosphere was one of interest, not hostility. He made a brief presentation, inviting questions and comments as he went along.

> First let me say that I can well appreciate that some of you may have very strong feelings about being "studied" or being "checked up on." I can assure you that I had other things in mind than investing two weeks of my life in checking up on one ward in one VA NP hospital. I might also add that the VA lacks the funds, the interest, and the trained personnel to do systematic checking on all its wards. Well, then, what was I doing?
>
> I'll explain by saying that I really am the patient whom you knew as David Kent. Or at least a part of me is that patient. I'm sure you know that the differences between normal people and abnormal ones are, for the most part, differences of degree, not of kind. There is some paranoia, some depression, some mania in all of us. I drew on and exaggerated the depressive side of my character, and I became that patient, David Kent.
>
> I thought the experience was important enough to undertake the risks involved. I hope I can convince you that it was important and worthwhile as I am convinced that it was. It is my conviction that

what I call experiential research is an extremely valuable tool in understanding man. By experiencing the depressed suicidal patient's life (or something much like it) I have an emphatic perspective that would be hard to come by any other way. Now, let me share some of what I learned from my experience with you. Then I'll need some help from you in interpreting what went on during my hospitalization.

I'll ask you some questions such as: How was I like other depressed patients? How was I different? What did you like about the way I was treated? What would you have done differently?

You see, any single viewpoint, by itself, is distorted. Only by bringing several perspectives to bear on the same events can we begin to get a truly accurate picture of what really went on.

One of the areas we wanted to explore in our research was the area of privacy and personal space for a suicidal patient on special status. Does he experience discomfort and pressure because he is being watched? Does a lack of personal freedom in the real world prod him to escape into the free world of unreality — his fantasies?

My experience indicates that for the severely depressed patient privacy need not be a major concern in our planning. During the first few days of my hospital experience my "world" was only slightly larger than the space my body occupied. My world was almost wholly private and internally oriented. What came through to me from the outside was not faces, or names, or specific explanations of interpretations of my difficulties, but more intangible emotion-tinged gestalts: people sitting quietly beside me, people introducing themselves in a friendly way, people showing concern over my condition, a hand on my arm, a warm "good night." I couldn't respond to these gestures; I honestly couldn't remember names or faces later. Often I didn't even "see" what was going on and even though my hearing was sharper than my vision much of what I heard those days didn't register in my memory. Nevertheless, these experiences were directing me through my confusion toward a larger world "outside," a positive, a good, place for me to be if and when my depression lifted.

At this point I might insert the impression I picked up later that some staff members don't feel that foreign nurses can be effective with patients because they are not completely familiar with our lifeways and our language. In my deep depression it made no difference who offered nurturance, concern, and warmth. These human qualities came through as clearly from the foreign-born as from the native-born, from the blacks as from the whites, from the males as from the females, and at every level of staff these nonverbal communications of concern touched me.

As my psychomotor depression lifted matters of physical privacy and space became more important. I appreciated the aides' taking care not to "press" me. They watched, but from across the dayroom. I could enter the bathroom without an escort, and so forth. There needs to be a balance here, though, between giving the patient a sense of freedom and trust on the one hand, and giving him the feeling that he is being ignored and unprotected on the other. Feelings of abandonment were uppermost in my mind on the evening when I faked a suicide attempt in the hospital. Perhaps now is a good time to talk with you about that experience. It's hard to communicate the deep feelings of frustration and anger that I felt on that evening. [See pp. 000-000 for a description of that event.]

You had spent four days communicating to me that you wanted me to get better. But you must see those four positive days in the light of the months and years in which people hadn't communicated much concern for me at all. I was coming out of my sorrow and self-pity, drawn out by medication and by your interest. Then, suddenly, I "realized" that no one "really" cared whether I lived or died. I felt as if I'd been "suckered" out of that miserable yet failure-proof world by a false hope. I wanted to show you that I hadn't been fooled; I wanted to punish the aides who weren't taking care of me as they should have; and I wanted an escape from these thunderheads of feeling.

All this may sound artificial but I assure you that these feelings were genuine and very strong. In fact, the reality-oriented side of me became frightened that I might actually do myself harm. That's why I broke the rope *before* I put the noose around my neck. That way I felt safer from any wild impulse that might emerge as I rubbed the rope back and forth around my neck in order to make chafing marks there.

The opposite side of that coin is that there were shifts when certain ward personnel were on duty during which I wouldn't have made an attempt even if I had felt like killing myself. We had developed so strong a relationship that I couldn't bear to disappoint them or get them in trouble.

There followed a generally profitable exchange of information. We were relieved to find the communications fairly free, even on potentially touchy subjects. Staff members showed a minor defensiveness, but as they perceived from our responses and inquiries that we were not interested in assigning blame or focusing on faults but rather had found the hospital experience to be, on the whole, a positive one, their defensiveness diminished further and still more opening occurred.

Discussion topics included the special insights obtainable through experiential techniques, problems of foreign-born psychiatric nurses, the nonpressuring stance of nursing assistants toward patients on suicide status, the advantages and disadvantages of administratively keeping suicidal patients together, the VA policy regarding suicidal precautions, techniques for concealing medication, staff responsibilities for balancing trust and caution, the usefulness of written orientation material for the new patient, initial interviewing procedures in the ward, rules and rule bending, the trauma of admissions staffing, delays in psychological testing and social service contacts, dangers that appear as depression lifts, Kent's prognosis and discharge planning, and plans for future staff meetings and individual contacts. The meeting broke up only because some of those attending had other commitments, but the discussion and exchange of information could have extended on into the evening. The ward psychiatrist in charge of psychodrama was not present at this meeting, but he was contacted personally later.

## Second Staff Meeting

By the time of the second meeting some of the staff members had had time to mobilize defenses against the possibility that they had been conned. The first part of the meeting was spent dealing with the issues of whether or not they had actually been taken in and whether or not it was possible for Kent to have had genuine feelings of suicidal depression. Some of the staff members openly admitted that they had perceived Kent as severely depressed. The psychologist who had analyzed the psychological tests presented her findings. The building supervisor attested to the validity of Kent's identity change. We presented hospital records that indicated the convincing nature of Kent's presentation. The researcher offered some information about his psychological and physiological states and raised the issue of the indirect means by which we determine that any person is depressed and suicidal. Some of the remarks from that second meeting follow.

> Psychologist: "My only concern on this testing when I skimmed through it when it was first done was when his depression lifted would we discover we had a paranoid schizophrenic on our hands."
> Psychiatrist: "But you just sat there apologizing for being you or for being there or being alive."
> Psychologist: "I selected him for my evening group. I was planning that he was going to stay in the area and it made me very angry when I found out on Tuesday [sic] that he was discharged that day

before I had a chance to talk to him. That was how completely I was fooled. I still think he would've been a fine addition to the group.''

Psychiatric consultant: "Well, it sounds as if, based on the psychological testing, on the ward workup, the ward observation, and so on, that you pulled it off very well, although there may have been a few things some people thought were a little unusual, like being too observant for someone purportedly being so depressed. Your simulation of depression was quite expert.''

Social worker: "Dr. F., I want to react to your comment and to the comment I made to you, Dr. Reynolds. I felt angry as you indicated, and I told you this yesterday. My first reaction when I first heard about it was anger. We were duped. I was duped individually. But I understand since yesterday how he pulled it off, because as he talked and gestured about his experiences I guess I felt that he was not playacting. Partly it's just intuition and partly it's the way he responded and the way he reported what happened. I can remember the names of the people he mentioned on the ward and how they responded and what it meant to him. And it wasn't so much clinical as it was human. And it stuck in my mind because Mr. D. (a nursing assistant) and I talked, and Mr. D. had said, 'We talk about his relationship with the patients, and he apparently felt it, too.' Again, not clinically but as a human being. I'm not angry any more.''

Nursing assistant: "Now that I look back on some of my notes, I saw him as a depressed person but not as a suicide. Because, as it was mentioned over and over, he was too alert to be so suicidal. I didn't have any suspicion of him really. . . . I just saw him as a person who needed help." [Did you react to him any differently, do you think, from most patients who would generally fall into this category?] "No.''

Building supervisor: "You see, the thing that I was mentioning to you, David. You really picked it up in the discharge staff, that my feeling was that everybody was kind of mad at you for leaving the hospital. They had spent an awful lot of time with you, they'd worked out plans, they wanted to help you very much on a lot of different things. I remember that Mr. F. [the social worker] said, 'He'll be back.' ''

Psychiatrist: "I had that feeling. I felt you were leaving prematurely and I remarked to Miss J., 'Mr. Kent will make another attempt. I really don't feel he's been here long enough.' ''

During the meeting various issues were discussed, including status distinctions between nurses and nursing assistants, posthospital contacts with patients, and differing conceptions of suicidality among the various role groups in the ward. Amid laughter a psychiatrist raised the question of whether Dr. Reynolds was "simulating so well, or maybe there really is some reason for concern." A social worker added, "I guess what he's saying is you're always welcome to come back." Much of the meeting, in addition to the information exchange, can be seen in terms of individuals' efforts to accept the fact that they had been deceived. After some initial denial and anger (which served to direct attention away from the deception and toward the staff member's inner emotional condition), two "acceptable" interpretations emerged. Either Kent was very skillful at simulating depression or he was genuinely disturbed. Either way, the deception was understandable and nonthreatening. The mental squirming had produced a comfortable psychological fit.

*Meeting with Social Workers*

On August 12, 1971, we met with the ward social workers. After some preliminary discussion of the research we focused on the one (and only) contact Kent had with the two social workers, Miss C. and Mr. F. Kent's impression that the social workers were somewhat disorganized in their contact with him that last day was confirmed. They were mildly angry that Kent was to be discharged since they perceived him to have minimal resources for a return to society. Particularly after hearing that the afternoon before he had been taken apart in psychodrama without having been put together again, they were uncomfortable with the fact of his leaving.

One social worker considered that since many suicide gestures are aimed in anger at a significant other, Kent had possibly aimed his hospital suicide gesture at his friend, Larry, to whom the young veteran was returning on discharge. Furthermore, the prospect of getting a loan from Larry depended on Kent's getting a job. With such considerations in mind, the social worker felt that Kent's prospects were none too good and predicted that he would soon return to the hospital.

The social workers were all relatively new to the ward when Kent was admitted (the most experienced one having been there only two weeks). They were still not well organized, not yet acquainted with ward procedures, unsure about their patient loads, and so forth. These circumstances explain the lack of contact with Kent until his final hospital day.

The person who contacted Kent on the third or fourth day of his hospitalization was a volunteer worker from social service. She said that she would try to get him some money, but she wasn't heard from again. The social workers told us that such a contact involves duplication of effort, so steps were taken to eliminate it in the future.

We discussed the need to offer one's professionally based strength and stability to the patient in solving his problems, the need for staff-patient contact in the ward, the possibilities of using alternate shifts to spread therapy beyond the morning hours, the usefulness of various discharge programs, the use of advanced patients as cotherapists, and the feelings surrounding Kent's pseudo suicide attempt.

One social worker admitted to some surprise, then laughter, then anger, at discovery of the research. He then balanced the aroused feelings with what was learned from the project. Another social worker had read Caudill's article and had noted his evaluation of the unethical nature of this type of research. Still, she felt curiosity about the purpose and the findings of the study.

The social workers felt that their role was ambiguous in the ward, that the ward as it existed could probably function without their services, and that they are still only beginning to find their functional niche as well as learning effective tactics in achieving their goals. We emphasized the positive potential of ambiguous roles, calling for creativity and a clear perception of the patients' needs.

Again the discussion ended only because of some of those present had other commitments. We were invited to speak before a general meeting of social workers at the hospital.

## Meeting with Occupational Therapy Trainees

During the interview on August 4, 1971, Dr. Reynolds spoke with the two occupational therapy trainees who had supervised his vocational testing and evaluation. They felt somewhat caught between their impulses toward youthful opennesss and friendliness on the one hand and pressures toward professionalism on the other. For example, they were required to wear uniforms (other VA hospitals no longer require uniforms, and changes are supposedly on the way at this hospital also). They had been instructed not to engage in personal conversations with patients, nor were they to use first names when dealing with patients.

One trainee remarked that the uniform did provide her with a necessary feeling of security when she first came on the job. Later on, however, the minimal advantages of self-concealment and of not having to decide what to wear each morning were overshadowed by the desire to dress more freely. The other trainee commented that she had caught herself using Kent's first name once and thought, "Uh, oh, I'm not supposed to do that."

The human qualities of personal concern and interest in broader areas than simply measuring dexterity, perception skills, and perseverance seemed to be stifled by the restrictions of professionalism. It was our impression that what the occupational therapy testing offered in its best sense was the human personal contact and that it was weakest in its reporting of technical results from the testing.

There were two general problem areas that the trainees saw in their handling of Kent's case. One was that they felt a stronger need to give Kent specific information regarding test results. They felt they should have had more opportunity to counsel with him regarding his aptitudes and interests. This was closely tied to the second problem, which involved the lack of coordinated effort and communication among the wards, occupational therapy vocational testing, and psychology service vocational counseling. We discussed the possibility of having an occupational therapy representative visit each of the wards and participate in team meetings to provide additional immediate input in overall treatment planning for the patients.

The trainees noted many areas in which Kent was a typical patient. Particularly, his probing for more direction and advice on his last visit to the clinic seemed very much like that of other insecure, inadequate, depressed patients. Such probing, however, can also be seen as a realistic human response to the occupational therapist's initial limited information output in a critical area of living. When the researcher came to the clinic to interview them, the trainees both believed Kent had returned to tell them he had obtained a job. They were surprised he had found work so fast.

On thinking back they could see some ways in which Kent was unlike other patients. He had conversed more than many. Also, he seemed more alert and more aware of his surroundings than most of the patients, particularly in view of his diagnosis of depression.

## Ward Visits

Several other visits were made to the ward during the posthospital period. Personnel on the morning and evening shifts were contacted.

Individual meetings with the ward psychiatrist, the chief nurse, and the building supervisor were held. The tone of the meetings was one of good humor and mutual interest. Handshaking and laughter were common. The purpose of the research was made clear to everyone, and our observations were communicated to those who could use the information to create a more human setting for both patients and staff.

A form letter (see Appendix E) signed by the building supervisor and the chief of the Central Research Unit (NLF) served as DKR's introduction to those VA employees who had not yet heard about the research. On presenting the letter, the anthropologist immediately received full cooperation from clerical and professional staff.

# REFLECTION

## GENERAL ISSUES

Clearly there is a problem in generalizing from the highly personal insights acquired in experiential research. The raw data may be interesting from a humanistic standpoint and valuable in generating testable hypotheses; but their status as nonpublic, nonreplicable information limits their usefulness within the traditionally accepted domain of scientific knowledge. We are well aware that our tentative generalizations in this section require further validation before they can inspire scientific confidence. Theories built inductively on experiential research would require a number of "calibrated" investigators living in a variety of sampled settings. The end result might be a validated comparative theory of the effects of elements of social systems (and patterned combinations of those elements) on personality functioning or, more specifically, on suicidal ideation and behavior.

### Some Thoughts about Identity

Perhaps one of the most remarkable insights attained through this study and supported by the experientially based writings of others who have undertaken similar endeavors is the eminently social construction of one's identity. When others reflect back toward a researcher their expectations, attitudes, and understandings, all of which take for granted his sick pseudo identity, real symptoms begin to appear. The investigator is no longer playing a role; his depression, his paranoia, his anxiety, are genuine.

It may be, of course, that those who engage in such research are uniformly atypical. In some way, perhaps, they are more sensitive to social cues or more ready to permit such feelings and percepts to emerge. We doubt that such an explanation is sufficient. The fragile nature of one's self-concept and of one's construction of reality is well documented in the literature dealing with efforts — from hypnosis to brainwashing to psychoanalysis — to remold them. And, on a less encompassing level, the reader may well consult his own experience for social situations in which he participated as a stranger and found himself misidentified and therefore taking great pains to establish an appropriately recognizable identity, feeling rather uncomfortable until he had accomplished his purpose.

Rokeach (1964) reports his own experience and that of several colleagues with experimental name reversals in children. Calling a child by another name or pretending he is some creature other than himself can be quite disturbing to him. His taken-for-granted identity is called into question. Of course, a child has not had the long-term social experience or the varieties of social support (including indirect written social support, such as ID cards, badges, etc.) which adults accumulate. Nevertheless, with all their protective encrustments adults find themselves vulnerable to the primitive anxiety brought forth by identity questioning and misidentification. Such vulnerability seems to be related, in part, to the mass, faceless urban sociocultural setting in which we function.

DKR, after engaging in the suicide research experiment, expressed his views on it at the Death Research Conference held in Berkeley in 1973:

> To be quite open and honest I must admit that we claim more than entry into a setting in order to observe. There is a sense in which the experiential researcher really becomes another person. Inconceivable? Trivial? Merely a word game? Perhaps not. For a long time we in the social sciences have operated on the assumption that a normal human being is or has a single enduring identity or personality. The fact that I recognize that I *am* David Reynolds (with even a named label) provides some continuity to my existence as it evolves over time. But, now, on the basis of my research experience, I have also been David Kent and David Randolph [in a subsequent research project, to be reported by Reynolds and Farberow], both of whom felt and behaved in ways that David Reynolds never has.
>
> David Kent's characteristics were products of the convergence of

potentialities within "me" and the social-system pressures exerted on me. He was at times depressed, suicidal, callous, constipated, self-centered, and self-indulgent. It is not that David Reynolds lacks such qualities altogether now, but there are notable differences in degree if not in kind. There was evidence of some overlap in identities, as well. For example, Kent had an irresistible impulse to teach, and he appeared to others to be fairly intelligent.

The best phenomenological description of what I experienced would have to use the concept of oscillation. There were times when I was David Kent; then I'd flip over into my David Reynolds identity to observe Kent; then I would slip back into Kent's lonely spiraling world. Now, as I write of him my pen begins to slow, my head rests on my arm, and I experience a behavioral reminder of who I was.

My experience raises the issues of the usefulness and the meaning of a static, unitary concept such as "identity," the wisdom, and even the possibility, of incorporating actual and ideal images of the self into a single integrated self-concept, the importance of the social world in not only creating the self (a la G. H. Mead) or selves but also in sustaining it or them.

My position is similar to Gergen's [1972] whose research over the past few years casts doubt on conceptions of a single fixed sense of self as the foundation for a healthy personality. His work suggests that the social situation influences the interpersonal presentation of self to others and the intrapersonal self-concept as well. As he puts it [1972, p. 64]; "We are made of soft plastic, and molded by social circumstances."

The primary conceptual unit of our research is what one might call a "situated identity" or a "situated self." It comprises the behavior, thoughts, and feelings that are called forth by the setting in which a person is functioning. The concept serves to underscore our interest in the interrelationship of person and environment, including the social environment. In our experiential research the situations that prompted suicidal thought and behavior were those in which the depressed person's self-concept had been undermined by communications from others emphasizing impotence, unimportance, and an empty future. In a sense, these communications were social validations of and elaborations on themes that were already part of the patient's conceptual baggage (learned, presumably, in earlier settings from other alters).

We recognize that this way of thinking about the situational (especially the social situational) construction of the self assumes a rather passive model of man in the moment-by-moment evolution of his self-concept, for he is seen as reactor more than actor. The model seems to hold for children (G. H. Mead, Cooley, Rokeach, etc.), and we would prefer at this time not to push it beyond the subclass of depressed suicidal adults. But the ease with which we assumed other identities, were taken to be other persons, and felt ourselves to be other persons forces us to be aware of the fragile latticework of selves of which we are but momentary expressions.

## Suicide, Self-Esteem, and Powerlessness

An essential precursor of suicidal behavior is a sense of powerlessness. There may be an overlay of anger or despair, confusion or sharp clarity, isolation or overinvolvement in a relationship. But the basic conceptual state underlying suicide centers is the understanding that one has no control over the personal loss, or the voices, or the illness or the feelings, or the occupational failure, or one's life course, or whatever. When people speak of the common associations between hopelessness and suicide or between despondency and suicide they are referring, in part, to their shared feature, powerlessness. For what is hopelessness but a recognition (right or wrong) that a solution to one's dilemma will come neither from within nor from without? And despondency implies the acceptance of the unchangeable nature of one's predicament.

Personal control over one's existence is an important element in the development of a healthy self-concept. Clearly, such control characterizes the assertive, independent individual. Control is equally important, however, for the passive, dependent person who exerts it indirectly through others. For this reason the loss of a strong significant other may provoke a suicide attempt in a dependent person; that is, his mechanism for control over his life has withdrawn itself and other sources of indirect access to potency seem inaccessible or inappropriate.

What is being argued here is that persons with strong dependency needs have just as large a stake in maintaining a sense of personal power and control over their lives as do strongly independent persons. Only the channels to power are different, direct and indirect, by degrees. A good illustration of this perspective may be found in the Japanese. When the senior author went to Japan he was expecting to find a people much more ready to accept dependency needs and passivity than Westerners. What he found was a strongly hierarchical society in which the power of others over one's own life is more or less accepted, but, in addition, he discovered a plethora of tactics and strategies for influencing social superiors so that they provide the goods and services their social inferiors want. In other words, those low in the power structure still had a large number of means by which they could control their own existence through their superiors. Whether it is the humble housewife or the newest office clerk, there are leverage points by which to pressure those who are in formal control over an inferior. Dependency does not imply foregoing control over one's life. And we submit that it is precisely when one's leverage on life, whether applied directly or indirectly, becomes ineffective that suicide may occur.

There is an intermediate variable, we think, between powerlessness and suicide. We call it a "comparative life concept." By "life concept" we mean something more than self-concept and something less than a world view. Life concept includes one's view of himself, but also one's conception of the sort of life he is leading. By "comparative" we mean a cognitive matching of one's life concept with one's life-style in the past, one's expectable life-style in the future, other peoples' life-styles, and the expectations one has of nonlife, that is, of death. Simply put, when powerlessness is perceived as part of one's comparative life concept the continuation of life becomes devalued and death, through suicide or other means, becomes a positive alternative state.

Now, why do we need this intermediate concept between powerlessness and suicidality? Partly we need the comparative life concept in order to handle the kinds of events that are commonly thought to precipitate suicide. Often these events seem to have impact as they are compared with events in the suicidal person's past or future. Partly we need the concept because it is clear that some persons who are in positions of impotency do not try to kill themselves; presumably they have accepted impotence as part of their comparative life concept. And partly we need the intermediate concept to give us a conceptual foothold for treating people without necessarily changing their objective impotence (something over which we do not always have control) or physically restraining them from self-destruction.

A person who foresees no control over important aspects of his life can expect only want, misery, and humiliation. Such a life may not be considered worth continuing. The implications of this perspective for our study of suicide in mental hospitals and aftercare facilities become apparent as soon as we realize that, along with the pervasive boredom and stigmatization in institutions, the very sense of powerlessness is the principal existential condition of patients and ex-patients. Our own and others' experiential research studies underscore the mental patient's realistic appraisal that he has little or no control over many important aspects of his life.

We have found that one of the overwhelming impressions of patienthood in the literature of experiential research is the sense of powerlessness. Procedures happen to the patient; he does not initiate them. His life is dictated by schedules punctuated by decisions of others regarding his case. At first he has no knowledge of what is routine and expectable and what is not. His absorption in conversations or books or television is constantly intruded upon by the staff. For example, one evening several of us patients were engrossed in the all-star basketball game on television. We were interrupted by movie call. Because the movie was the scheduled entertainment, everyone was required to go. In another instance we watched a hostile patient who had angered an aide being put in his place. He was required to answer loud personal questions publicly; he was embarrassed publicly; he was forced to sit in a particular chair in the cafeteria, to put his empty tray in the rack at a particular time in a particular slot, and so forth. His feeling of autonomy was systematically strangled by the aroused aide. The sense of powerlessness combined with other demeaning aspects of patienthood contributes to or, more accurately, provokes suicidal behavior in institutional settings.

A mental hospital is in some ways a degrading and demeaning place in which to live. The blows to independence and self-esteem (and, we believe, a minimal degree of autonomy and self-esteem are corelated in every culture) are felt by all patients, but particularly by the suicidal patient. The suicidal patient is debating whether or not his "self" is worth keeping alive. Given these circumstances, it is surprising that there are not more suicides. We attribute the lack of suicides in the hospital setting to several factors: (1) successful efforts by staff members to get patients to accept impotence as part of the comparative life concept; (2) relationships supportive of self-esteem which counteract the effects of powerlessness on the patient's comparative life concept; and (3) the incompleteness of the impotence, or, in other words, the existence of channels through which patients can exert minimal control over their lives.

1) *Accepting impotence.* — Our impression is that those whose powerlessness is externally imposed can be coerced or helped to accept their impotence if they can be convinced that (*a*) authority is

concerned about them personally; (b) authority is responsive to their needs either through direct requests or by indirectly inferring the needs; (c) their peers are impotent, too; (d) impotency is not important (in comparison with, say, piety and humility in monasteries or staying alive in concentration camps); (e) there is a reason or a purpose for accepting impotency (e.g., "You're going to get better by doing this"). Alternatively, those who feel powerless can be helped if the staff (a) sedates them enough so that they are unaware of or unconcerned about their lack of control over life; (b) provides psychological escape through redirection of attention away from impotence via books, movies, and other recreational pursuits; (c) keeps them so busy and physically so tired that they have no time or energy to devote to thoughts of powerlessness.

2) *Relationships supportive of self-esteem.* — Other people help us define and value who we are. Even though a patient's comparative life concept includes awareness of powerlessness, he may come to see himself positively as a worthwhile individual, provided others in his social world view him in this way. Friendships among patients and between patients and staff lay the groundwork for maintenance of self-esteem in the hospital (see Rowland, 1939). In two earlier reports we suggest that suicide observation status in one VA mental hospital may save lives, not by preventing access to the means for killing oneself (there are numerous ways to commit suicide while on S-status), but by putting nursing assistants in continuous one-to-one contact with suicidal patients, thus providing an opportunity for a life-sustaining personal relationship to develop.

Such relationships also give a patient informal access to control over his hospital world. If he is friendly with an aide, he can request special favors and privileges. If his friendship ties are with another patient, he can participate in dyadic exchanges of various kinds. It is to these indirect tactics and long-term strategies of self-determination that we turn now.

3) *Channels of power accessible to patients.* — Despite the pervasive staff control over institutional life, patients have ways of symbolically demonstrating that they are not absolutely impotent. (See the journal for details.) Patients can force aides to wait, to move, to repeat instructions, to search for them, and to give individual orders. Patients can counteract unwelcome authority with violence, confusion, and disorder or with escape, detachment, and withdrawal.

Patients also assert a modicum of autonomy through collective action. Exchanges of cigarettes, information, praise, and small gifts are common between patients. There is a conspiracy of silence which conceals vandalism, suicide attempts, and rule breaking. Goffman (1961a), too, has written of ways to "work the system" in a mental institution.

The difficulty with coercing patients to accept impotence and with the means patients utilize to exert pressure on their world is that they are both inefficient and destructive. Coercive tactics for keeping people oppressed and passive are not necessarily successful because (a) it is difficult, given the shifting moods of humans and the mass-care pressures on the institution, to keep patients convinced that administration and staff really care about them personally (a breakdown in this area contributed to Kent's near suicide attempt); (b) needs cannot always be perceived or met, given the large numbers of patients and the low staff-to-patient ratio in most mental institutions; (c) patients realize that there is wide leeway in the amount of life control permitted to their peers, for favorites may be given a great deal of personal freedom by their staff allies; (d) since the traditional emphasis in the United States on independence and self-determination is currently yielding to emphasis on restoring power equilibria to the oppressed, it is extremely difficult to convince patients that impotency is unimportant in such a cultural milieu; and (e) assigning meaning and purpose to impotence is only initially effective as a tactic for keeping patients dependent and dominated, for as they learn that progress is slow or nonexistent and as they discover the personal costs of patienthood they become disenchanted with the proposed purpose. Staff efforts to aid the powerless may also fail because (a) most psychiatrists believe that minimal medication is best and that when a patient is placed on reduced medication or becomes adapted to his high-level dosage the sedation tactic becomes less effective; and (b) motivating patients to engage in work or recreational escape on a full-time basis is extremely difficult since powerlessness tends to breed apathy and inactivity which subvert this tactic. The point is, quite simply, that the attempt to impose long-term deprivation of independence on patients with our Western cultural background and support it with indirect tactics aimed at making such deprivation acceptable is ineffective and may be dangerous.

At this point it may be useful to consider the costs and rewards to hospital administration and staff members of placing more power in the hands of patients. It has been argued that keeping patients powerless has both psychological and social advantages for a hospital staff. When patients are kept in a restricted, dependent position, attendants can trade small privileges for work and cooperation (Goldman et al., 1970). Similarly, when patients are seen as incompetent and unable to care for themselves staff members can project some of their own inadequacies onto the patients. By emphasizing the difference between themselves and the patients, they generate self-esteem within their own comparative life concept. On the other hand, when legitimate access to control over one's life is destroyed the result is likely to be withdrawal and apathy, subversion through confusion and disorder, and possibly suicide.

Various alternatives to traditional roles and practices in mental hospitals are currently undergoing the test of practice. In general, we support innovations that humanize the hospital system in ways that permit patients to assume a higher degree of control over their lives. Later on we make specific suggestions for change which we think would reduce the frequency of suicides in mental hospitals.

Thus far we have written as if patients were the hapless dupes of a concerted effort to rob them of their sense of control over their own lives. For some patients there is, in fact, a clear-cut complicity in the effort. Such patients collude with staff members in giving up much of their leverage on life because by doing so they also escape from responsibility. An extreme case is that of a board-and-care resident, W. C., who admitted that he had done some pretty bad things in his life but planned to escape divine retribution on Judgment Day by "pleading insanity." He saw that method as his "only chance." Another suicidal patient dared not improve within the hospital because improvement would lead to discharge, and he feared above all being out on his own. We are not arguing that giving patients more freedom to make important decisions will eradicate collusive impotence. Some patients cannot or will not take advantage of increased freedom. On the other hand, restricting patients who are capable of moving toward self-determination contributes to their suicide potential.

When a suicidal person enters the hospital after a dyadic crisis he may be extremely concerned about control over his own interpersonal world while seeming to care little about other aspects of his life. (We would argue that he perceives access to other aspects of life to be through his significant other — figuratively, a bottleneck that has become clogged.) Admittedly he may not take advantage of the personal control allotted to him in the redesigned mental hospital. But if the access to potency is not available if and when he becomes ready to utilize it, he must choose either the path of accepting impotence (leading to institutionalization and chronicity) or the path of rebellion (leading, ultimately, to some form of self-destructive behavior). He should be given the more constructive option of guided movement toward self-governed activity.

Humans need validation of esteem and worth, particularly when occupying a stigmatized status. We are all vulnerable to messages of disinterest which communicate how unimportant we are to others. Mental patients by and large share the same disparaging attitudes toward insanity found in the general public. Praise and interest from normal staff members are especially coveted. Fellow patients, however, form a taken-for-granted support system that one can usually fall back on when expressions of worth are not forthcoming from the normal world. Following the expression of staff disinterest it was the breakdown in this minimal peer support system which precipitated Kent's pseudo suicide attempt. If even his disturbed fellows did not consider him worth saving, why should he think he was?

## Phenomenological Support for Beck's Analysis of Depression and Suicide

After the hospitalization phase of our research, we came across Beck's book, *Depression* (1967). His description of depression (pp. 253-267) accurately mirrored Kent's depressive experience.

Beck's primary triad of depression — construing experiences in a negative way, viewing the self in a negative way, and viewing the future in a negative way — fitted Kent's experience. Similarly, his detailed descriptions of these phenomena clearly paralleled Kent's depression. "The depressed patient selectively or inappropriately interprets his experiences as detracting from him in some substantive way. He tailors the facts to fit his preformed negative conclusions. He may, furthermore, exaggerate the significance of any actual loss, thwarting, or depreciation he encounters" (p. 256). On his very first hospital day Kent noticed that he was interpreting the behavior of others so as to confirm his own feelings of worthlessness. According to Beck, obstacles to goals are exaggerated and failure is anticipated in achievement-oriented situations. Kent's conception of the stairstep phenomenon, in which each success was interpreted as a step toward a more serious failure, is one expression of the anticipation of failure. Again, Beck notes that the "depressed patient is prone to read insults, ridicule or disparagement into what other people say to him. He often interprets neutral remarks as directed against him in some way" (p. 258). Kent, too, thought that ridiculing and disparaging remarks made by aides were directed toward him and other special status patients. Beck finds that a "striking feature of the depressed patient is his tendency to generalize from a particular behavior to a character trait. Any single deviation from a high level of performance is assumed to represent a major shortcoming" (p. 259). Kent was bothered by his forgetfulness. He saw the few instances in which he mislaid or overlooked something as evidence of a severe pathology. He even sought reassurance from nursing personnel that his brain was without visible abnormality on the X rays taken. According to Beck, the depressed person anticipates the same negative experiences of the present to extend unchanged into the future. He expects difficulties, unhappiness, and the continuation of hopelessness. Again, these observations were confirmed by Kent's experience.

One of Beck's most interesting statements enunciates his position that the affect accompanying depression is a consequence of the cognitive stance the depressed person has taken toward his world. In our techniques for bringing forth Kent we, too, began with cognition. The feeling state seemed to follow cognitive and behavioral changes rather than preceding them. Of course, ours was a special endeavor to intentionally bring about the depressive state, but it is certainly one pathway to depression, if not the only one.

Beck sees changes in motivation also as a result of depressed cognition. Apathy comes from the patient's evaluation of a hopeless future. Suicide reveals a desire to escape from a painful, futile existence: "He cannot visualize any way of improving things. He does not believe it is possible to get better. Suicide under these conditions seems to the patient to be a rational solution" (p. 264). Increased dependency during depression is seen as a combination of the person's own sense of inadequacy and his overestimation of potential complexities and difficulties. Thus the depressed person seeks a strong significant other who can take on the responsibilities of living for him. Physical symptoms seem related to cognition, too, from Beck's perspective. Passivity is a correlate of resignation, and agitation is an attempt to escape from a seemingly unsolvable situation through frenzied motor activity.

In general, Beck's formulations made sense in terms of our understanding of depression obtained through experiential research. The confirmation appears to be two-edged, serving to validate both Beck's conceptualization and the genuineness of Kent's experience.

## Privacy and Personal Space

Our culturally shared values include privacy, independence, and personal space (see Lee, 1948; Sommer, 1969; Hall, 1959). In a social setting in which these valued items are perceived to be depleted or lacking altogether, one might expect that efforts would be made to change either the inner or outer world so as to bring about more acceptable levels of perceived privacy, independence, and personal space. More specifically, when a patient perceives these values to be seriously restricted by his being on suicide observation status in a VA neuropsychiatric hospital, he may either withdraw behind psychological bastions (fantasy, cynicism, game playing, catatonia, etc.) so that his self will have more freedom and space, or he may try to gain more independence and privacy through manipulations of people and objects in his external environment. Manipulations may include communications that he is "better," establishing positive relationships with those who guard him, escape attempts, negotiations for transfer, and so on.

What have we learned about the limitations of privacy and personal space which follow the patient's being placed on suicide status? Our hypotheses show we expected the patient to find these limitations irksome and to react by withdrawal or by efforts to remove the limitations, but Kent's experience shows that we must modify our views. When Kent was in deep depression, his phenomenological world had diminished until it became only slightly larger than the space occupied by his body. People were "no more than trousers and shoes. And the ground that he walked on was blurred and dirty and unimportant." In a sense his world was indeed private, despite the presence of others, whose efforts to intrude into the ruminative privacy of his thoughts provoked resentment. Still, the physical presence of others was comforting at times.

As the psychomotor retardation lifted, Kent began to be concerned with the limitations of his environment. He began to test the degree to which he was permitted unsupervised activity. During this period he found the limits reasonable. Nursing assistants, young black males for the most part, were careful not to press the patient.

Normally the patient was observed from across the dayroom; he was discreetly allowed a short period in the bathroom without supervision. He was not bodily confined. He even found periods in which no one was watching him at all. And in such circumstances of isolation, he felt cheated, neglected, and abandoned. Nevertheless, Kent found the limitations on movement and privacy increasingly irksome. The environment was boring, the locked ward was confining, especially since recurring doubts about his own sanity made living in close quarters with other patients, who were obviously insane, difficult to endure. He wasn't like them — or was he?

The annoyance at confinement was shared by most patients in the locked ward. They felt no sense of control over their lives. They were forced to live by schedule, which was often interrupted or changed around at the convenience of the nursing aides. Events happened at such unexpected moments that becoming involved in any activity (such as a television program or a conversation) was useless. Detachment and withdrawal began again to permeate Kent's posture.

To give some sense of the importance of symbols of privacy, we repeat a short account of an event that occurred a few days after Kent's admission. For administrative purposes he was transferred, along with two other patients, to a three-bed seclusion room. There was no explanation; he was simply told to make the switch. In the new room there were no lockers. This lack seemed unimportant to the nursing assistant who helped them move, but it was very important to the three patients. A locker represented privacy and some measure of self-determination and self-expression. One could arrange his belongings inside the locker in any way he wished. Even though the lockers had no locks and offered no genuine protection for possessions, and even though they may have been inspected while patients were absent from the ward at meals or for recreational activities, they nevertheless had real meaning. Their symbolic function was sorely missed by the new inhabitants of the seclusion room.

In sum, considerations of privacy and personal space are likely to become issues only after the patient has begun to make genuine progress in emerging from his depressed state. At that point he is motivated to enter into negotiations with staff members for increased freedom, exchanging assurances that he will contact hospital personnel before engaging in self-destructive activity.

*Differing Perspectives among Ward Role Groups*

Two important findings in both our insider and outsider research were (1) the different perspectives on suicide risk among psychiatrists on the one hand and nursing assistants on the other, and (2) the relative importance of the patient's own estimation of his suicidal state.

In essence, it was clear that the psychiatrists we encountered tended to view suicide from a perspective in which the personality was considered to be relatively unchanging over time and strongly rooted in the emotional and interpersonal orientations of early childhood. Psychiatrists were usually conservative in evaluting suicide. Their estimations were based on (1) brief and infrequent personal contacts with the patient, and (2) records and nursing staff reports. The suicidal patient was presumed to be in need of basic personality readjustments.

The nursing assistants saw man as much more flexible and situationally responsive. His suicidal state might fluctuate from day to day and hour to hour. He was suicidal as a response to practical problems of living (money problems, job problems, woman problems, etc.) similar to those we all encounter. If helped to handle these problems, the patient would no longer be suicidal, the aides felt. Their estimation of suicidal risk was based upon their observations while living alongside the patient and upon down-to-earth talks which included advice giving and presumed problem solving. Remotivation groups tended to emphasize practical problems of living inside the hospital, such as care of clothing, obtaining grounds passes, and work assignments. Hospital records tended to be devalued by nursing assistants, at least in part, because they presented an inflexible picture of the patient. Aides really regarded any difficulty in this live-in ward, suicidality or some other disorder, as a response to practical problems. For the psychiatrists whom Kent encountered the difficulties were not related to practical problems but to the patient's orientation to life and his personality makeup. The views of psychiatrists and aides supplement each other when the two role groups are willing to exchange information and accept the relevance of the other's perceptions.

As noted above, psychiatrists and nursing assistants (with nurses as intermediaries) held implicit models of man and suicide which were consistent with the sources of data avilable to them and their formal and informal educational backgrounds. They behaved consistently with these models and tended to ignore or reinterpret information inconsistent with their own perspectives. For example, for the nursing assistants one of the most frustrating and hostility-producing patients in the ward was the suicidal Mr. W., who apparently had a long-term character disorder. No amount of reality discussion was able to break through his tears and his hopelessness. Eventually, staff communications of anger and abandonment contributed to Mr. W's self-destruction about a month after Kent's discharge.

Both groups relied heavily on the patient's verbalizations about his suicide potential. Often the most reliable cue that the patient intended to kill himself was his own statement to that effect. Staff members at all levels were aware of the credibility problem. Some patients who threatened suicide were not genuinely suicidal; they were simply manipulators. Conversely, some patients who denied suicidal ideation had a high potential for self-destruction; they might be called dissemblers. Negotiations for determining the truth value of verbalizations of both manipulators and dissemblers were fraught with pitfalls. To challenge a potential manipulator might provoke him to suicide. To confront a potential dissembler might undermine the trust that had been built up in the relationship between staff member and patient.

The sense of trust was one of the criteria by which staff members evaluated a patient's communications about his suicidal potential. Another criterion was observation of the patient's actions. Experienced staff members at every level made efforts to establish and sustain a social relationship with suicidal patients which permitted the patient some freedom in exchange for assurances that he would tell them before attempting to harm himself. In effect, what amounted to a social contract was established between patient and staff person. Uncertainty as to suicidal intent was usually interpreted conservatively. For example, from the record of David Kent, the doctor's progress notes state: "Some slight improvement noted this morning; however, still requires observation in view of his uncertainty and ambivalence."

One of the clearest revelations of the difference between the world views of staff and patients came every Monday morning. "How was your weekend?" staff members would ask, failing to realize that patients have no weekends. Weekends are breaks in the workweek;

they are getting out and seeing new sights and being with the family and sleeping in late and generally sloughing off the past week and readying oneself to start a new one. For the patient, however, Saturday and Sunday are just like Monday and Tuesday and Wednesday — more tedium, more routine, more of the same dying faces and anemic walls, more TV and dozing and waiting for dinner. Skeleton staff on weekends? Skeleton patients, too.

## Manipulating Staff Perceptions of Suicidality

Our question, "What do staff members perceive as cues in uncovering suicidal intent, and what do they interpret as signs of improvement?" was not specifically directed toward the cues that patients give before serious suicide attempts, although there is probably a relationship between classes of cues given and classes of cues perceived. This research question on which we focused is, however, important in that it reveals cues to which the staff responds and so makes these cues available for critical examination.

Initially we planned to have Kent use the "cues to suicidal intent" and "cues to improvement" listed below (1) to manipulate estimations of his suicidal intent by different shifts so that marked differences in evaluation would be shown by morning and evening shifts; and (2) to manipulate evaluations by individual staff members of his suicidal intent in the same way. He was then to reverse the cues several times, but once in the hospital setting he was so caught up in the flow of his feelings that it was impossible for him to control his presentation of self in an orderly way.

How does one go about presenting a suicidal self to the staff of a VA neuropsychiatric hospital? It helps to be on suicide status or to have a record of past suicidal thoughts and behavior, so that one begins with a social reputation of being suicidal. Then one engages in certain behaviors that are interpreted by staff as external reflections of suicidal thoughts and planning. We have formulated the following list of these cues to suicidal intent, based on experience.

1) Observations: checking locks, windows, and cords in the ward.
2) Preparations: loosening bolts, tearing sheets, accumulating drugs, obtaining razor blades, concealing knives.
3) Inquiries: asking about death and about the relative pain, quickness, and accessibility of various suicide methods.

4) Self-destructive activity: self-mutilation and suicide attempts.

5) Inactivity: withdrawal, quietness, asociality.

6) Requests: for aid in obtaining suicide tools, for escape, and to be killed.

7) Farewells: remarks of finality, and of appreciation; notes and wills; the giving away of personal possessions.

8) Displays of extreme emotion: tears, agitation.

9) Uncooperativeness: negativism, secretiveness, refusing medication and/or food.

10) Insomnia, real or imagined.

11) Loss of contact.

On the other hand, how does one communicate wellness? How does one achieve removal from suicide observation status? What kind of self is it necessary to present? When a patient enters the hospital with a reputation for suicide the staff is prepared for cues of a suicidal nature, so that the patient initially placed on suicide observation status would find it relatively easy to communicate suicidal intent. In other words, the staff would be sensitized to pick up cues that confirm the identity already imposed upon the patient. The patient who wishes to remake his identity must find it something of an uphill climb. There is a whole gamut of nonconforming behaviors that might be interpreted as cues to suicidal intent but a much narrower range of conforming actions that communicate the diminution of suicidal intent. The latter acts include:

1) Maintaining a neat, clean appearance.

2) Displaying sociability and openness.

3) Engaging in insightful, hopeful talk about problems.

4) Cooperating with ward routine.

5) Offering encouragement and proper advice to other patients.

6) Working actively.

7) Planning for the short-term as well as the long-term future.

8) Good appetite and ability to sleep.

9) Spurning all behaviors that can be construed as cues to suicidal intent.

We found it was not easy to manipulate staff members' perceptions of Kent's suicidal status. In part, the difficulty stemmed from Kent's inability to present various social images simultaneously and his lack of control over expressions of suicidality at night. Nursing notes contained references to his alertness and his ability to sleep well, phenomena not altogether consistent with other aspects of his depression. At other times, purposely presented cues were not picked up by personnel and therefore did not find their way into the records. Kent's examinations of barred windows and his agitated pacing were a few of the cues that busy personnel failed to pass on to others, or at least to record on the chart.

Rockwell (1971) mentions two factors that seem to retard the immediate and accurate communication of worsened conditions of patients: (1) inertia, which is the staff's tendency to see the patient as continuously improving; (2) leveling, which is the tendency to dilute and neutralize messages as they pass from staff member to staff member. In Kent's case we also found a Pollyannaish tendency to distort and even to conceal information that did not jibe with a positive and hopeful prognosis for the young veteran. The tendency increased in scope and strength as Kent's discharge day drew near. Considerable agitation and publicly expressed doubts were under-played in the reports, possibly because staff members failed to notice such expressions during Kent's last hospital days. We suspect that nursing personnel were responding not so much to the blinders of a positive set as to their awareness of the permanency of and routine distortions contained in the records. They knew that mood shifts often level out over time, that complaints diminish, that crises fade. Nursing personnel constantly had to make judgments about whether or not to enter an incident in the record and whether to tone it down somewhat as they passed the word along to other staff members, either verbally or in writing. It is likely that omissions in hospital records are also related to limitations of time and energy and to the degree of involvement of nursing personnel. Time, energy, and in-volvement are important variables, but so far we have discovered no simple, accurate way of measuring them.

Yet, given the busyness of staff members, the number of patients under their supervision, and the many opportunities Kent had to manufacture his cues to suicidal intent and his cues to improvement, the staff did pick up and report a large number and variety of them. Seven types of cues to suicidal intent which Kent displayed were noted and recorded. They were preparations for suicide, self-destruc-tive activity, inactivity, requests for aid in obtaining a lethal dose of medication, displays of extreme emotion, uncooperativeness, insom-nia, carelessness in personal appearance, and slumped posture. Cues given by Kent but unreported included observations (of windows, broken glass, a rope), inquiries (of a chaplain) concerning death and suicide, farewells (in a letter to Kent's wife which was reported but not in a context indicating recognition of its potential as a cue to suicide), and, of course, the accumulation of sufficient medication for a lethal dose. Loss of contact was never purposefully projected except in sleep, and then it was reported.

All nine types of cues to improvement were offered by Kent, and eight were perceived and recorded by personnel: neat, clean appearance; sociability and openness; insightful, hopeful talk about problems; cooperativeness in ward routine; working actively; short- and long-term future planning; increasing appetite; and the avoidance of behavioral cues to suicidal intent. The remaining cue, encouraging and advising other patients, was observed and given verbal approval by staff members, yet such activity was not noted in Kent's records.

We learned that communications of improvement were likely to get positive verbal feedback from staff members. Unless signals of suicidality were overt and demanded an immediate reaction from the staff, however, they were less likely to be picked up and communicated back to the patient. In fact, aides pretended to ignore some cues (e.g., the coat hanger) but reported them to other aides. The notion that, once a suicidal identity had been established, communications of wellness would be less likely to be noted than communications of suicidal intent was not borne out. Staff members were eager to discern evidence of improvement and less likely to perceive and report minor setbacks. Thus, in the extreme case, the onus is on the manipulator to furnish a stream of cues in order to maintain his suicidal identity and the rewards it brings him.

*Notes on Suicide Observation Status*

To his surprise, Kent found himself with numerous opportunities to kill himself while on S-status. Methods were available (razors, broken glass, pills, a rope, nails, moving vehicles, heights, a hanger, etc.). Time was ample, particularly in the early morning, during disruptions of routine, en route to appointments, and during recreational periods. If S-status does not effectively protect a patient from killing himself by eliminating opportunity, then what justification has it? We think the key to understanding S-status is recognition that it forces staff members to have contact with and pay attention to suicidal patients. In other words, the staff member must remain near the patient and must keep aware of the patient's behavior, and the necessary contact can lead to the building of human concern and a genuine relationship. We believe that it is people, not tactics, that keep other people alive.

If it is true that S-status effectively protects the patient by providing him with a corps of people who express concern for him, then we face the need to reorient ourselves and to develop a whole set of tactics for implementing S-status. From this new perspective the staff member should not be constantly fearful and cautious and should not focus exclusively on preventive measures. Rather, he should employ positive methods, such as expressing genuine interest, establishing mutual trust, and participating in ward life as a knowledgeable companion. By the negative approach, staff members can at best break even: that is, they can keep the patient alive. With a positive methodology keeping the patient alive is a by-product; the real achievement is establishing a mutually satisfying relationship.

As noted in the journal, Kent once talked with an aide about keeping a patient alive while the patient was on S-status. The aide said, "You know, nobody can keep a patient alive whether he's on S-status or not." He went on, "Nobody really cares about whether you live or die. If you die, then the next day somebody will come and say, "Where's Kent?' And somebody will say, 'He's dead.' And he'll say, 'Oh.' And they'll forget about you right then. They might make a big fuss and show, but down inside nobody really cares." Perhaps that assessment is the realistic one. Certainly we expect a great deal from a staff member when we ask him to invest himself in a sequence of patients who come in, stay briefly, and go out again. But some have found the investment worth making.


## SUGGESTIONS FOR REDUCING THE SUICIDE RATE IN PSYCHIATRIC HOSPITALS

Most studies of suicide in psychiatric facilities emphasize diagnosis and medication as precipitators of self-destruction. A few touch on the role of staff members in creating a social milieu that inhibits or provokes suicide. We feel that an important factor previously uninvestigated is the effect other patients have on the suicidal patient's life and death. When the staff is hostile or indifferent and mutual support among patients collapses, it may indeed look like the end of the world to a depressed patient.

Our recommendations to the institutions in which we have carried out experiential research are both general and specific. Broadly speaking, we reinforce existing structural features and suggest changes that would make the facility a more human, more supportive, place in which to live. When the quality of life is improved, extending life chronologically becomes less of a problem. This idea is neither profound nor novel, but through experiential research we can offer specific concrete suggestions for improving the environment in NP hospitals.

The trauma of "staffing" for patients was somewhat reduced in one ward by having only two or three staff members talk informally with a patient in the dayroom (i.e., on his own turf) over a cup of coffee. Previously, a patient was brought to a meeting room where numerous medical authorities directed personal questions at him prior to deciding his fate. It is hard for anyone to look undisturbed in such circumstances. We suggested that the professional staff stagger their shifts so that some consultations and therapy appointments could be scheduled for the late afternoon or the evening when patients have little to do. The new arrangement would have the added benefit of reducing competition among staff members for the desirable late-morning appointments with newly admitted patients.

When Kent left the hospital he took with him only a single telephone number to use if and when he had difficulties on the outside. His contacts with friendly staff members and fellow patients were effectively cut. He did not know whether he was eligible for outpatient treatment; no plans had been made for follow-up contact. He had no job and only a minimal amount of money. He had only one friend outside the hospital. It is not surprising that the suicide rate of neuropsychiatric patients jumps in the period after they have left the hospital (Farberow et al., 1971). They leave familiarity and a kind of "success" to face an impersonal and competitive world. We have discussed the possibility of sending patients out in pairs and groups. We recommended regular follow-up contact and an open-door policy for revisiting the hospital. Day care and overnight lodging in time of crisis can sharply reduce the discharged patient's feelings of having been abandoned, but he must be made aware of these resources and told how to avail himself of them. We are investigating styles of follow-up contact (discussed briefly below and in more detail in a forthcoming publication) which might reduce suicides among discharged veterans. We have also completed experiential research on the lives and conduct of recently discharged suicidal patients.

We found the staff's expectation that the patient's hospitalization would be brief to be good, on the whole. From Kent's first day people were asking him about his plans for returning to society. His stay was seen as one of limited duration, a sort of tiding-over period until he got his feet on the ground again. We can now contrast this policy with that of some aftercare facilities and some psychiatric hospitals of the past whose staff members let a patient know that he could expect to stay in the facility for a long time, probably for the rest of his life. It is important, however, to balance the optimistic expectation of early discharge with a sensitive desire not to push the patient too hard. The patient who presents cues that he is not ready to leave as discharge time approaches must be dealt with carefully and compassionately. Mr. W., for example, could not afford to get well because he perceived that staff members were eager to discharge him, to turn him loose in a world where the resources he could reasonably expect to depend upon had long since been exhausted.

The team approach to patient care trickled down to the patient level as the recognition that certain staff people were directly responsible for Kent's care and specifically concerned with his welfare. He did not distinguish between his group leader and his team leader, and the niceties of having several specialized services provided by the team to which he was assigned were not clearly understood by him, but the overall impact of the team approach was positive.

We have outlined the different perspectives of man and suicide adopted by various staff role groups and have emphasized that they are complementary. Staff members should be made aware, however, that the patient receives advice and instruction from persons with differing viewpoints. They should strive not to undercut other perspectives and not to depreciate the patient should he ask questions or otherwise indicate that he is inappropriately responding to a particular staff member's viewpoint.

Simple gestures that we suggested to help humanize a ward include staff members' thanking patients for volunteered work, conscientiously returning change owed to patients, taking patients' complaints about living conditions seriously, acknowledging the correctness of a patient's assertion even if it had to be checked first, including the patient in decision making, and so forth. The list, of course, could be extended. The thrust of our argument is that overtly or covertly we convey to others what we think they are worth. When we let the suicidal person know that we genuinely value him, we help him to value himself. To the person who is debating within himself whether he is worth keeping alive, a message of concerned human support is the most important message we can send.

## SUMMARY AND PROSPECTS

*An Overview*

The research topic was suicide observation status, that is, the protective watch placed on potentially suicidal patients in most VA wards. The research approach was to obtain complementary perspectives on the subject. First, the staff and patients in a local VA hospital were interviewed and observed intermittently over a three-month period. Then the researcher took on the identity of a suicidal patient and lived in another VA hospital for a two-week period. This book is concerned with both phases of the research: the observation period and the live-in experience.

Ethical and safety problems were weighed against the usefulness of the information likely to be gained by the experiential method. Staff members were informed that an unidentified researcher would be coming into the hospital at an unspecified time within the next year. After Kent had spent two weeks in the hospital, meetings were held with both individuals and groups to enlist staff support in interpreting the experiences of the researcher. Staff members' initial surprise, restraint, and anger gave way to acceptance of the goals and the methods of this particular research project.

All indirect measures suggest that the research anthropologist was able to develop within himself a feeling closely approximating if not identical with genuine depression. Nursing notes, doctors' reports, naively taken and blindly scored psychological tests, introspective reports, and psychophysiological changes uniformly indicate that the anthropologist was successful in getting into a depression. No one on the ward staff suspected his research identity during his hospital stay.

The hospitalization period included a week of S-status in a locked ward followed by a week in an open ward and, finally, discharge after receiving "maximum hospital benefits." Experiences within the hospital comprised psychodrama, a frighteningly real pseudo suicide attempt, vocational testing, and the trauma of disposition staff meetings. We concluced that phenomenological accounts by persons trained in psychology, sociology, and anthropology can provide a useful experiential basis for integrating these disciplinary perspectives. Such fieldwork may be called "experiential research" and can be used as a tool for bridging the gap between experiential knowledge and rational-scientific knowledge.

With regard to the specific research topic, suicide in a mental hospital, we suggested that there are numerous ways to kill oneself while under suicidal observation. It may well be that suicide observation status does more than prevent self-destruction by limiting the opportunities to accomplish it, for it also forces nursing assistants and nurses into sustained one-to-one contact with depressed patients, thus establishing life-sustaining social relationships.

The more traditional research strategy of observation, interviewing, and record analysis and the experiential research strategy provided sometimes confirmatory, sometimes contradictory, information. Notably, the different role groups' perspectives on suicidal man emerged clearly in both research areas. On the other hand, the numerous suicide opportunities available to the patient on suicide observation status became apparent only during experiential research. On the basis of interviewing alone, we were skeptical of patient claims that there were many ways to kill oneself in the ward, perceiving the patients to be fantasizing out of their impotence.

The different approaches allowed us to draw on complementary categories of data. The anthropologist role provided many opportunities for questioning others but inhibited their willingness to reply freely. The patient role allowed unrestricted observation of otherwise inaccessible phenomena (e.g., internal states of a patient) but limited spatial mobility and curtailed the number and kinds of questions the researcher as patient could ask. Record analysis allowed manipulation of an unchanging but severely restricted data set. Some combination of research strategies and personal perspectives would seem to be most useful in dealing with the type of research problem undertaken in our project.

Our findings are easily summarized. Humanized settings are likely to build self-esteem, and increased self-esteem is likely to deter some suicides. Psychiatric wards where patients' self-images are undermined are preparing fertile ground for the burgeoning of suicidal thoughts and acts.

*Prospects*

We have completed experiential research in several aftercare facilities for former mental patients and are currently writing up the results. In that research we probed the experiences of depressed patients in the first weeks following discharge from a psychiatric hospital. Some refinements in technique were necessary. In one facility we arranged for a second researcher, a female graduate student in clinical psychology, to enter at the same time that Kent did. She, too, adopted a depressed suicidal identity. The similarities and differences in their experience helped us to "calibrate" our human instruments. As in our hospital research, in order to get complementary perspectives on Kent's behavior we utilized staff members' written records and verbal descriptions of his stay, both during the live-in phase and during special debriefing sessions afterward. At the beginning of the first debriefing session at each aftercare facility, staff members were asked if they could guess which patient was also a researcher. Their guesses (never unanimous but sometimes correct) and the reasons for them provide important information about Kent's social presentation of depression and suicidality.

Another forthcoming publication deals with the experiences of a depressed patient (with a history of several suicide attempts, at least two of which should have been lethal) during the twenty-five days between his discharge, relapse, and readmission to a VA mental hospital. The research tactic we call "shadowing" was employed. It requires the researcher to live alongside his subject during virtually all the subject's waking hours, even to the point of sleeping on the living room rug of the family apartment so as to be ready to observe and record the moment the subject got up in the morning.

These innovative research tactics offer new perspectives on the interrelationships among psychological functioning, situation, and behavior. They provide another foothold for the important task of helping the suicidal person recreate a life he finds worth continuing.

# APPENDIX A

# SECURITY MEASURES
# AND
# SUICIDE PRECAUTIONS

A Veterans Administration Hospital

Professional Information
Bulletin 70-23
May 7, 1970

## SECURITY MEASURES

I.  Purpose
    *a.*  To update policy and procedures pertaining to the security of patients.
II.  Policy and Procedures
    *a.*  All employees will maintain close observation of patients who have known or suspected suicidal, assaultive, convulsive, or elopement tendencies, and will report any such apparent tendencies promptly to the physician-in-charge, nurse, or other professional personnel.
    *b.*  *Check of Closed Ward Patients Leaving and Returning to Wards*
        1)  Closed ward patients being conducted from the ward to other parts of the hospital will be counted and identified by the employees accompanying them upon their departure and return, to insure the presence or account for the whereabouts of each patient in the group. Detail Sheet (V.A. Form 10-2338), prepared in duplicate, will be signed by the ward nurse. The employee-in-charge of the group will retain the original and leave the duplicate on

the ward. The following code designation will be used to identify patients' tendencies, when such tendencies are known or suspected:

E . . . . . . . Eloper
S . . . . . . . Suicidal
A . . . . . . . Assaultive
C . . . . . . . Convulsive

Both copies of V.A. Form 10-2338 will be disposed of when all patients in the group have returned or are accounted for.

2) In escorting patients outside the ward, employees will have all patients in view at all times. The group will be kept together as a relatively compact unit, and straggling or loitering will NOT be permitted. Convulsive patients and patients inclined to suicide, elopement, or assaultive behavior will be placed where closest supervision may be provided.

3) *Security of Escorted Patients while involved in Ancillary Treatment Programs*
Nursing Service personnel WILL be responsible for the security of patients during their movement to and from clinic and treatment areas. The therapist-in-charge WILL be responsible for the security measures and protection while in the clinic and treatment areas. However, Nursing Service personnel remaining with the patient in the clinic and treatment areas WILL assist the therapist in maintaining security measures.

c. *Patient Count as Shift Changes and Bedtime.* A count of all patients on the ward will be made jointly by the ward nurse or her designee going off duty and the one coming on duty. The names of the patients as they are identified or accounted for will be checked off on Patient Count, V.A. Form 10-2384, which will be initialed by both employees making the check. This form will be prepared by the ward secretary, who will enter the patients' names alphabetically, and the code designations described in subparagraph *b*(1) above, after the name of each convulsive patient and each patient known to have tendencies toward elopement, suicide, or assault. If any doubt exists as to a patient's presence or whereabouts, a recheck will be made. A count will be taken again at bedtime by the ward nurse or her designee as prescribed above, at which time particular attention will be given to insure the identity of each patient in his assigned bed. After all spaces on the form have been used, it will be retained for 30 days and then disposed of in accordance with M3-8, V.A. Disposal Bulletin.

## SUICIDE PRECAUTIONS

When a patient drops clues such as "life is no longer worth living, I caused the last war," alert yourself to observe patient further. Make your report to the nurse. If patient's doctor feels patient is contemplating suicide, he may write an order placing patient on Suicidal Status.

Your responsibility then would be:

1. To make the environment safe. Remove articles that could be harmful such as glass vase, ceramic ash tray, cords, etc. Replace with articles that are less harmful. Be alert to solutions kept in housekeeping cupboards; check equipment left out in treatment room; check bathroom and shower room. Use common sense. Remember, you could take everything away, and if a patient wanted to, he could still harm himself. Be alert to your window screens, that they are locked at all times.

2. To be alert to use of utensils in the dining room. Allow patient to use knife, fork, spoon, china plate, glass, etc., but observe his handling of them. If his actions indicate misuse, step forward and quietly put it back in place. Allow your patient to be as other patients. Don't leave suggestion that you expect him to harm himself. Most patients are ambivalent; they want to live and they want to die. Try to give them more reason to want to live.

3. To be alert to use of tools at activities, especially O.T. If patient is using sharp tools, sit next to him working on some object yourself. Do not become so preoccupied with your work that you forget the patient. If you notice his behavior indicates possible misuse, reach over and place the tool in its proper place. Talk with the patient and others at the table. When occupied with group, patient is less likely to think of attempting suicide. Check that tools are replaced before leaving the clinic.

4. When escorting outside, be alert to roadways and walkways. Do not allow your patient to be the first one standing on the curb. Keep him more in the middle of the group. If escorting alone, time your stride so you arrive at the curb after cars have passed. When walking on sidewalks that have walls on one side, keep patient to the opposite side. Sometimes the wall tempts the patient and he jumps over the wall, falling to the ground below. Seldom have our patients who attempted this actually killed themselves, but they have sustained injuries such as broken ankles, heels, shoulders, and arms.

5. Supervise the use of sharps on the ward. Example: Patient asks to use the scissors. Ask what he plans to do with them. If you feel he can handle the scissors, then let him have them, but follow and observe his use of them. Chat with him. If you feel he is too impulsive, then go with him and tactfully use the scissors yourself. Sharps would be scissors, nail file, toe nail clippers, can opener, bottle opener, needle. These articles are kept in the Nursing Office in a locked cabinet.

6. Observe what patient picks up when you are escorting him. Patients see many things you and I would miss. Feel free to ask him what he has and take those things that qualify as contraband. Example: Sometimes a patient stops and picks up something from the ground. You step up and say, "What did you find?" Patient shows you a rusty razor blade. "Oh, that would cut someone's foot, it's good you saw it. We'll put it in a can so it can be safely discarded." What you say and how you say it is very important. If you notice patients are finding syringes and needles on the grounds, report this immediately to your nurse.

7. To be alert to patient when he is in the bathroom. Some patients plan to drown themselves in the lavatory. This means they will have to plug the sink. Drowning is difficult, so many patients plan to hit their heads against the faucet, hoping to become unconscious and face fall in the water. If patient's behavior indicates this type of thought, unplug sink and suggest they clean the sink. You are not expected to enter the individual closed commode area when such is present, but you observe the patient's feet which are showing. Example: Metal door is usually cut off about 2 1/2 feet from the floor. As long as patient's toes are facing you, or his heels, he's probably using the commode for the intended purpose; but if the sole of his shoe is showing, then

investigate for the possibility that he may be trying to drown himself in the commode.

8.  To be alert to your patient at medication time to see if he's saving medication. Example: Station yourself ahead of the patient if he's in a medication line. As he leaves line, observe movements of his arms as he walks away from you. If elbow bends and arm comes up, there is a possibility he may be spitting the medication out to save. When you make your report to Nurse, state you *suspect* the patient is not taking his medication. Role playing is used to demonstrate the approaches for effective use of safety precautions. Class is asked to suggest others not mentioned so far.

9.  Close observation. Be aware of your patient — where he is, what he is doing. Try to keep him involved in activities or in area where others are present. Involve patient in your ward duties when possible. If you have been assigned to a special patient on suicidal status, he is your responsibility. Follow through on your safety precautions.

    You do not need to breathe down his neck or hold on to him, but you need to be aware of where he is and what he is doing. If you have to leave the area, ask someone else to assume your specialing. Verbal and written reports of your observations and patient clues are very important to the doctor and the nurse. Display a genuine interest in your patient as a person.

    Problem Solving: You have been assigned to *special* an actively suicidal patient on status. Describe three additional safety precautions you would use.

    Remember — Suicide is most likely to occur when the depression begins to lift.

Note:  Permission was obtained for publication of this bulletin.

# DAVID KENT'S
# HOSPITAL RECORDS

*Application for Medical Benefits*

Type of Benefit Applied for: Hospital Treatment

Name: Kent, David Randolph

Social Security No.: 569 51 8544

Sex: Male

Religion: Protestant

Date and Place of Birth: 9/28/40, Dayton, Ohio

Marital Status: Separated

Active Military Service and Record of Active Duty Status: Navy; service no., 588 21 51; date entered service, 9/20/58; date separated, 9/6/61.

The following person designated to receive possession of all of applicant's property left on the premises under the control of the V.A. after leaving such place or at the time of his death: Sharon H. Kent, 2227 8th Street, South St. Petersburg, Florida 33704; Telephone — none (813 area code); relationship, wife.

Applicant's Home Address: 3752 Sawtelle Boulevard, Los Angeles 90066

Occupation: Unemployed

Applicant does not believe this need for care is related to his employment. He is financially able to pay cost of his transportation to and from hospital at time of admission and discharge. He does not believe his need for hospital care is due to an accident caused by another person. He hereby swears that he is unable to defray the necessary expenses of the hospital treatment (or domiciliary care) for which he is applying.

Condition for which applicant desires treatment: Depression

Signed: David R. Kent                    Date: July 8, 1971

*Report of Contact*

I received a call from the Los Angeles Suicide Prevention Center regarding Veteran David Randolph Kent.

Mr. Kent's friend had contacted the Prevention Center for help, stating that Mr. Kent had recently made a suicidal attempt and that today he had found him quite depressed and confused. He was still talking about wanting to die.

There is a history of recent rejection by the wife. The Suicide Prevention Center recommended that Mr. Kent's friend bring him to B Hospital for evaluation and/or admission.

I request that this patient be admitted to Ward 207B.

*Clinical Record — History*

Date of Admission: 7/8/71

A 30-year-old male, unemployed, separated, first admission.

Vet was brought to the hospital by a friend. Patient attempted suicide on 7/5/71 with an overdose of Seconal, stomach pumped at Emergency Hospital, has been wandering and "just sitting around" since. He is thinking of suicide.

This patient came to California from Florida last August to get a job in the aerospace industry. His wife was to follow when he got settled. He was unable to get work. He called his wife on Monday, the 5th, their wedding anniversary. She told him they were through — she had found someone else. He took the Seconal in what appears to be a genuine suicide attempt.

Patient has a history of a previous depressive reaction to the death of his mother in 1963 and a possible depression during his tour of duty in the Navy in '60 or '61.

Veteran has worked in clothing sales, clerk-typist, parking lot attendant, gas station, etc. No job lasted very long. Was a radioman in the Navy.

He doesn't smoke or drink. A few weeks before admission he got a prescription for Seconal from a local GP. He got them for anxiety, insomnia, and headaches. He used them in his suicide attempt. No other drugs.

His father left the house when Vet was 6 or 7, never to be heard from again. Mother died of cancer in 1963. Wife living with her mother in Florida. No children.

Usual childhood illnesses, no adult illnesses or injuries. No known allergies.

## System Review

Mental Status on Admission: The patient is oriented X3 and in good contact. However, his affect is extremely depressed and he shows evidence of psychomotor retardation. Although he answers questions willingly, he does so in affirmative or negative monosyllables. He appears to be of average intelligence, with fair insight into his problem. He expresses ambivalence about suicide as a solution.

## Physical Examination

General Appearance: Patient is a 30-year-old white male, who is well developed and well nourished. He has brown hair, brown beard, and blue eyes. Patient is depressed, lethargic; he is oriented in time and space; he must be prodded to talk. He is cooperative.

Head, Face, Scalp & Neck: Head — normocephalic, no exostosis. No enlargement of submaxillary and submental glands. Scalp — no alopecia. Eyes — no papilledema; no inflammation. Ears — no perforation of tympanic membranes; no inflammation. Oral cavity — no tonsils (palatine); no gingivitis. Throat — no tracheal obstruction; no thyroid enlargement. Nose — no septal deviation; no discharge.

Chest & Thoracic Contents: Chest is symmetrical on expansion. Heart — no arrhythmia; no bradycardia; no murmurs of pulmonic, aortic, mitral, tricuspid valves. Pulmonary lungs — clear to auscultation and percussion; no rales or rhonchi.

Abdomen & Viscera: Gastro-intestinal — Abdomen — supple, soft, no tenderness; active bowel sounds. No bruit. Liver, spleen, kidneys — non-palpable. Genito-Urinary — circumcised; testes descended into scrotal sac; no inguinal hernia. Prostrate normal and of normal consistency.

Extremities: Upper/lower — no varicosities, no edema, no scars, no flaccidity.

Back & Other Musculoskeletal: No deviation of vertebral column. Musculoskeletal — no masses, no flaccidity.

Neurological: Deep tendon reflexes are active. Babinski & Romberg signs are absent. Cranial nerves II-XII are intact.

*Medical Certificate and History*

A 30-year-old male, unemployed, separated, first NP admission.

Patient was brought to the hospital by a friend following a suicide attempt a couple of days prior. Patient is thinking of suicide. He exhibits signs of physiological/psychological depression.

7/8/71 0730 Vet. arrived here at 7:00 A.M. and appears very withdrawn and depressed. Lives alone, wife has told vet. she will not come and join him. Married 1968, no children. Previous marital problems, unable to hold job; "She did not think I was much of a man." Wife left him 1970. She called "cops," he came to California in August '70 and unable to find work.

Mother died at 63 from cancer. One sister, younger, who lives in Atlanta, Georgia. Good health.

Vet. is oriented and feels hopeless. Retarded thought processes and body movement. Sleeps poorly; appetite poor.

Evaluation: Depressive reaction, severe.

Recommend admit on "S" status and expedite to Ward 207B as requested in report of contact.

*Doctor's Progress Notes*

7/9/71 Admissions staff: Patient is 30, unemployed, separated (to be divorced as of the date of his overdose on Seconal). He has lived alone for a year. He has had 2 years of college. In Florida he was employed for 2 years as a clothing store clerk but was fired as too unaggressive. He came to Los Angeles to find work but has worked only briefly (such as 2 weeks parking cars). This is his first neuro-psychiatric hospitalization, but he has had 2 previous depressive episodes. He will be given vocational counselling while here. He told nursing personnel he wanted to stay here only long enough to get enough pills to end it all. He was able to sleep last night, but he still is quite depressed, with a "wait and see" attitude toward his future, not knowing whether he still wants suicide. He will be treated in psychodrama. When he took the overdose, he took all he had, but also he "hoped" his friend might come over that night. He feels he really wanted to die. He says he has never been that depressed before; though he was "really down" when his mother died. (He has not seen his father since age 5.)

History as above. Some slight improvement noted this morning. However, still requires observation in view of uncertainty and am-

bivalence. After he is restabilized sufficiently reconstituted vocational counselling may be indicated.

7/14/71 Staff: Patient no longer considered to be suicidal. Remove from "S" status.

7/20/71 Staff: Regular discharge 7/21/71. Patient asking to leave
and is making own plans.

*Radiographic Reports*

7/9/71

Routine PA and right lateral views of the skull: Reveals the
calvarium appears intact. The pineal is not calcified. There are no
abnormal intracranial calcifications seen. The petrous and sphenoid
ridges and sella turcica are within normal limits.

Conclusion: Negative skull.

Routine PA and left lateral views of the chest: Reveals the heart,
mediastinum, hilar shadows, pulmonary parenchyma, and bony
thorax are within normal limits.

Conclusion: Negative chest.

KUB: Radiographs of the abdomen reveal the osseous structures
are within normal limits. The renal and psoas shadows are normal
bilaterally. The liver and spleen are not enlarged. There is no evidence of intestinal distention.

Conclusion: Negative KUB.

*Doctor's Orders*

7/8/71

"S" status; regular diet; Elavil 50 mg b.i.d. [twice daily] ; Quaa-
lude 300 mg. Hexovitamins II q.d. [every day].

7/9/71 — Discontinued TPR & B/P.

7/12/71 — Reduced Elavil 25 mg b.i.d.

7/14/71 — Remove from "S" status.

7/15/71 — 7-10 privilege card; Occupational Therapy Building
254.

7/17/71 — Elavil 25 mg; 6:30 A.M.-11:00 A.M.

7/20/71 — Regular discharge effective 7/21/71.

*Nursing Notes*

7/8/71 — 8:00 A.M.

Patient expedited to Ward 207B as emergent. Reportedly first neuropsychiatric hospitalization. "S" status. Evaluation: depressive reaction, acute. Patient is 30 years old, Caucasion male. Appears unkempt, unshaven. Sits with head lowered, eyes cast downward. Appears acutely depressed. Non-responsive to verbal requests. Refuse to eat regular diet offered. Replies to suggestion to drink juice for "body fluids." "I don't give a damn about body fluids." Shakes head to acknowledge staff introductions, but doesn't respond. Patient informed by Miss Johnson of nature of "S" status. Patient remained nonverbal. Complied with request to remove personal effects from pockets. Checked for contraband. Dr. S. notified. Patient slowly states "I have not been feeling well for a long time. The other day when I called my wife and asked her to come out. She said she wasn't going to come out and she wanted a divorce. It was our anniversary." States he has been separated from wife since last summer. Agrees by shaking head that telephone call to wife on Monday, 7/5/71 compounded the feelings. Patient asks in slow voice, "Can we do this some other time?" Asks, "If you want to help me you can get me a bottle of these pills." (Patient reportedly took Seconal capsules on 7/5/71, and was treated for overdose at Emergency Hospital.) Patient oriented X3.

8:40 A.M. — Seen by Dr. S. Patient states "I feel like I want to die." "I can't get a job, and my wife doesn't want me and I can't even kill myself right." "I felt this way when my mother died" (1963). Agrees that he got rundown feeling. Lasted approximately 3 months. Replies, "I just sat around." "Felt bad on ship for couple of days. Doctor said take these pills. I did and felt better" (1961). Patient states he received an honorable discharge. Attended school for a while, then mother died, and patient states he didn't return to junior college. Longest job he ever held was 2 years as clothing clerk in Florida. Met wife there (married in 1968). Patient states he was fired from job. "I wasn't aggressive enough." Remarks to question regarding marital problems onset, "About the time I got fired." Shakes head no to question regarding sexual incompatibility.

*Interview Nursing*

7/8/71

   Mr. Kent is 30 years of age. Was born in Dayton, Ohio. Religion none. Patient lives alone for past year. Patient is married but presently separated and possible divorce. Patient states "he doesn't know why he got married." Married in 1969; this is patient's first and only marriage. There are no children. Relationship with wife — not good. Patient hasn't seen wife since last August. She presently resides in Florida. Patient's mother is deceased. Hasn't seen father since age 5. Has a sister who lives in Atlanta. No recent contact with her. Last time about 2 years ago. Patient had two years of college in Florida. Wife completed high school.

   Patient unemployed. Last job was parking cars 2 hours weekly in Santa Monica in May 1971. Longest period of employment was a clerk in a clothing store for two years. Wife working and is a cashier. No income at present time. Had part-time job and occasionally wife would send money.

   Patient volunteered into the service in 1958-1961. Petty officer, radioman third class. Overseas duty — Pacific. Received honorable discharge.

   Patient's first neuropsychiatric hospitalization; no out-patient care.

   Patient unable to sleep. Went to a doctor who gave him some red pills to sleep. First medication was in the Navy, given by Navy doctor for depression and disability to sleep.

   Friend called the Suicide Prevention Center and they suggested patient come here for admission.

   Patient would like to help with his depression and some vocational guidance.

   No hospitalization for physical problems.

   The most important person to Mr. Kent as he states it "she's dead" (mother).

   Read paper during spare time and walk and watch T.V. and look for job. Patient has one friend, otherwise a loner. Sees friend occasionally. At first fairly frequently, now sporadically.

   Patient does not drink, no drugs, no known allergies. No police record.

   Patient expects to stay here only long enough to get pills to end it all, that is the way he feels today.

No present plans for the future. Patient was very slow in response to questioning. Kept head down, and supported chin with hand. Did smile once during the interview. He appeared very depressed but more than that very helpless. Expressed only a desire to die. Became very bored with interview, but tried to be cooperative. Assigned to Team I and personally assigned to Mr. D., Nursing Assistant.

7/8/71 — 3:15 P.M.

Patient appears quite depressed. Sat with head down and eyes open most of day in day room. Did not appear to be watching T.V. He answers questions put to him by nodding his head or with a direct yes or no. He ate very little lunch. Just dabble on his potatoes. Stated he was not very hungry. He attended off ward activity in Building 210 patio but did not participate. He appeared to be sleeping while others played volleyball. Mr. D., Nursing Assistant.

7/8/71

Before dinner Mr. Kent sat in day room with eyes closed or head down. Sometimes both as though trying to sleep or avoid contact with others. He appeared to be aware of the activity around him. Went to dining room with closed ward. And ate well. Stated, "I ate more this evening than at lunch because I was hungry." Went for a walk after dinner with ward. He appeared to be all right walking, but unable to stand still for long due to apparent weak knees or legs. He sat on the ground once, and squatted once. Stated he was all right, just tired. When at ballfield, he appeared to be watching at times and head down at times. After returning to ward he sat in chair with eyes closed as though asleep. He did not initiate any conversation. But was responsive on approach. Was pleasant and no management problem on 1 to 1. Mr. W., Nursing Assistant.

7/9/71 — 6:00 A.M.

Up once otherwise slept well. Friendly and sociable. No management problem. Does not appear depressed.

7:15 A.M.

While observing Mr. Kent in the mess hall he ate a good breakfast and sitting with his head up and looking around at the others in the mess hall. Does not appear depressed but very quiet. Patient G. M. was walking with arms around patient attempting to talk to him. Patient answers question with a direct answer. Does not elaborate.

10:30 A.M.

Seen in admissions staff. Sits upright in chair and looks interviewer directly in eye. States he is feeling much better today. "I was able to sleep last night — that helped." Answers questions with monosyllables. States he feels like he wants to "wait and see" before trying to kill himself. Dr. S. explained to patient that he would like him to attend the psychodrama group on ward. Stated he had taken 10 or 12 reds — "I wanted to die." Stated he knew that his friend would be coming to the house.

Patient appears more alert today. He was observed sitting in day room occasionally watching T.V. His walking gate is a bit more pert. He continues to communicate by moving his head and occasionally verbal. When asked what his plans were when he leaves the hospital he stated "to find a job." He was given a physical, an X-ray and seen by the Contact Man. He accompanied the therapist to Building 210 patio. Ate good lunch; fish, potatoes, salad and ice cream. Mr. D told me patient gave him a coat hanger.

4:00 P.M.

Patient appeared less depressed today. He appeared more alert and his conversation appears less stressful. Breathing did not appear exaggerated as he did upon admission. Patient still needs to be encouraged to get involved as he has and shows no interests. Now looks up when spoken to, head not bowed. Appears totally aware of surroundings.

9:30 P.M.

Mr. Kent appeared less depressed this evening. Appears more alert. Said he felt better. Ate well at supper. Went with a group to the volleyball field. Didn't participate.

7/10/71 — 7:00 A.M.

Appeared to sleep well.

12:45 P.M.

Patient ate a good breakfast holding his head up and looking around at others in the dining hall. Appears well aware of what is going on around him. After returning from breakfast sat in chair in the rear of day room reading or glancing through magazines. Went to the patio with group and laid under the tree. Also went to canteen with group. Does not appear depressed. Ate a good lunch. Watched the ball game on T.V. and read a magazine afterwards. Voiced no complaints.

Mr. Kent seems to be feeling much better. Takes some interest in what is going on around him. Eats well. Went to the theater tonight.

7/11/71 — 6:00 A.M.

Slept all night. No complaints in the morning. Non-socializing but does not appear depressed.

Spent a quiet day on intensive treatment unit. Stayed to himself and did some reading. He appears suspicious and occasionally writes notes in his notebook. Was no ward problem and voiced no complaints.

7:00 P.M.

Patient went to afternoon activities. Was lying on the grass when I approached. I asked patient if he wanted to participate in volleyball game. Stated "no, but I play basketball." Stated he would rather shoot a few baskets alone, as he doesn't play so well. Other patients did come up and participate; along with Mr. W. Patient stated he started feeling better yesterday. Says he does a lot of thinking and has come to a conclusion that he'll have to forget his wife and get a job. Patient states that if he should go through another crisis his resources will be a job and friends. Says his coping techniques before when he had problems was to just forget. Says that resolved the problem. States he can't blame his wife for leaving because she's been supporting him most of their married life, which is 3 years.

7/12/71 — 6:00 A.M.

Slept all night. No complaints in morning. No change in behavior.

Patient appears much more relaxed today. He has been reading a novel most of the day. Played chess with nurse. Stated he had a nice weekend. Attended group this morning but did not take part in conversations. He showed concern about Mr. W's inability to sleep at night and asked if something couldn't be done about his bed.

Afternoon

Patient looked depressed but more outgoing today. He played chess most of early evening. To the patio with intensive therapy unit. He played basketball a few minutes. He played chess upon returning to ward.

7/13/71 — 6:00 A.M.

Slept well. No complaints in the morning. Behavior remains flat. More pacing this morning than usual. No management problem.

10:30 P.M.

Seen in staff: States that he feels better. Says medications have helped him to sleep. Also states that he no longer wants to kill himself but would like to remain on "S" status for a couple of more days. Patient continues to speak in a soft tone of voice but seems very alert. Does not appear to be depressed. To remain on "S" status and be re-evaluated on 7/17/71.

Patient quite alert today. No display of depression. Talked with personnel and other patients. Was staffed to come off "S" status but asked to remain longer. Attended psychodrama.

4:12 P.M.

Patient seemed more relaxed and outgoing. Played chess most of early evening. Groom his beard. To Building 210 for a movie. He said he enjoyed the movie.

7/14/71 — 6:00 A.M.

Slept well all night. No complaints.

Patient quite cheerful all day. Socialized with other patients. Played pool and chess. Asked to be removed from "S" status. Was seen by Dr. C and removed from "S."

7/15/71

Patient has shown remarkable improvement in his overall appearance and behavior. Appears very alert and aware of what is going on. Patient has had problems with past employment. He was granted 7-10 privilege card and assigned to Tower Vocational Training Program in Building 259. To see Mr. D daily.

11:00 P.M.

Visited by friend.

7/16/71

Patient complained of inability to sleep. Was concerned about lack of sleep causing low feeling. A long conversation regarding several areas were discussed. Patient was concerned about his X-ray findings. They were reviewed with him. Patient thinks that the patient sleeping next to him, snoring, caused some of his inability to sleep. Patient's medication has been adjusted and efforts will be made to reassign a bed in another area. Patient made nurse a promise that if he started feeling too bad that he would inform someone. Seen by Dr. L.

Visited by friend, and clothing was left.

10:00 P.M.

Played chess. Washed his clothes. Went to Bingo party with closed unit. Mr. Kent appeared to be in good spirits. He is always friendly, pleasant with a smile on his face. Stated he took a test, which helped him to know what work he is capable of doing. And now he doesn't think he will be here but about 5 more days. After his discharge, he plans to seek a job he can handle. He spoke of how depressed he was when admitted. And how he was helped. His conversation indicates he is happily looking forward to returning to community living.

7/18/71 — 10:30 A.M.

Patient discussed with Mr. B. about his suicidal thought on 7/11/71, which he discussed with one of the personnel on the evening tour. He explained the method of attempted suicide by placing a rope over a tree in the Building 210 patio area. The rope was apparently rotten and broke. He then decided he did not want to take his life. Conversation with Mr. B. continued. Patient states he is not depressed at this time. Patient does not appear depressed. His plan is to remain in the hospital a few more days. Patient appears more outgoing and socializes well with others.

7/19/71

Summary — Patient came to the hospital 7/8/71 in what appeared to be a deep depression. He remained this way for a few days, then started to interact with other patients and personnel, stating "that he would have to work his problem out." As time passed he stated he no longer felt like doing away with himself. He was removed from "S" status and appears to be making good adjustment with things that affect him. He now states he is ready to leave the hospital and return to the community. He says he will live in his apartment and will look for work. In my opinion patient should be considered for discharge with hospital follow-up.

7/20/71 A.M.

Seen in discharge staff. States that he cannot stand to live in the hospital any longer and wants to be discharged. Approved for regular discharge. Patient wants to leave tomorrow.

9:15 P.M.

Was not seen on or around building until medication call at 9:00 P.M. at which time he told me good-bye, and that he is leaving in the morning. He knows where he is going but doesn't know how long he will be there. Stated he was sorry he could not play chess with me this evening, but he did not feel very good. He went to psychodrama and it was kind of strong. Stated he was in the middle. He managed to smile during part of our conversation. At the same time he didn't seem happy. Went to bed right after medication.

7/21/71 A.M.

Will return to apartment and find a job. Regular discharge.

*Physical Medicine Rehabilitation Progress Report*

David Kent, 30, was referred to O.T. 259 and scheduled to report on July 15, 1971, for the pre-vocational job sample and TOWER clerical tests.

The patient generally performed well on structured tests, but his scores were mediocre on the unstructured tests. TOWER clerical tests revealed superior ability in spelling, filing and typing; but scores on arithmetic, abbreviations, computing a payroll and record keeping were low. In a workshop situation, Mr. Kent appears suited for those structured activities requiring discrimination and organization such as sorting and inspection; but he should also function well on packaging and assembly tasks of a repetitive nature. His highest aptitude and interest, however, seem to lie in clerical tasks like typing and filing, in which his scores were superior.

The patient was neat in appearance, quiet in manner and prompt in attendance. He was polite, cooperative and coyly friendly. He seemed alert and intelligent. Mr. K. is able to follow both oral and written directions, and attention span and frustration tolerance appear within normal limit. Work was neat, organized and accurate.

## Report of Serologic Procedure

| Test Name | Results | Range | Test Name | Results | Range |
|---|---|---|---|---|---|
| Calcium | 10.2 | 8.5-10.5 | Protein | 8.0 | 6.0-8.0 |
| Phosph. Inorganic | 4.0 | 2.5-4.5 | Albumin | 4.6 | 3.5-5.0 |
| Glucose | 100.0 | 65-110 | Bilirubin, Total | 0.9 | 0.15-1.0 |
| Urea Nitrogen | 17 | 10-20 | Phosphatase, Alk | 30 | 30-85 |
| Uric Acid | 7.4 | 2.5-8.0 | LDH | 130 | 90-200 |
| Cholesterol | 240 | 150-300 | SGOT | 44 | 10-50 |

# APPENDIX C HOSPITAL RULES

## WELCOME TO BUILDING 207B

The ward team consists of your nursing assistants, nurses, social worker, psychologist, and psychiatrist. You will be given a list of persons on your team.

The nursing assistants assigned to you will help you become acquainted with the ward and its procedures. Talk with them often. Discuss any problems and questions with them, and if they cannot help you, they will refer you to the psychiatrist or other team members.

Your ability to assume responsibilities, show initiative and co-operation with ward policies are important in showing that you are ready for privilege card status or pass. When you feel that you are ready for more privileges than you have, discuss your request with nursing team members who will recommend you when you are ready. Discuss your activity assignments with them.

You will be assigned to a ward group which meets MONDAY and WEDNESDAY from 8:45 A.M. to 9:15 A.M. The purpose of the group is for you to get to know each other better and to discuss whatever concerns you. The staff group leaders are nursing personnel on your team. Each group selects a group representative and an alternate who serves as patient group leaders and also as your representative to the PATIENTS COUNCIL.

The Patients Assembly meets Tuesday from 8:15 A.M. to no later than 9:00 A.M. You are expected to attend this meeting which is aimed at improving ward conditions. The Patients Council consists of the officers who conduct the meeting, the group representatives and alternates, several members at large, and the coffee chairman. You are encouraged to become a group representative or alternate, or if your group already has them, to run for member at large when vacancies occur. The chairman, vice-chairman, and secretary are elected from the council members.

Everyone is expected to make his own bed and to help keep the ward clean.

NO SMOKING IN BED or where NO SMOKING signs are posted.

Drinking alcoholic beverages or bringing them on the ward is not permitted. Violation of this rule will result in loss of certain privileges and possible reduction of your allowance.

Appointments are handed out each morning. If you have a privilege card, you are expected to appear for your appointment on your own. If you're on the Intensive Therapy Unit, you will be escorted. The schedule of daily ward activities, special staff's recreational activities, mail call, paymaster visits, visiting hours, etc., is posted on bulletin boards located on both floors. Please check the bulletin board often.

REMEMBER: GO TO YOUR NURSING TEAM MEMBER FIRST, IF HE OR SHE CANNOT HELP YOU, THEY WILL REFER YOU TO THE PROPER PERSON.


WARD ROUTINE: Everyone is expected to make his own bed and to help in cleaning and in keeping the ward areas clean. NO SMOKING signs are to be observed at all times.

| | |
|---|---|
| 6:00 A.M. | Morning call and shaving — Intensive Therapy Unit |
| 6:15 A.M. | Morning call and shaving — Self-Supervision Unit |
| 6:20 A.M. | Cigarette call in dayrooms |
| 6:30 A.M. | Medications (passed on B Floor) |
| 7:05 A.M. | Breakfast — Intensive Therapy Unit |
| 7:20 A.M. | Breakfast — Self-Supervision Unit |
| 8:55 A.M. | Privilege Card patients leave for details (9:00 A.M. details may attend group meeting first) |
| 9:15 A.M. | Intensive Therapy Unit patients either: Socialization clinic, Corrective Therapy or ward housekeeping |
| 11:00 A.M. | Showers ($207B_1$-$207B_2$) |

| | |
|---|---|
| 11:00 A.M.-11:30 A.M. | Medications given out in treatment room #212 ("B" Floor) |
| 12:05 P.M. | Lunch — Intensive Therapy Unit |
| 12:20 P.M. | Lunch — Self-Supervision Unit |
| 12:55 P.M. | Privilege card patients leave for details Intensive Therapy Unit patients to canteen on Mondays for one-half hour except the last Monday of the month — which is to attend Mrs. E.'s monthly show |
| 1:15 P.M. | Intensive therapy unit patients to sports, recreation or occupational therapy |
| 4:00 P.M.-5:00 P.M. | Showers daily for self-supervision unit (if not taken in A.M.) A-1 shower to be used |
| 4:30 P.M. | Medications |
| 5:05 P.M. | Supper — Intensive Therapy Unit |
| 5:20 P.M. | Supper — Self-Supervision Unit |
| 9:00 P.M. | Bedtime medications |
| 9:45 P.M. | Lights out and bedtime for Intensive Therapy Unit |
| 10:00 P.M. | Privilege Cards end |
| 10:30 P.M. | Lights out and bedtime, except weekends and night before holidays |
| | |
| SPECIAL STAFF | Screening of all new patients 9:30 A.M. except Tuesday and Thursday Discharge staff (and unaccompanied pass) Tuesday, 9:30 A.M. Group meeting Monday and Wednesday, 8:45 A.M.-9:15 A.M. |

*Veterans Administration Reference Slip*

Your team leaders are: Miss B., R.N.; Miss N., R.N.; Mrs. Q.; Mrs. C., R.N.

The head nurse is: Miss J., R.N.

Your social worker is: ?

Your doctor is Dr.: S.

Remarks: Mr. Kent, David, you have been assigned to Group A on Mondays and Remotivation Group on Wednesdays. The groups meet at 8:15 A.M. to 9:15 A.M. Your group leaders are: Days, you are assigned to personally Mr. D., Miss B.; PM s: Mr. C., Mr. W; Nights: Mr. R., Mr. C. If you have any problems or requests, please talk to the nursing assistant assigned to you. If he or she isn't available, please ask the next one on your list.

# PSYCHOLOGICAL TESTS

I. Sentence Choice Questionnaire

INSTRUCTIONS: For each pair of statements, circle A if you are more likely to agree with the statement lettered A, and circle B if you are more likely to agree with the statement lettered B. If you agree with both statements, choose the statement you agree with more (or disagree with less). [Kent's choice is indicated by parentheses.]

1. A. I would like a job which would require a lot of traveling.
   (B.) I would prefer a job in one location.
2. A. I am invigorated by a brisk, cold day.
   (B.) I can't wait to get into the indoors on a cold day.
3. A. I often wish I could be a mountain climber.
   (B.) I can't understand people who risk their necks climbing mountains.
4. (A.) I dislike all body odors.
   B. I like some of the earthy body smells.
5. A. I get bored seeing the same old faces.
   (B.) I like the comfortable familiarity of everyday friends.
6. (A.) I like to explore a strange city or section of town by myself, even if it means getting lost.
   B. I prefer a guide when I am in a place I don't know well.
7. A. I sometimes like to do things that are a little frightening.
   (B.) A sensible person avoids activities that are dangerous.
8. A. I would like to take up the sport of water skiing.
   (B.) I would not like to take up water skiing.
9. (A.) When I go on a trip I prefer to plan my route and timetable fairly carefully.

B. I prefer to take off on a trip with no preplanned or definite routes, or timetables.
10. A. I would like to learn to fly an airplane.
(B.) I would not like to learn to fly an airplane.
11. (A.) I would not like to be hypnotized.
B. I would like to have the experience of being hypnotized.
12. A. The most important goal of life is to live it to the fullest and experience as much of it as you can.
(B.) The most important goal of life is to find peace and happiness.
13. A. I prefer friends who are excitingly unpredictable.
(B.) I prefer friends who are reliable and predictable.
14. (A.) When I go on a vacation I prefer the comfort of a good room and bed.
B. When I go on a vacation I would prefer the change of camping out.
15. A. I prefer people who are emotionally expressive even if they are a bit unstable.
(B.) I prefer people who are calm and even tempered.
16. A. Children get into trouble because their parents punish them too much.
(B.) The trouble with most children nowadays is that their parents are too easy with them.
17. A. Many of the unhappy things in people's lives are partly due to bad luck.
(B.) People's misfortunes result from the mistakes they make.
18. A. One of the major reasons why we have wars is because people don't take enough interest in politics.
(B.) There will always be wars, no matter how hard people try to prevent them.
19. A. In the long run people get the respect they deserve in this world.
(B.) Unfortunately, an individual's worth often passes unrecognized no matter how hard he tries.
20. A. The idea that teachers are unfair to students is nonsense.
(B.) Most students don't realize the extent to which their grades are influenced by accidental happenings.
21. (A.) Without the right breaks one cannot be an effective leader.
B. Capable people who fail to become leaders have not taken advantage of their opportunities.

22. (A.) No matter how hard you try some people just don't like you.

    B. People who can't get others to like them don't understand how to get along with others.

23. A. Heredity plays the major role in determining one's personality.

    (B.) It is one's experiences in life which determine what they're like.

24. (A.) I have often found that what is going to happen will happen.

    B. Trusting to fate has never turned out as well for me as making a decision to take a definite course of action.

25. (A.) In the case of the well-prepared student there is rarely if ever such a thing as an unfair test.

    B. Many times exam questions tend to be so unrelated to course work that studying is really useless.

26. A. Becoming a success is a matter of hard work; luck has little or nothing to do with it.

    (B.) Getting a good job depends mainly on being in the right place at the right time.

27. A. The average citizen can have an influence in government decisions.

    (B.) This world is run by the few people in power, and there is not much the little guy can do about it.

28. A. When I make plans, I am almost certain that I can make them work.

    (B.) It is not always wise to plan too far ahead because many things turn out to be a matter of good or bad fortune anyhow.

29. A. There are certain people who are just no good.

    (B.) There is some good in everybody.

30. (A.) In my case getting what I want has little or nothing to do with luck.

    B. Many times we might just as well decide what to do by flipping a coin.

31. A. Who gets to be the boss often depends on who was lucky enough to be in the right place first.

    (B.) Getting people to do the right thing depends upon ability; luck has little or nothing to do with it.

32. (A.) As far as world affairs are concerned, most of us are the victims of forces we can neither understand, nor control.
    B. By taking an active part in political and social affairs the people can control world events.
33. (A.) Most people don't realize the extent to which their lives are controlled by accidental happenings.
    B. There really is no such thing as "luck."
34. (A.) One should always be willing to admit mistakes.
    B. It is usually best to cover up one's mistakes.
35. A. It is hard to know whether or not a person really likes you.
    (B.) How many friends you have depends upon how nice a person you are.
36. (A.) In the long run the bad things that happen to us are balanced by the good ones.
    B. Most misfortunes are the result of lack of ability, ignorance, laziness, or all three.
37. A. With enough effort we can wipe out political corruption.
    (B.) It is difficult for people to have much control over the things politicians do in office.
38. (A.) Sometimes I can't understand how teachers arrive at the grades they give.
    B. There is a direct connection between how hard I study and the grades I get.
39. A. A good leader expects people to decide for themselves what they should do.
    (B.) A good leader makes it clear to everybody what their jobs are.
40. (A.) Many times I feel that I have little influence over the things that happen to me.
    B. It is impossible for me to believe that chance or luck plays an important role in my life.
41. A. People are lonely because they don't try to be friendly.
    (B.) There's not much use in trying too hard to please people, if they like you, they like you.
42. (A.) There is too much emphasis on athletics in high school.
    B. Team sports are an excellent way to build character.
43. A. What happens to me is my own doing.
    (B.) Sometimes I feel that I don't have enough control over the direction my life is taking.

44. (A.) Most of the time I can't understand why politicians behave the way they do.
    B. In the long run the people are responsible for bad government on a national as well as on a local level.

## II. Saxe Sentence Completion Test (Form M)

NAME  David Kent                          DATE

COMPLETE THESE SENTENCES AS RAPIDLY AS YOU CAN

1. I pleased my friends when  *I was good*
2. My secret desire is  *stop failing*
3. Even though I loved her, she  *left me*
4. I thought of myself as  *not worth a dime*
5. A husband has a right to  *fail*
6. I would make enemies if  *I tried too hard*
7. I don't like women who  *give up*
8. I gave in because  *she wanted it*
9. I could not love her because  *she couldn't make up her mind*
10. I wish my friends would  *like me*
11. My body is  *O.K.*
12. When she refused me, it meant  *the end*
13. I like men who  *are tough*
14. My friends don't understand that  *I am sick*
15. Sometimes sex  *is fine*
16. When nobody cares, I  *lose hope*
17. I like myself when  *I succeed*
18. I was really loved by  *my mother*
19. Sometimes marriage  *is too much pressure*
20. I was annoyed by people who  *pushed me*
21. I feel worse if  *people push me*
22. When she began flirting with me, I  *got scared*
23. Making friends is hard if  *you're shy*
24. It isn't right for a child to  *lose his father*
25. I wanted my mother to  *live*
26. When I was punished, I  *cried*
27. I don't like to  *die*
28. I almost lost hope when  *she said we were through*
29. Nobody could force me to  *live*
30. When my parents argued, I  *they didn't*
31. What I have to do is  *get well and get a job*

32. When I lost my temper, I  *got cold inside*
33. My father annoyed me when  *he left*
34. I always worried about  *my mother*
35. If only my mother  *were alive*
36. I would get better if  *I could get a job*
37. I am scared by  *ropes*
38. My father should have  *stayed around*
39. When something worries me, I  *close up*
40. Being told what to do is  *all right*
41. My mother annoyed me when  *she cried*
42. I was undecided so  *I wouldn't do anything*
43. I watch people for  *to see what they want me to do*
44. I wanted my father to  *play with me*
45. I was criticized when I  *didn't get good grades*
46. My mother should have  *stayed alive*
47. I would feel lost if  *I had nothing to hold on to*
48. When upset, I  *just sit*
49. The worst thing about getting older is  *you die*
50. I suppose I want to  *stay alive*

ADD ANYTHING ELSE YOU WISH TO SAY:

III. Admissions Questionnaire

Name *David Kent*  Age *30*  Race *Caucasian*  Religion *Prot.*  Sex *M*
Marital Status:  Single  Married  Divorced  Widowed  *X* Separated
Children (Number, age & custody) *0*
Dates of service *1958-1961*  Military occupation *—*
Any combat service? *No*  WWII ____ Korea ____ Vietnam _____
Civilian occupation *Sales*  Education *2 years J.C.*
Number of previous NP hospitalizations, if any *None*
How long ago were you last discharged? *No*
Why did you come to the hospital? *Depression — attempted suicide*

What symptoms or problems do you want treatment for? _Depression_
  _attempted suicide_

How old were you when you first realized you had any mental or
emotional problems? _30_

How long do you expect to be hospitalized? _2 weeks_

Immediately before you came in the hospital, were you living (check
one):

_X_ alone           ____ with friends        ____ Domiciliary
____ with wife/husband   ____ boarding house   ____ other
____ with parents        ____ family care

Do you plan to return to this living arrangement when you leave the
hospital? _Yes_

Have you ever seriously thought of suicide? _Yes_ Attempted
  suicide? _Yes_

Were you employed when you entered the hospital? _No_

  If yes, do you still have the job? _—_

  If not, how long has it been since you have worked stead-
  ily? _1968_

What other income do you have (pension, Social Security,
etc.)? _None_

          Source _____ Amount _____

Have you ever used tobacco? _No_ How old were you when you first
tried it? _—_

  Do you still use it? _No_ How much? _—_ How often? _—_

Have you ever used alcohol? _No_ How old were you when you first
tried it? _—_

  Do you still use it? _—_ How much? _—_ How often? _—_

Have you ever used marijuana? _No_ How old were you when you
first tried it? _—_

  Do you still use it? _—_ How much? _—_ How often? _—_

Have you ever used barbiturates (downers)? _No_ How old were you
  when you first tried it? _—_ Do you still use it? _—_ How
  much? _—_ How often? _—_

Have you ever used amphetamines (pep pills, speed)? _No_ How old
  were you when you first tried it? _—_ Do you still use
  it? _—_ How much? _—_ How often? _—_

Have you ever used hallucinogens (LSD, STP, peyote, etc.)? _No_
  How old were you when you first tried it? _—_ Do you still use
  it? _—_ How much _—_ How often? _—_

Have you ever used heroin (or other hard drugs)? _No_ How old were you when you first tried it?_—_ Do you still use it?_—_ How much?_—_ How often?_—_

IV. Minnesota Multiphasic Personality Inventory Profile

| | |
|---|---|
| L 6 | Mf 40 |
| F 14 | Pa 16 |
| K 13 | Pt 28 |
| Hs 8 | Pt + 1K 41 |
| Hs + .5K 15 | Sc 25 |
| D 41 | Sc + 1K 38 |
| Hy 18 | Ma 12 |
| Pd 22 | Ma + .2K 15 |
| Pd + .4K 27 | Si 57 |

# APPENDIX E

# LETTER OF INTRODUCTION

VETERANS ADMINISTRATION HOSPITAL

July 20, 1971

To whom it may concern:

This is to introduce David Kent Reynolds, Ph.D., a cultural anthropologist, who was admitted to this hospital as a patient under the pseudonym, David Kent, for purposes of research. In the second phase of this research, Dr. Reynolds is seeking information about reactions to him as a patient. Please give him your full cooperation in order to provide us with several perspectives on his hospital experience.

Sincerely,


(Signed)     N. L. Farberow, Ph.D.
             Principal Investigator
             Central Research Unit


(Signed)     J. T. C., M.D.
             Chief, Psychiatry Service I

# BIBLIOGRAPHY

Banen, D. M. Suicide by psychotics. *Journal of Nervous and Mental Disease,* *120,* 349-357, 1954.

Barry, Anne. *Bellevue Is a State of Mind.* New York: Berkley, 1971.

Beck, A. T. *Depression.* New York: Harper and Row, 1967.

Beisser, Arnold R., and Blanchette, James E. A study of suicides in a mental hospital. *Diseases of the Nervous System, 22,* 365-369, 1961.

Boisen, Anton. *Out of the Depths.* New York: Harper and Row, 1960.

Bowen, Elenore S. *Return to Laughter.* New York: Harper, 1954.

Braginsky, Benjamin M., et al. *Methods of Madness.* New York: Holt, Rinehart and Winston, 1969.

Caudill, W. *The Psychiatric Hospital as a Small Society.* Cambridge: Harvard University Press, 1958.

Caudill, W., et al. Social structure and interaction processes on a psychiatric ward. *American Journal of Orthopsychiatry, 22,* 314-334, 1952.

Caudill, W., and Stainbrook, E. Some covert effects of communication difficulties in a psychiatric hospital. *Psychiatry, 17,* 27-40, 1954.

Chagnon, Napoleon A. *Yanomamo: The Fierce People.* New York: Holt, Rinehart and Winston, 1968.

Chapman, Richard F. Suicide during psychiatric hospitalization. *Bulletin of the Menninger Clinic, 29*(2), 35-44, 1965.

Cooley, C. H. *Human Nature and the Social Order.* New York: Scribner's, 1922.

Dean, R. A., et al. Prediction of suicide in a psychiatric hospital. *Journal of Clinical Psychology, 23,* 296-301, 1967.

Deane, William N. Reactions of a nonpatient to a stay on a mental hospital ward. *Psychiatry, 24,* 61-68, 1961.

Farberow, Norman L., et al. Suicide among schizophrenic mental hospital patients. In Farberow, Norman L., and Shneidman, Edwin S., eds. *The Cry for Help.* New York: McGraw-Hill, 1961.

Farberow, Norman L., and McEvoy, Theodore L. Suicide among patients with diagnoses of auxiety reaction in general medical and surgical hospitals. *Journal of Abnormal Psychology, 71,* 287-299, 1966.

Farberow, Norman L., Shneidman, Edwin S., and Neuringer, Charles. Case history and hospitalization factors in suicides of neuropsychiatric hospital patients. *Journal of Nervous and Mental Disease, 142,* 32-44, 1966.

Farberow, Norman L., et al. An eight-year survey of hospital suicides. *Life Threatening Behavior, 1,* 184-202, 1971.

Farberow, Norman L., and Reynolds, D. K. Dyadic crisis suicides in mental hospital patients. *Journal of Abnormal Psychology, 78*(1), 77-85, 1971.

Farberow, Norman L. *Bibliography on Suicide and Suicide Prevention.* 1897-1957, 1958-1970. DHEW Publication (HSM) 72-9080, 1972.

Gergen, Kenneth J. The healthy happy human being wears many masks. *Psychology Today,* 31-66, May, 1972.

Goffman, E. *The Presentation of Self in Everyday Life.* New York: Doubleday Anchor, 1959.

_____. *Asylums.* New York: Doubleday, 1961*a.*

_____. *Encounters.* Indianapolis: Bobbs-Merrill, 1961*b.*

_____. *Behavior in Public Places.* Illinois: Glencoe Free Press, 1963*a.*

_____. *Stigma.* Englewood Cliffs, N.J.: Prentice-Hall, 1963*b.*

Goldman, Arnold R., et al. On posing as mental patients: Reminiscences and recommendations. *Professional Psychology, 1,* 427-434, 1970.

Green, H. *I Never Promised You a Rose Garden.* New York: Holt, Rinehart and Winston, 1964.

Hall, E. T. *The Silent Language.* New York: Doubleday, 1959.

Hyde, R. W. *Experiencing the Patient's Day.* New York: G. P. Putnam's Sons, 1955.

Jackson, D. D. *The Etiology of Schizophrenia.* New York: Basic Books, 1960.

Kahne, M. J. Suicide research: A critical review of strategies and potentialities in mental hospitals. *International Journal of Social Psychiatry, 12,* 120-129, 1966.

Kamano, D. K., and Crawford, C. S. Self-evaluations of suicidal mental hospital patients. *Journal of Clinical Psychology, 22,* 278-279, 1966.

Kaplan, B., ed. *The Inner World of Mental Illness.* New York: Harper and Row, 1964.

Kesey, K. *One Flew over the Cuckoo's Nest.* New York: Signet Books, 1962.

Kobler, Arthur L., and Stotland, Ezra. *The End of Hope: A Social-Clinical Study of Suicide.* New York: Free Press, 1964.

Laing, R. D. *The Divided Self.* London: Tavistock, 1960.

_____. *Sanity, Madness and the Family.* London: Tavistock, 1961.

Lee, Dorothy. Are basic needs ultimate? *Journal of Abnormal and Social Psychology, 43,* 391-395, 1948.

_____. *Freedom and Culture.* Englewood Cliffs, N.J.: Prentice-Hall, 1959.

Levinson, D. J., and Gallagher, E. B. *Patienthood in the Mental Hospital.* Boston: Houghton Mifflin, 1964.

Levy, S., and Southcombe, R. H. Suicide in a state hospital for the mentally ill. *Journal of Nervous and Mental Disease, 117,* 504-514, 1953.

Lipschutz, L. S. Some administrative aspects of suicide in mental hospitals. *American Journal of Psychiatry, 99,* 181-187, 1942.

MacAndrew, C., and Edgerton, R. B. *Drunken Comportment: A Social Explanation.* Chicago: Aldine, 1969.

Mead, G. H. *Mind, Self and Society.* Chicago: University of Chicago Press, 1934.

Menninger, Karl. *The Vital Balance.* New York: Viking, 1963.

Miller, Dorothy, and Goodman, D. Predicting post-release risk among hospitalized suicide attempters. *Omega, 1,* 71-74, 1970.

Mills, C. W. Situated actions and vocabularies of motive. *American Sociological Review, 5,* 904-913, 1940.

Mueller, Betty S., and Sherman, Clinton C. Nurses' experiences as psychiatric patients. *Hospital and Community Psychiatry, 20*(1), 40-41, 1969.

Neuringer, C. Reactions to interpersonal crises in suicidal individuals. *Journal of General Psychology, 71*(1), 47-55, 1964.

Peters, F. *The World Next Door.* New York: Farrar, Straus, 1949.

Pokorny, Alex D. Characteristics of 44 patients who subsequently committed suicide. *Archives of General Psychiatry, 2,* 314-323, 1960.

Redlich, Fritz. The anthropologist as observer. *Journal of Nervous and Mental Disease, 157,* 313-319, 1973.

Reynolds, David K. Directed behavior change: Japanese psychotherapy in a private mental hospital. Ph.D. dissertation, University of California, Los Angeles, 1969.

Reynolds, David K., and Farberow, Norman L. Experiential research: An inside perspective on suicide and social systems. *Life Threatening Behavior, 3,* 261-269, 1973*a.*

————. The suicidal patient: An inside view. *Omega, 4,* 229-241, 1973*b.*

Riley, M. W. *Sociological Research: A Case Approach.* New York: Harcourt, Brace and World, 1963.

Rockwell, Don A. Some observations on "living in." *Psychiatry, 34,* 214-223, 1971.

Rokeach, Milton. *The Three Christs of Ypsilanti.* New York: Knopf, 1964.

Rosenhan, D. L. On being sane in insane places. *Science, 179,* 250-258, 1973.

Rotov, Michail. Death by suicide in the hospital: An analysis of 20 therapeutic failures. *American Journal of Psychotherapy, 25,* 216-227, 1970.

Rowland, H. Friendship patterns in a state mental hospital. *Psychiatry, 2,* 363-373, 1939.

Salisbury, R. F. *Structures of Custodial Care.* University of California Publications in Culture and Society, vol. 8, 1962.

Sletten, Ivan W., et al. Suicide in mental hospital patients. *Diseases of the Nervous System, 33,* 328-334, 1972.

Snavely, H. R. Factors underlying clinician bias in decisions about suicide potential. Ph.D. dissertation, University of California, Los Angeles, 1968.

Sommer, R. *Personal Space.* Englewood Cliffs, N.J.: Prentice-Hall, 1969.

Stanton, Alfred H., and Schwartz, Morris S. *The Mental Hospital.* New York: Basic Books, 1954.

Sudnow, D. *Passing On.* Englewood Cliffs, N.J.: Prentice-Hall, 1967.

Tabachnick, N. Interpersonal relations in suicidal attempts: Some psychodynamic considerations and implications for treatment. *Archives of General Psychiatry, 4,* 16-21, 1961.

Weitz, William A. Experiencing the role of a hospitalized psychiatric patient: A professional's view from the other side. *Professional Psychology, 3,* 151-154, 1972.

Wellmet Project Proposal. Mimeographed. Boston, 1969.

# INDEX